I0824077

A DEGREE IN A BOOK
SOCIOLOGY

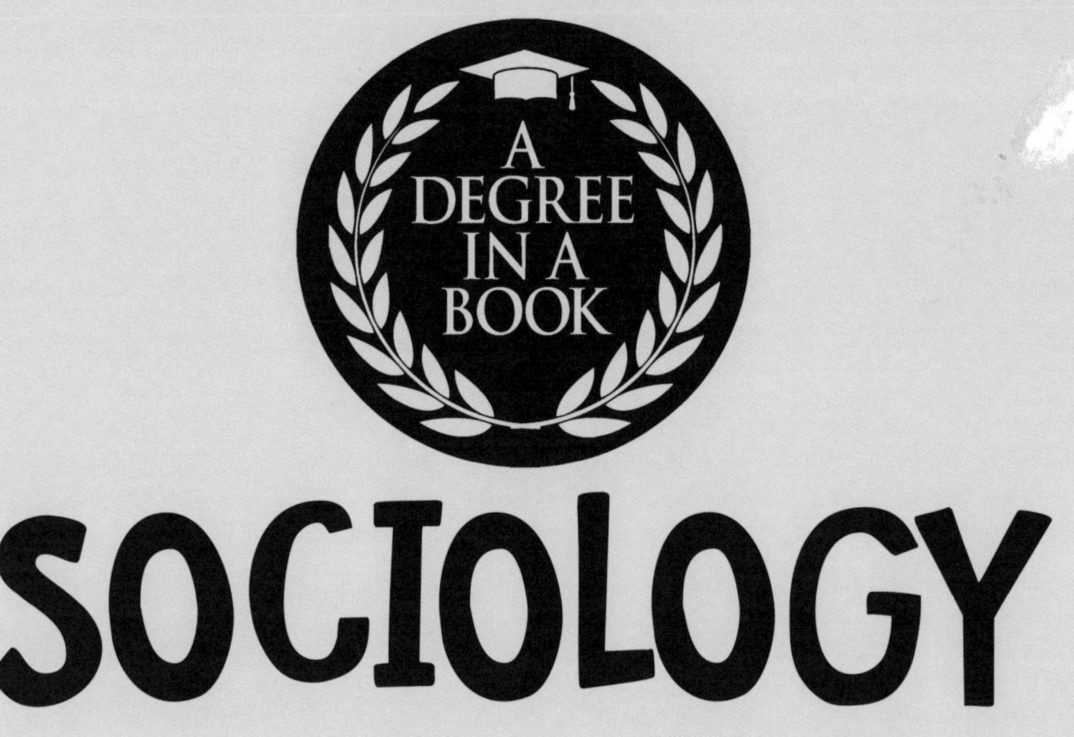

MEGAN TODD

Dr Megan Todd is a sociologist with over two decades of experience in higher education, most recently as course leader and senior lecturer at the University of Lancashire. Before that, she taught English literature and language in secondary schools. Her research explores sexualities, gender and violence, and, more recently, their intersection with climate change and human-animal relationships. Megan's book *Sexualities and Society: An Introduction* brings these passions together. She's committed to making complex ideas approachable and relevant, especially for curious minds diving into sociology for the first time. In her spare time, she enjoys walking the fells of Cumbria.

This edition published in 2026 by Sirius Publishing, a division of
Arcturus Publishing Limited,
26/27 Bickel s Yard, 151–153 Bermondsey Street,
London SE1 3HA

ISBN: 978-1-3988-6844-1
AD010855UK
Supplier 29, Date 0226, PI 00009105

Printed in China

CONTENTS

INTRODUCTION

Sociology is a vibrant and challenging discipline, not least because its subject – the social world – is so vast and ever-changing. Sociology asks the big (and small) questions about society, in such a way as to help us understand, not just the world around us but also our place within it, our relationship to others and our identities. The plural of identity is key here – throughout the book, we will start to think about the ways in which we all have a variety of identities including social class, ethnicity, sexuality, age and gender, and how these interconnect to shape social experiences and structures.

This book will not only introduce you to the key ideas, theories and methods within sociology but, perhaps most importantly, it will help you to develop your own sociological imagination. This is something that is really useful, especially in a world that changes as fast as ours does. Having the ability to think critically, from a sociological perspective, on the huge array of topics you might be passionate about, or concerned with, will be a valuable life skill!

A Degree in a Book: Sociology introduces you to an exciting selection of topics typically covered on an undergraduate course. To begin with, in the first section of the book we're going to consider what sociology is and why it emerged, before moving on to think about some key theories and ways of thinking; this is crucial because theory is actually very exciting as well as being very important – theories might be seen as the tools which help us solve a puzzle. This is then followed by a chapter on how we 'do' sociology, focusing on a few popular methods for conducting research. It might be useful to read these chapters first, to get an understanding of the subject and its uses. The rest of the book then covers some of the issues with which sociology has been, and will be, concerned. These chapters can be read in any order. Throughout, you will be introduced to key thinkers in, and pieces of research on, particular areas. These give you a taste of the promise of sociology. At the end of the book, there is a glossary of key terms (indicated in bold italics in the text) and also some suggested readings; hopefully, your interest will be suitably piqued, so that you feel inspired to explore the richness of sociological thought.

Whatever has brought you to this book, by the end, if it has been successful, you will be persuaded of sociology's importance, not just for understanding our social world but also for helping to change it for the better. As you embark on this journey through the sociological landscape, remember that sociology is not just about understanding society – it's about engaging with it. The insights you gain from this book will equip you to become a more informed, empathetic and active participant in your social worlds.

So, let's begin our exploration of sociology – a subject that might just change the way you see yourself, others,and the complex web of social relations that surrounds us all.

Society is dynamic, as depicted here in Liberty Leading the People *by Eugène Delacroix. Sociology aims to respond to that change.*

Raphael's The School of Athens *shows many Greek philosophers and scholars. Sociology, interdisciplinary in nature, has its roots in philosophical enquiry.*

Chapter One

WHAT IS SOCIOLOGY?

A 'social science' – Social 'science'? – A 'social' science? – The emergence of sociology – Founding fathers – A limited and limiting explanation – A black belt in sociology – Developing a sociological imagination – Sociological ways of knowing – Timeline of sociology's development

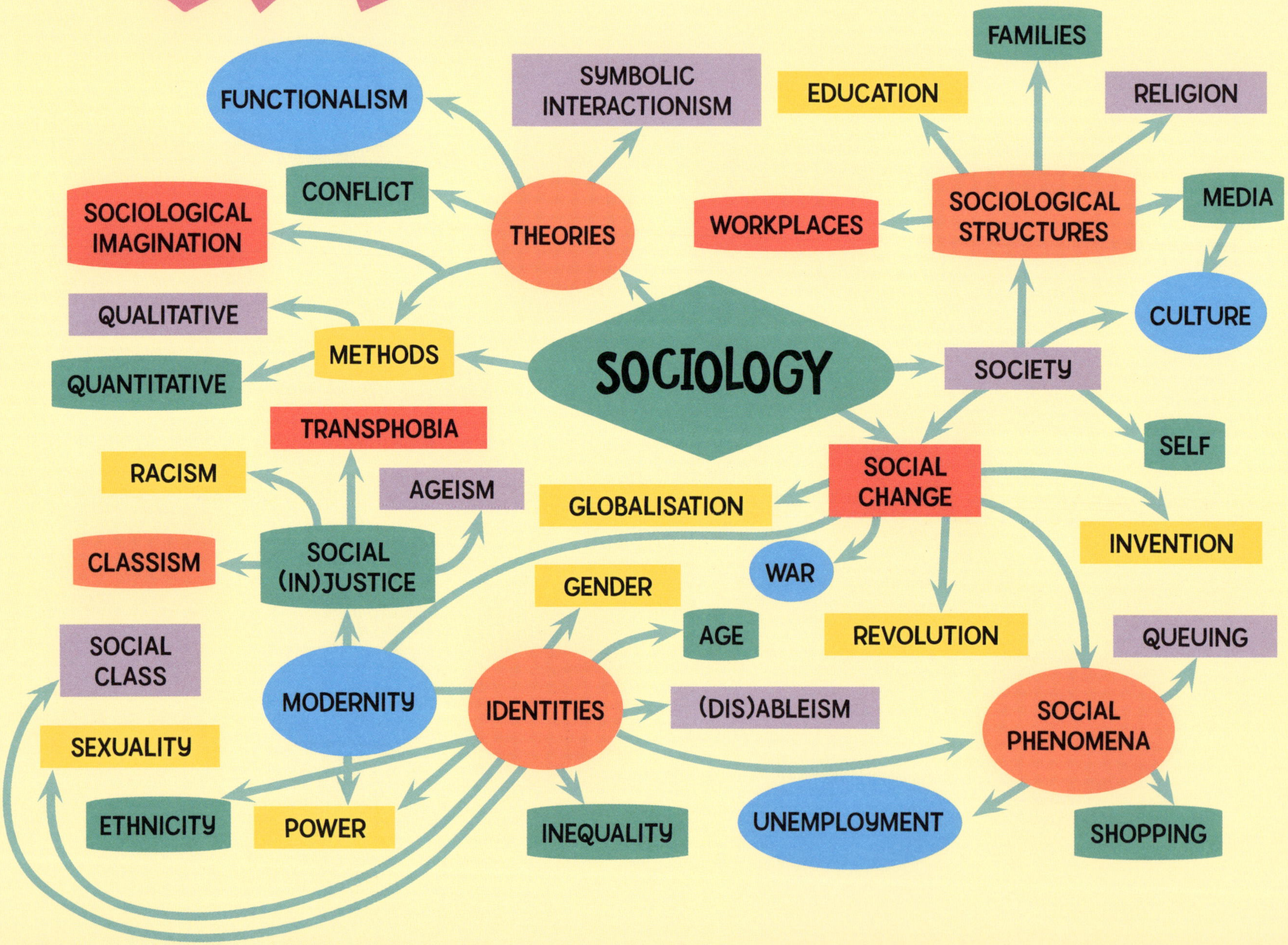

SOCIOLOGY

THEORIES
FUNCTIONALISM
SYMBOLIC INTERACTIONISM
CONFLICT
SOCIOLOGICAL IMAGINATION

METHODS
QUALITATIVE
QUANTITATIVE

SOCIETY
SOCIOLOGICAL STRUCTURES
EDUCATION
FAMILIES
RELIGION
MEDIA
WORKPLACES
CULTURE
SELF

SOCIAL CHANGE
GLOBALISATION
INVENTION
WAR
REVOLUTION

SOCIAL (IN)JUSTICE
TRANSPHOBIA
RACISM
AGEISM
CLASSISM

MODERNITY

IDENTITIES
GENDER
AGE
(DIS)ABLEISM
SOCIAL CLASS
SEXUALITY
ETHNICITY
POWER
INEQUALITY

SOCIAL PHENOMENA
QUEUING
UNEMPLOYMENT
SHOPPING

We live in 'interesting times', so this is a great moment to begin your sociological journey. Sociology can be broadly understood as a lens through which we study society, yet defining it can be tricky. Labels are powerful, as many academics, such as Howard Becker (1928–2023), have argued; they shape how we think about things. There are some fairly standard ways of defining and understanding sociology but perhaps they raise as many questio ns as they answer. Far from being a problem, though, this reflects the ways in which sociology is a fascinating and diverse subject.

A 'SOCIAL SCIENCE'?

Sociology is one of a range of subjects understood in the broad category 'social sciences' that study the activities of societies and people; other subjects include criminology, anthropology, social policy and so on. These are very often differentiated from humanities subjects such as history, philosophy and languages (disciplines often perceived as being more abstract), or so-called hard sciences like chemistry, biology, engineering and mathematics, which look at natural processes. It should be noted that there is no universal agreement as to which subjects belong under these umbrella terms. However, sociology, like many other subjects, shares commonalities with a variety of disciplines – we can see elements of many of those mentioned, and more, within sociological thinking and research – thus in many ways, it is interdisciplinary. Arguably, this is its strength, or superpower. Some have gone so far as to suggest that these disciplinary 'silos' are arbitrary and to the detriment of critical thinking. As you go through this book, you might consider which aspects of sociology are distinct from some of the other disciplines mentioned.

SOCIAL 'SCIENCE'?

The fact that subjects such as sociology associate themselves with science is in itself interesting and tells us something about how society values science, perhaps above other disciplines. This is something the French thinker Michel Foucault (1926–1984) was interested in. It begs the questions what do we mean by 'scientific', in what ways is sociology scientific and why are some so keen to align the discipline with science? As we shall see, some early sociological explorations of the 19th century were influenced by the natural sciences – 'rigorous', 'objective' ***methods*** were used to reveal social 'facts' or truths. This approach has been called ***positivism***. Positioning itself as a science perhaps gave credence to this new subject as it was establishing. Indeed, the word 'sociology' is a hybrid of the Latin *socius*, meaning 'companion', and the addition of *ology* meaning 'study of', from the Greek *logos* – 'knowledge'. Many summarize this to mean the systematic study of human societies but this, perhaps, doesn't do justice to the scale of sociology and its potential. Nevertheless, perhaps we *can* say that a sociological endeavour is one that is either concerned with generating and analyzing empirical data in order to understand a particular phenomenon and/or draws from theories in order to advance understanding.

A 'SOCIAL' SCIENCE?

The 'socio' of sociology, however, points to the ways in which the subject is concerned with social relations, structures, patterns and problems. An early statement in this chapter was that sociology might be thought of as the study of society. You are probably anticipating the next question – what do we mean by 'society'? (You're already beginning to think like a sociologist!) Margaret Thatcher (1925–2013), a UK Conservative prime minister, controversially stated in 1987 that there was 'no such thing as society', yet most sociologists would disagree. If we think of society as comprising a group of people who share a common culture and structured relations and ***institutions***, we can see that far from there being no society, we need to start thinking in the plural. Sociology is interested in the connection between individuals and the societ(ies) they live in, and the relationship between different societies. These relationships will be informed by rules, regulations, ***norms*** and values, and are in a constant state of flux – which is what makes sociology so interesting.

SOCIAL NORMS ▶ ***those rules that govern interactions. Generally, these are informal – such as covering our mouths when we cough – though sometimes they become more formalized. Covid-19, for instance, prompted some changes in rules of behaviour.***

Not all agree about the focus on society though: Norbert Elias (1897–1990) argued for a sociology that considered social processes and shifting relationships, beyond the level of society. John Urry (1946–2016) argued that ***globalization*** has meant that society and national identity is less meaningful now – instead we should think in terms of mobilities. These are debates to bear in mind as you read on; for instance, political rhetoric and media reports about asylum seekers and refugees might suggest that many are still very much invested in 'society' and 'national identity'. These debates also point to the fact that society changes, sometimes rapidly, and sociology is concerned with mapping these changes and responding to them.

THE EMERGENCE OF SOCIOLOGY

Standard explanations for the history of sociology are frequently presented in the following way. The 18th and 19th centuries saw a period of immense social change and upheaval prompted by three revolutions. The ***Industrial Revolution***, for instance, triggered changes in the way goods were produced and resulted in a move from largely rural, agrarian, ways of life, to urban working and dwelling. With it came changing economies and ***capitalism*** quickly established itself as the dominant form of transaction and living in many areas across the globe. The rapid economic transformation relied on the continuation of European empire-building, exploiting raw materials and labour through economic and political domination. A scientific, or intellectual, revolution, influenced by the ***Enlightenment*** – or Age of Reason as it's sometimes known – changed ways of thinking: many began to question the role of traditional authorities and previous explanations for the world that were based on religion and instead were drawn to the use of reason, logic and science as methods to explain the world.

This was a period that grappled with ideas about human rights and freedoms – concerns that are still with us today. Often looking back to the ancient Greeks, questions were asked about what it is to be human, what is society and how should it be ruled, and what is knowledge – conundrums sociology still wrestles with. At times, it was self-congratulatory, positing Europe as the epicentre of '***modernity***' and progress. It was propelled by radical thinkers like the English political theorist and philosopher John Locke (1632–1704), who developed the concept of the ***social contract*** – an agreement between a government and the majority of people to be ruled by consent. Another prominent thinker was the German philosopher Georg Hegel (1770–1831), a true 'child of the Enlightenment', influenced by figures such as Jean-Jacques Rousseau (1712–1778) in particular. Hegel contributed to the development of sociology when he began to analyze the role of social institutions, particularly religion and government, in bringing about social change. It should be noted that some academics – such as Theodor Adorno (1903–1969) and Max Horkheimer (1895–1973) – were critical of this rational, optimistic view of the world, arguing that it enabled surveillance society.

THE ENLIGHTENMENT ▶ ***an intellectual movement of 18th-century Europe that valued reason and observation over religious explanations for the world.***

The French Revolution (1789–1799), in part inspired by some of the ideas of the likes of Rousseau, saw the overthrow of the monarchy and generated radical ideas about the state, giving rise to new social orders, concepts and modes of thought – democracy, citizenship and equality. These dramatic changes provoked thinkers to seek new ways to understand the rapidly transforming social world.

FOUNDING FATHERS?

Among those thinkers inspired by, and concerned with, these events was Auguste Comte (1798–1857), who coined the term 'sociology' in 1838. Influenced by the emerging science disciplines, he thought it was possible to use a 'scientific' approach to study human society. Much like there were natural laws that governed life on earth, such as gravity, he thought sociology could reveal the laws of society, thus, he is often referred to as a positivist. Others included Herbert Spencer (1820–1903) and Ferdinand Tönnies (1855–1936).

But there are three scholars who are most often cited as being foundational for sociology. Perhaps the most famous of the early pioneers was the radical and prolific German thinker Karl Marx (1818–1883), who, often in collaboration with his friend Friedrich Engels (1820–1895), argued that history was propelled onwards by conflict between different ***social classes***. He witnessed, and was angered by, the exploitation, powerlessness and isolation that the new working classes experienced within the industrial system; he called this ***alienation***.

Émile Durkheim (1858–1917), a French sociologist, was motivated by a belief, like Marx, that modern society was damaging for many people but that the social bond was a stabilizing influence. In the 1890s Durkheim established an early

NAMES TO KNOW: KEY SOCIOLOGICAL THINKERS

Auguste Comte *(1798–1857)*

Karl Marx *(1818–1883)*

Émile Durkheim *(1858–1917)*

Max Weber *(1864–1920)*

Harriet Martineau *(1802–1876)*

W.E.B. Du Bois *(1868–1963)*

university course in sociology, effectively institutionalizing it, so that now it is taught in universities across the globe.

Another prominent early sociologist was the German scholar Max Weber (1864–1920). One of his most influential theories was based on his observations of the development of industrial capitalism. Such societies, he argued, inevitably saw a rise in ***bureaucracy*** and ***rationalization*** as a mode of thinking.

These thinkers are often described as the 'founding fathers' of sociology, a subject born out of social upheaval. Not all of them would have necessarily considered themselves to be sociologists, but they all asked the big questions that gave sociology its identity – though, as we shall see, they often provided different answers.

A LIMITED AND LIMITING EXPLANATION

However, the above narrative of sociology's emergence is as much disputable, or at least incomplete, as is the very definition of sociology. The account provided, for instance, focuses largely on the Global North and the scholars cited above tend to be white, middle-class men with beards. Yet that ignores a wealth of contributions from scholars across the globe. It also reflects the broader history of domination, ***colonialism*** and ***patriarchy***. We can see traces of what might be considered sociological thinking in the work of the Greek philosophers like Aristotle (384–322 BCE), the Chinese historian Ma Duanlin's (1245–1322) consideration of social dynamics and the work of Tunisian scholar Ibn Khaldun (1332–1406). We also frequently see a failure to recognize the contributions of academics such as Harriet Martineau (1802–76), W.E.B. Du Bois (1868–1963) and Marianne Weber (1870–1954).

Engels visited Manchester and wrote The Condition of the Working Class in England *(1845) after seeing the poverty there. Angel Meadow, in particular, he described as 'Hell on earth'. Millions of people who had converged on the great industrial cities lived in slum conditions like this.*

Where Du Bois is mentioned, it is frequently only in relation to his work on the role of slavery and ***racism*** in the shaping of ***modernity***. This was crucial work, yet it underplays his role in establishing an early and pioneering sociological research centre. Similarly, Martineau is often cited only with regard to feminism and scholarly work that focuses on the role of women; certainly, her work did look at this but arguably she also played a role in bringing Comte's ideas to the UK, through her translations. So good were they, he had them as his 'official' versions. She also preceded Durkheim in studying suicide, yet this is rarely mentioned. Marianne Weber is often only visible as Max Weber's wife, but she was an important sociologist in her own right, with her work continuing to influence many contemporary feminist sociologists. Thankfully, sociology has been able to turn its critical gaze inwards and increasingly, contributions from beyond the traditional 'canon' are recognized and valued.

A BLACK BELT IN SOCIOLOGY

Another way to understand what sociology is, is to consider what it can do, or its purpose. Marx wasn't just observing the world: he wanted to change it for the better. The French sociologist Pierre Bourdieu (1930–2002) argued that sociology is a martial art, whose role was to come to the aid of those less fortunate and to reveal domination, or ***inequality***, based on ***social class***, ***gender*** or ***ethnicity***, for instance. Zygmunt Bauman (1925–2017) agreed when he said sociology is there to help the individual; that, as sociologists, we must be in the service of freedom. To become justice warriors, Bourdieu states we have to 'reveal what is hidden'. The UK sociologist Laurie Taylor (1936) furthers this by stating that sociology 'disturbs conventional ways of thinking, breaks up solid categories and throws doubt on accepted truths'. These thinkers are pointing to a particular frame of analysis that requires thinking critically about taken-for-granted 'knowledge'. We can then ask questions such as is romantic love a 'natural' part of the human experience, and is capitalism inevitable or even desirable. This is often referred to as a ***sociological imagination***.

A sociological imagination helps us to understand human behaviour by linking social structures and processes to individual experiences.

DEVELOPING A SOCIOLOGICAL IMAGINATION

Employing our sociological imaginations is one of the most interesting and powerful ways that sociology can deepen our understanding of ourselves, the world around us and the ways in which ***social structures*** help to shape us. It's a mindset, one that uses ***theory*** and observation to reveal how things happening in our everyday lives are linked to the changing social structures and events in which we live. A sociological imagination asks us to think differently about what might seem obvious or familiar. We are encouraged to go beneath the surface to explore the social processes and structures that help to create, shape and maintain our social world. The concept was developed by a somewhat maverick US sociologist, Charles Wright Mills (1916–1962), and part of what he was requesting was an ability to link ***private troubles*** to ***public issues***. In other words, he was concerned to recognize the ways in which one person's misfortune, such as being homeless, was connected to a range of social structures and events shared by many others, such as an economic downturn or an increase in unemployment.

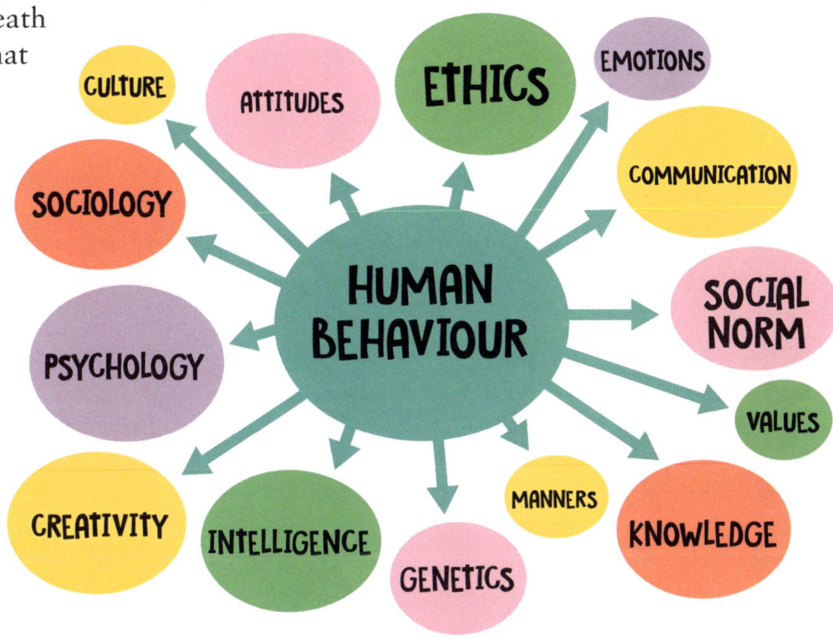

The sociological imagination encourages us to see the ways in which social inequalities such as those based on social class, gender and ethnicity are not inevitable or natural but instead products of the social world. It means we can say that human behaviour is not simply driven by biological impulse and we're not as individual

Charles Wright Mills saw the sociologist's tole as linking personal biography to social and historical events.

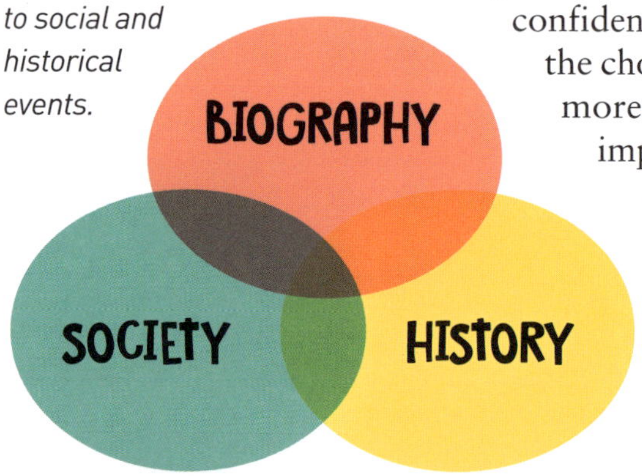

BIOGRAPHY

SOCIETY

HISTORY

as we might imagine (as the poet John Donne wrote, 'no man is an island'). Its task is to show us the various social forces that influence our lives. For instance, looking at statistics can reveal that being born in a lower socioeconomic class tends to lead to shorter life expectancy. Closer analysis begins to explain this by examining access to healthcare, quality of education provided and outcomes, confidence (or lack of) in navigating such systems, the impact of ***austerity*** measures, and the choices some might have to make between heating their homes and eating. An even more nuanced consideration will look at how ethnicity, age or (dis)ability further impacts life expectancy. This enables us to see the ways in which some groups have less ***power*** than others; they have fewer choices, or ***agency***, and more constraints than others.

Our agency, to some extent, is determined by social structures and ***institutions*** like legal, educational or healthcare systems. The power imbalances may change over time or differ from one nation to another, but sociology enables us to map the continuities and changes. Mills recognized that it's not always easy to do this – it is far easier to blame an individual than it is to look at structural causes. Indeed, perhaps we live in a society where the media, laws and governments might encourage us to blame individuals to avoid scrutiny themselves.

Francisco Goya's The Third of May 1808 *depicts a moment of conflict and reflects power dynamics – issues sociology is still concerned with.*

SOCIOLOGICAL WAYS OF KNOWING

Thus, sociology is more than just a descriptive endeavour. It's an analytical, often critical and sceptical approach to understanding social phenomena. Its use has been widely recognized – many sociological concepts have found their way into everyday language – '***moral panic***', 'gentrification' and '***social capital***'. A key insight from sociological thinking is that knowledge is

This diagram shows how sociology views individual behaviour as influenced by various social factors, e.g. family, education, media, economic systems and cultural norms.

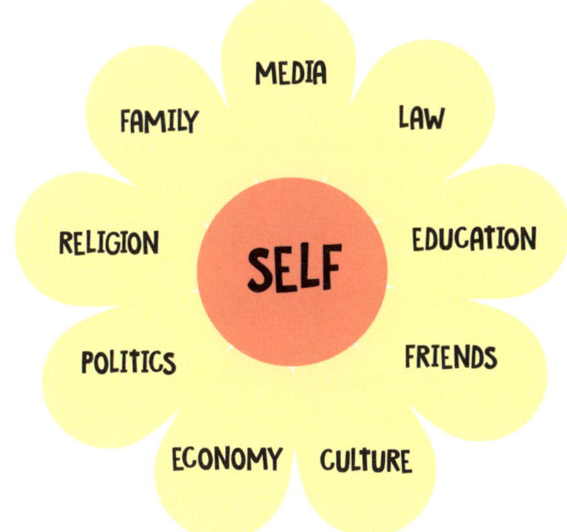

The painting American Gothic *by Grant Wood is a study of social norms, rural life, family structures, and the stock market crash.*

created in a social setting and as such, is always partial. Certain ways of thinking might become more valued than others at certain times, or in particular places. For example, we have already seen how the Enlightenment led to 'scientific' approaches being valorized, and that ideas from groups who are marginalized or 'othered' might be silenced or ignored. The recognition of the ***social construction*** of knowledge is referred to as social constructionism, another sociological perspective we will consider in the following chapters.

Sociologists strive not only to observe and document social realities but also to explain them, to uncover hidden patterns, and sometimes even offer a challenge to the status quo. In other words, perhaps as Kai Erikson (1931) suggests, what makes sociology distinct from other disciplines is not what is seen but the ways of seeing and knowing.

In the chapters that follow, you'll see that many of the ideas and themes that helped to shape sociology's origin are still relevant today; you might think others are less effective. Just as sociology emerged in response to new social phenomena, it continues to evolve in response to social shifts and changes. We'll delve deeper into the theories, methods and key areas of enquiry that make sociology such an exciting and vital field of study. Get ready to flex your sociological imagination ...

TIMELINE OF SOCIOLOGY'S DEVELOPMENT

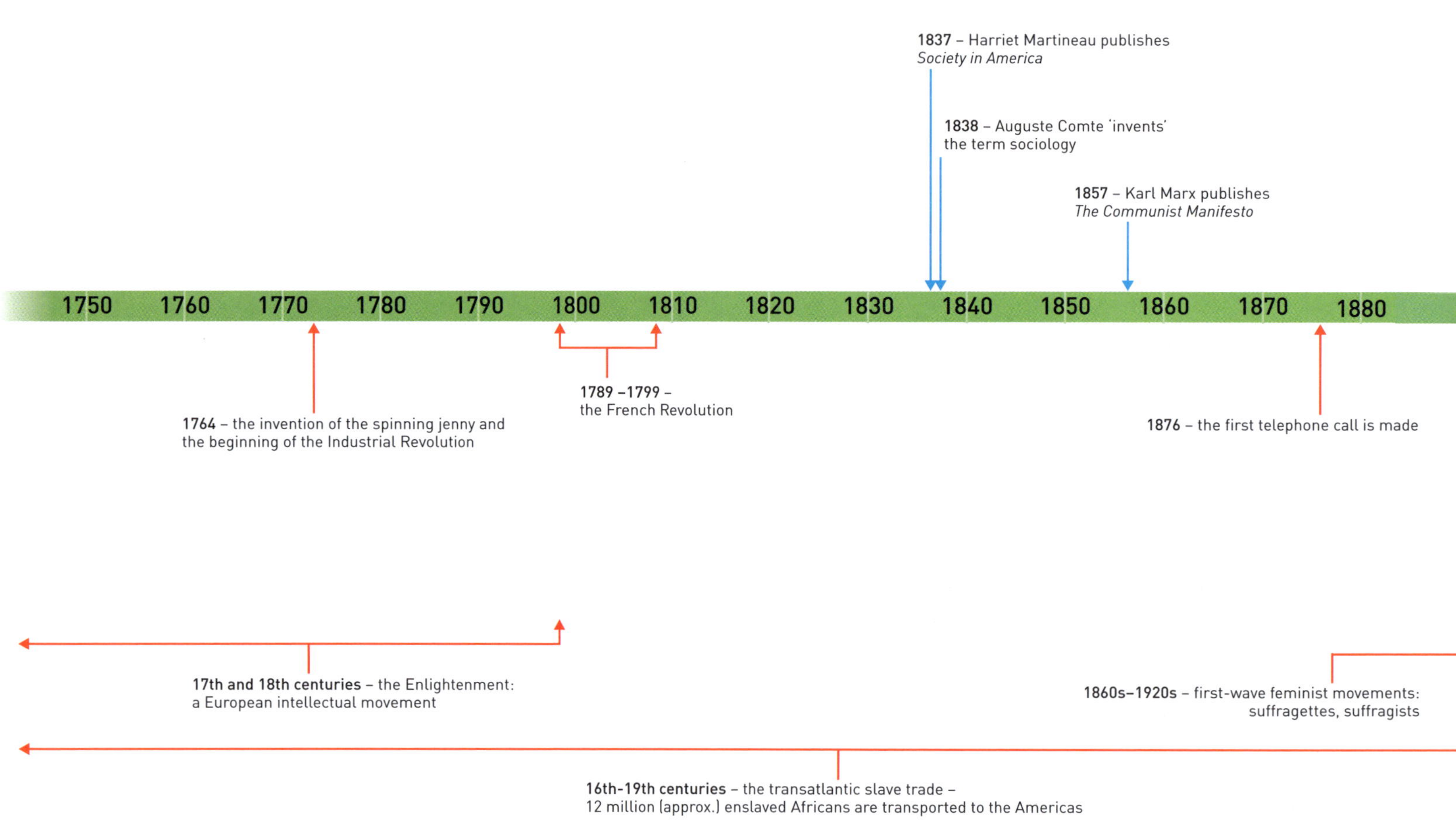

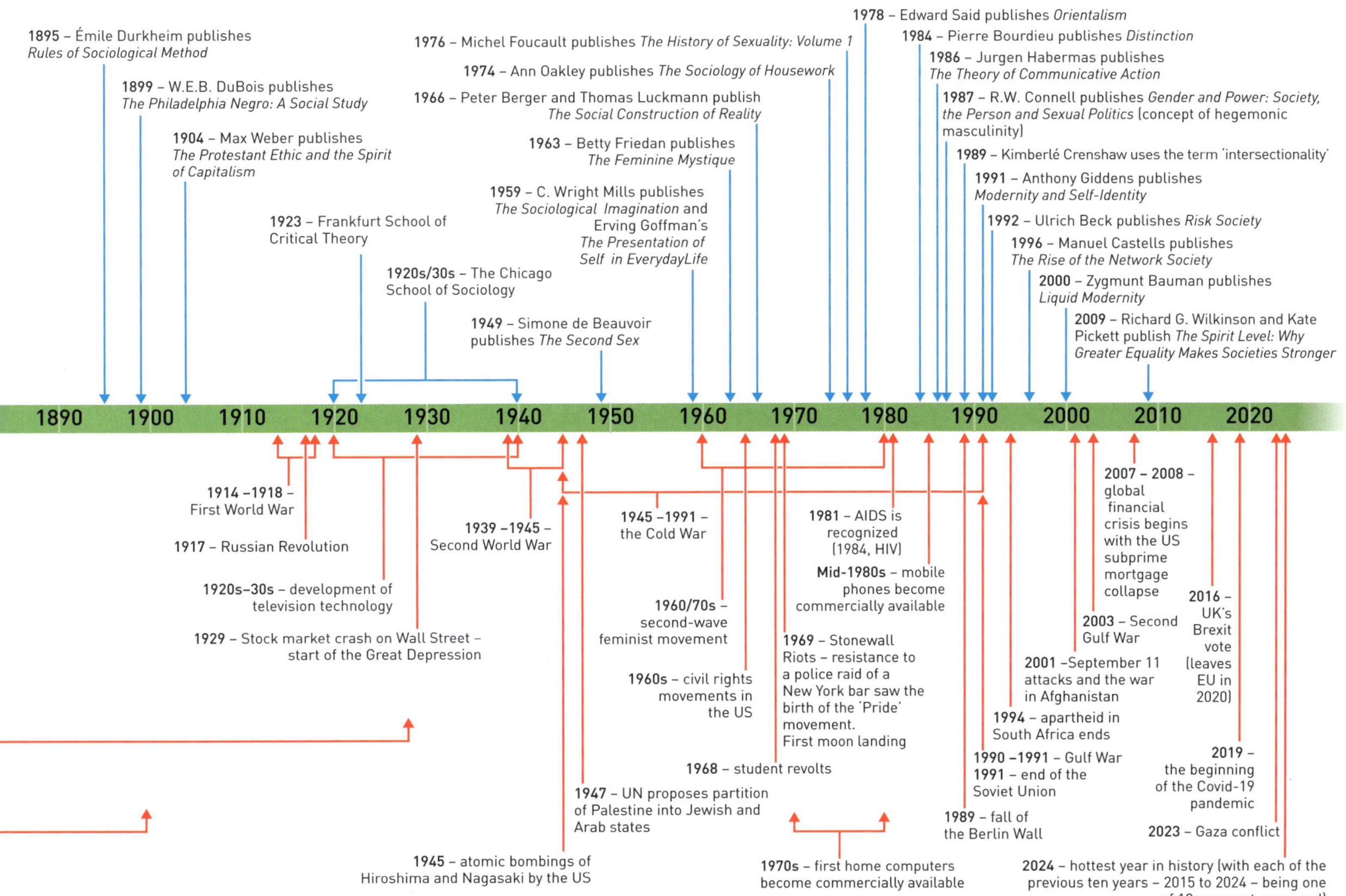
Sociology events
1895 – Émile Durkheim publishes *Rules of Sociological Method*
1899 – W.E.B. DuBois publishes *The Philadelphia Negro: A Social Study*
1904 – Max Weber publishes *The Protestant Ethic and the Spirit of Capitalism*
1923 – Frankfurt School of Critical Theory
1920s/30s – The Chicago School of Sociology
1949 – Simone de Beauvoir publishes *The Second Sex*
1959 – C. Wright Mills publishes *The Sociological Imagination* and Erving Goffman's *The Presentation of Self in EverydayLife*
1963 – Betty Friedan publishes *The Feminine Mystique*
1966 – Peter Berger and Thomas Luckmann publish *The Social Construction of Reality*
1974 – Ann Oakley publishes *The Sociology of Housework*
1976 – Michel Foucault publishes *The History of Sexuality: Volume 1*
1978 – Edward Said publishes *Orientalism*
1984 – Pierre Bourdieu publishes *Distinction*
1986 – Jurgen Habermas publishes *The Theory of Communicative Action*
1987 – R.W. Connell publishes *Gender and Power: Society, the Person and Sexual Politics* (concept of hegemonic masculinity)
1989 – Kimberlé Crenshaw uses the term 'intersectionality'
1991 – Anthony Giddens publishes *Modernity and Self-Identity*
1992 – Ulrich Beck publishes *Risk Society*
1996 – Manuel Castells publishes *The Rise of the Network Society*
2000 – Zygmunt Bauman publishes *Liquid Modernity*
2009 – Richard G. Wilkinson and Kate Pickett publish *The Spirit Level: Why Greater Equality Makes Societies Stronger*
1890
1900
1910
1920
1930
1940
1950
1960
1970
1980
1990
2000
2010
2020
1914 –1918 – First World War
1917 – Russian Revolution
1920s–30s – development of television technology
1929 – Stock market crash on Wall Street – start of the Great Depression
1939 –1945 – Second World War
1945 – atomic bombings of Hiroshima and Nagasaki by the US
1945 –1991 – the Cold War
1947 – UN proposes partition of Palestine into Jewish and Arab states
1960/70s – second-wave feminist movement
1960s – civil rights movements in the US
1968 – student revolts
1969 – Stonewall Riots – resistance to a police raid of a New York bar saw the birth of the 'Pride' movement. First moon landing
1970s – first home computers become commercially available
1981 – AIDS is recognized (1984, HIV)
Mid-1980s – mobile phones become commercially available
1989 – fall of the Berlin Wall
1990 –1991 – Gulf War
1991 – end of the Soviet Union
1994 – apartheid in South Africa ends
2001 –September 11 attacks and the war in Afghanistan
2003 – Second Gulf War
2007 – 2008 – global financial crisis begins with the US subprime mortgage collapse
2016 – UK's Brexit vote (leaves EU in 2020)
2019 – the beginning of the Covid-19 pandemic
2023 – Gaza conflict
2024 – hottest year in history (with each of the previous ten years – 2015 to 2024 – being one of 10 warmest on record)
Historical events

Chapter Two

SOCIOLOGICAL WAYS OF THINKING

Cracking the code – A tool not a fetish – Roots and branches – Beyond speculation – What are theories made of? – Concepts and statements – Variables and hypotheses– The 'big three' or 'the good ol' boys' – A matter of conflict – New warring classes – A functional society – Actions and interactions – The old in the new – The interrelation of structure and agency – Debates, disputes and new directions

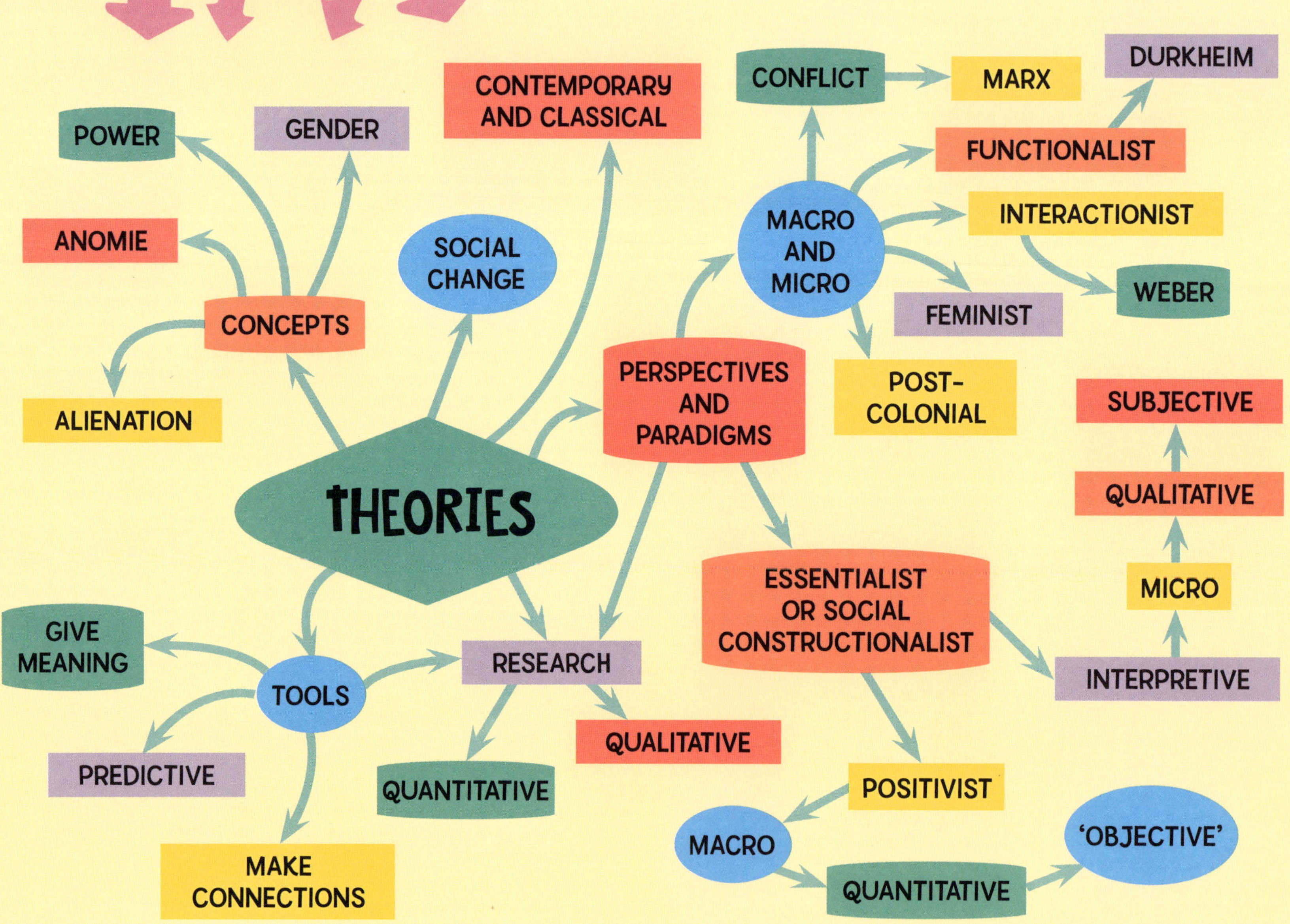

Sociological theory has a profound influence on the way we live: capitalism and democracy, for instance, are theoretical concepts. Sociologists are concerned with thinking critically about the things we often take for granted – things that are often themselves based on theories; theory is one of the ways in which sociologists attempt to make sense of the world.

CRACKING THE CODE

A common assumption about theory, usually held by those who perhaps haven't spent much time reading it, is that it is difficult, dusty and dry. Far from it! A good theory is a beautiful thing, one that might just shed light and meaning on to your own understanding of the world. It is a living, adaptable beast. Yes, occasionally scholars present their ideas in esoteric, abstract ways – but once you have that eureka moment and unearth their meaning, it makes the endeavour worthwhile. Think of them as codes to break. Once you have done, you can see parallels between different theories (even though many scholars might suggest their ideas are completely new) and can trace the history of ideas or 'archaeology of knowledge' as Michel Foucault (1969) puts it. It means that you can start to assess which schools of thought have relevance for a particular issue or moment in time.

Much as Sherlock Holmes used deductive reasoning to solve crimes, sociologists use theories to help solve or understand social conundrums.

A TOOL NOT A FETISH

A word of caution before we continue any further: a sociologist's goal is to understand the social world – theories are just one way in which that might be done. Most university courses will have modules devoted to theory, and separate ones concerned with methods. First, this distinction is one of convenience for teaching, but theories and methods often inform one another. Second, and more controversially, it might be said that a little too much emphasis is placed on the centrality of theories and methods to understanding social processes, to the extent that Ken Plummer (2010) has argued they are fetishized, when really, they are just tools. However, learning about how sociology understands itself, reading its own narrative, enables us to understand where it is now and perhaps gives us more insight into which bits are especially pertinent and useful.

ROOTS AND BRANCHES

Classical and contemprary theory

Theory within sociology is often divided into two distinct groups: classical and contemporary theory. Sometimes a third, 'modern', is slipped between the two. A common metaphor to distinguish them is a tree: the roots are classical theories, and contemporary theories form the branches. This being sociology, there is much (sometimes heated) debate about who falls into which camp and where the divide between the two falls. Classical is commonly understood to begin in the 1850s and runs until the 1920s or 1930s. Karl Marx, Max Weber and Émile Durkheim are the most oft-cited classicists but increasingly, others – such as Harriet Martineau, Georg Simmel (1858–1918), Herbert Spencer (1820–1903), Charlotte

Perkins Gilman (1860–1935) and W.E.B. Du Bois – are recognized in this group. All were responding to the rapidly changing times that gave rise to modernity.

Many of the issues they were concerned with continued to be a source of enquiry for later theorists. These contemporary thinkers (an odd word you might think, for ideas that are nearly a hundred years old), were charting and questioning social relations from the 1930s (or 1950s for some) onwards. Many see the crises of capitalism – such as the Wall Street Crash, the perceived failure and crisis of Marxism, together with the two world wars – as prompting a radical shift in thinking. But before we look at these in more detail, just what is social theory?

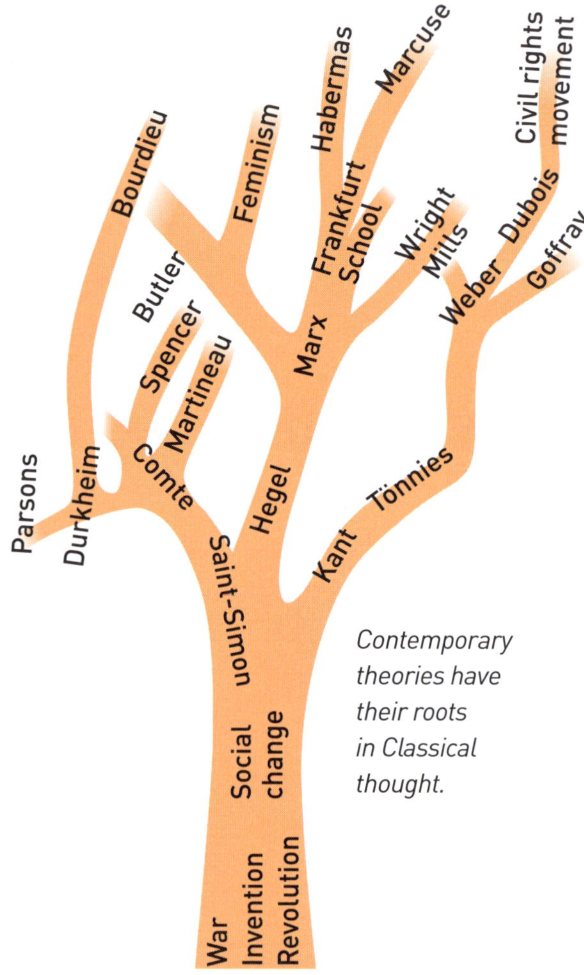

Contemporary theories have their roots in Classical thought.

BEYOND SPECULATION

Sociologists observe and ask questions of society, such as how and why so many people deny climate change is happening, despite ample and compelling evidence that it is. We might think, or speculate, that one explanation for this is fear. Theory goes beyond mere speculation, however. It might use previous theory (such as Stan Cohen's theory of ***denialism***) and build on it; it will look to evidence produced in research in order to connect events that might seem to be happening in isolation (as climate scientists did with floods, storms, wildfires, glacial melts etc.) and make connections between them. Once evidence is gathered, patterns may emerge and from this, theories might be used to predict future events or responses. Thus, theories are able to provide context for, and give meaning to, events. Part of the process of theory building is to assess how plausible it is as an explanation for the social world. In sum, theories:

- give meaning
- make connections
- are informed by previous theory and research
- are predictive
- are often a starting point for research

WHAT MAKES A GOOD THEORY?

We can start to put this all together by arguing that there are certain elements that are indicative of a good theory:

- Evidence
- Explanation
- Applicability
- Testability
- Predictability

WHAT ARE THEORIES MADE OF?

CONCEPTS AND STATEMENTS

As an intellectual endeavour that sets about developing ideas to explain social processes and interactions, a sociological theory may contain several elements. Yet again, there may be differences of opinion as to what these elements are! Several explanations agree that concepts are a key part, the building blocks, of many theories. To form a concept is to define something, thus 'gender' and 'ethnicity' are concepts, ones that different theorists might define slightly differently. '***Anomie***' is a concept from Durkheim's theory, while 'alienation' is a key concept within Marx's ***historical materialism*** theory; in addition, 'norm', 'power' and 'inequality' are other familiar sociological concepts. They enable others to 'see' what is being discussed and understand the ways in which it is being used.

These concepts within a theory are often linked to one other to form some sort of a statement or proposition. Many suggest that what makes a good theory is its ability to be proven wrong. Indeed, the philosopher Karl Popper (1902–1944) stated that 'every refutation should be regarded as a great success' – a statement that has been a source of comfort to many of us over the years! Thus, theoretical statements might be tested in some way, perhaps by using empirical evidence. For instance, Max Weber's (1905) proposition that Protestant ethics contributed to the development of capitalism in Western societies is one that can be challenged, or tested, in various ways.

VARIABLES AND HYPOTHESES

Related to this are the somewhat scientific terms ***variable*** and hypothesis. Variables can be understood as measurable aspects of concepts, which might vary in quantity or quality. For example, in studying social stratification, variables might include income, education level and occupational prestige (Blau and

UNDERSTANDING THE COMPONENTS OF THEORY

Durkheim's study of suicide (1897) is a useful way to see how the different components of theory work together.

The theory

- Social integration and regulation shape human behaviour, thus even seemingly personal acts like suicide are primarily influenced by social forces.

Key concepts

- **Social integration:** the strength of connections between individuals and social groups.
- **Social regulation:** how strongly societal rules shape individual behaviour.

Theoretical statements

- Different levels of social integration affect suicide rates.
- Societies vary in how strongly they regulate individual behaviour.

Variables

- **Independent variables:** social integration (measured by religion, marital status) and regulation (measured by economic stability).
- **Dependent variable:** suicide rates.

Hypotheses

- Protestant communities will have higher suicide rates than Catholic ones (less social integration).
- Married people will have lower suicide rates than single people (stronger social bonds).

How it all works together

Durkheim's theory about social forces led to specific concepts (integration, regulation), which he turned into measurable variables. He tested these through hypotheses, finding that suicide rates varied based on social factors. There have been many criticisms of the way he conducted his study and some of the conclusions he made. However, he did show that personal acts have social causes.

Hypothesis

Duncan, 1967). A hypothesis is a type of statement but is often one that tests the relationship between variables and might be more likely to be used to guide empirical research. For example, Robert Putnam's (2000) hypothesis that declining social capital leads to reduced civic engagement is testing the relationship between 'social capital' and 'civic engagement', both of which can be quantifiable.

THE 'BIG THREE' OR 'THE GOOD OL' BOYS'

Certain theories have proven to be particularly popular or longstanding. When scholars work with the same or similar premise, building on and developing previous theories, they become perspectives or ***paradigms***.

Classical theories are often divided into three broad approaches, frequently associated with the three founding fathers, or as Liz Stanley (2003) refers to them, 'the good ol' boys':

Marx, Durkheim and Weber

1. Conflict (Marx)
2. Functionalism (Durkheim)
3. Symbolic interactionism (Weber)

Women in early sociology

This grouping reflects power struggles more generally; the voices of the privileged get heard, even in subjects whose goal is social equity. A central concern of this early sociology was a focus on what we understand as the public domain – the economic and political structures of capitalism. This was a time of increasing separation of home and work; where previously men and women had worked alongside each other, women were being relegated to the so-called private sphere, in part because they were seen as a competition for jobs. Thus, theory focused, not necessarily consciously, on domains viewed as 'masculine' and academia itself was a male-dominated arena (women were not admitted into universities until the later 19th century). This narrow focus has been challenged now, and other classic theorists like Ida B. Wells (1862–1931) and Charlotte Perkins Gilman are recognized.

Yet sociology, as we understand it, is a subject developed on ideas emerging from the Global North, something that contemporary scholars are addressing. These theoretical perspectives are often described as being ***grand narratives***, which attempt to provide overarching explanations for the social world. They are also ***macro*** approaches, in that they look at large-scale social structures (though we see elements of the ***micro*** within Weber's work).

NAMES TO KNOW: KEY SOCIOLOGICAL THINKERS

Ida B. Wells *(1862–1931)*

Georg Simmel *(1858–1918)*

Herbert Spencer *(1820–1903)*

Charlotte Perkins Gilman *(1860–1935)*

A MATTER OF CONFLICT

Conflict theory is rooted in the work of Karl Marx, who was driven to chart the impact of the new capitalist economic system. He used French words for many of the concepts associated with his theories, probably because he lived in France for a number of years. He argued that (almost) all societies have been class societies, with a ruling class at the top, and then subordinate classes (whether serfs, peasants, slaves or workers). In *The Communist Manifesto* (1948), he and Engels wrote that 'the history of all hitherto existing society is the history of class struggles'. The term ***bourgeoisie***, for example, referred to the business owners, the class who invested money into privately owned factories; also known as the ruling class. This new ruling class needed workers who could sell their labour in the newly developed urban areas.

Bourgeoisie

NEW WARRING CLASSES

Where previously there had been a feudal system – lords ruled areas of land and the people who lived on it were forced to work it – the bourgeoisie were powerful enough to change the system. The peasants, or serfs, of the old system became the new class of the ***proletariat***, or the working class. These two classes, according to Marx, needed one another but were always in conflict. His main philosophical position was called historical materialism, which argued that it is the mode of production at any time that determines the economic, social and political institutions of any given society: the social and economic base influencing social superstructure activities and ideas. For Marx, the economic structure shapes other social institutions, including forming and moulding consciousness and knowledge formed by material conditions. Marx argued that this new system meant the people had very little control over their own lives. This leads to alienation. Workers undertake repetitive tasks, often making products they cannot afford to buy; they become mere cogs in the wheel. Capitalism also inevitably drives competition and pushes down wages; having to compete with one another for jobs is another form of alienation.

Proletariat

Factory work, often repetitive, with low wages, became the 'bread and butter' for the new working classes. Factory owners made profit from the labour of the workers.

'THE RULING IDEAS OF EACH AGE HAVE EVER BEEN THE IDEAS OF ITS RULING CLASS'

The ruling class are able to construct a world through ***ideology***, a way of thinking that reflects their views and also disguises the facts, which means that the workers live under a ***false consciousness***, unable to clearly see the inequality of the system they live in. He predicted that capitalism contained the seeds of its own destruction, however. The consequences of the pursuit of capital would lead to economic crises that in turn would create a ***class consciousness*** once the proletariat realized that the system was exploiting them; then comes the revolution.

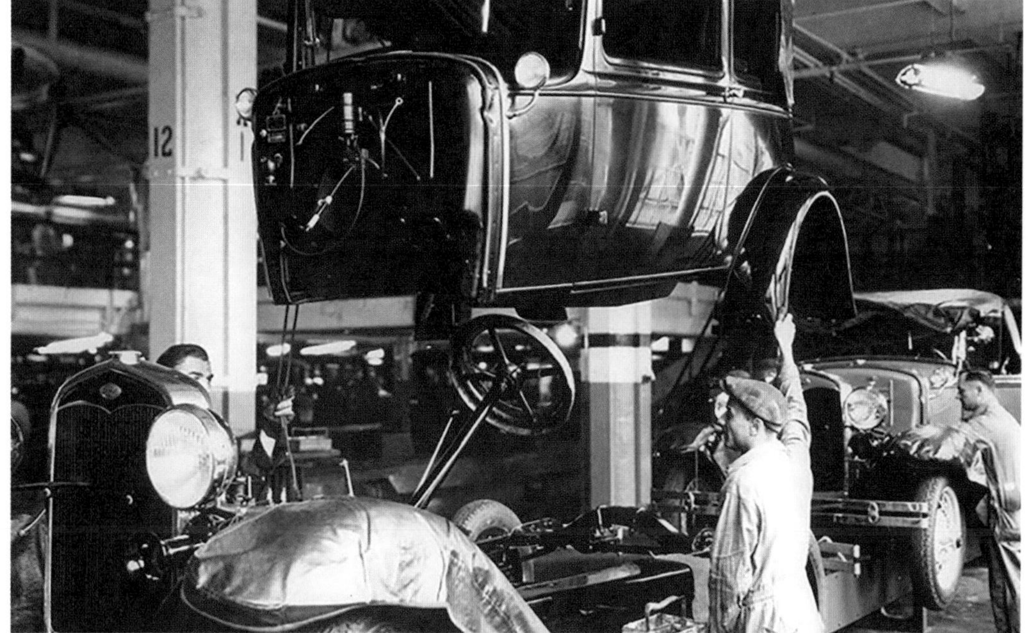

A FUNCTIONAL SOCIETY

Durkheim recognized what Marx was talking about in terms of the inequalities of capitalism but he was more optimistic: he thought the sophisticated ***division of labour*** would lead to more equal opportunities in society. He saw the shift to modern society as one from mechanical solidarity to what he called organic solidarity. Within smaller, more 'traditional' societies, mechanical solidarity is held together through a sense of shared beliefs and morality. The new industrial societies, for Durkheim, had a solidarity based on social relationships; increasing specialization unites members. Solidarity becomes a form of functional interdependence, rather than a moral consensus. He was interested in the role of social norms in keeping society functioning. These are things that exist for Durkheim as part of wider society; we perform our roles and obligations without really thinking about them. Even crime, an act of deviancy according to Durkheim, has a role to play in maintaining social order because it confirms norms of morality for wider society. When society becomes unstable, its norms and values weaken and under this condition, people may feel worthless, depressed – he called this anomie – and things like crime and suicide might increase. His study of suicide is famous, arguing that there were noticeable differences in rates between countries, which he put down to different religious norms and values, with for example Catholic countries having less suicide because it was seen as a sin.

ACTIONS AND INTERACTIONS

Like Marx, Weber looked at power and the centrality that capitalism had in the emerging new society. But he wasn't convinced that revolution was going to happen any time soon. He argued that religious values, in particular the work ethic of Protestantism, helped capitalism to emerge. Values such as self-denial, hard work and viewing excess spending as immoral were central to the religious traditions of Calvinist Protestantism. This ascetic Protestant lifestyle of discipline and frugality was also reflected in control over the body, such as not overeating or controlling ***sexuality***. In other words, the everyday actions of people become solidified into social structures (for instance marriage, saving and investing) and the ***Protestant work ethic*** becomes a central principle of everyday life in capitalist countries, whether or not you happen to be Protestant. Part of the spirit of the Protestant

Riots, for Durkhem, are a sign that social values have become weak and people experience anomie.

work ethic is an increased ***rationality***, such as a 'rational' use of time. As societies shift to becoming organized under industrial capitalism, they can experience ***disenchantment***, or an erosion of mystery and spontaneity. With rationality and efficiency as the central agenda comes increased bureaucracy, often suffocatingly dehumanizing, thus we become trapped in its iron cage.

These scholars were prolific writers, so these are only partial accounts of some of their key ideas. As ever, many sociologists would query the labels given to the schools of thought that developed from their ideas. All three thinkers worked beyond a narrow theoretical framework and these labels are perhaps too simple to explain their work fully. While it would be difficult to say there is a unifying aspect that unites them all, we can say they were making connections between aspects of society that might not, at first glance, seem obvious. We can also see these early thinkers as the roots of more contemporary sociological thinking.

Weber saw the bureaucracy of modernity creating a metaphorical cage which traps us, like animals in zoos.

THE OLD IN THE NEW: CONTEMPORARY THINKING

THE MACRO

By the 1920s and 1930s, theory, directly or indirectly influenced by the classicists, expanded into multiple paradigms in response to changing social worlds. Many of these continued the macro approach, being concerned with large social institutions and organizations. Antonio Gramsci (1891–1937) responded to creeping fascism in Europe, the failure of the Russian Revolution to spread and 'success' of capitalism, by revisiting Marx and adapting his ideas for the society he witnessed. He is particularly associated with the concept of ***hegemony***, to describe the ways in which, through cultural institutions, people are ruled by consent. Dominant ideologies, those of the ruling classes, appear natural, inevitable and beneficial, thus we can see parallels with Marx but Gramsci emphasizes the role of culture as much as economics.

Hegemony

The structural functionalist Talcott Parsons (1902–1979), another macro theorist, was grounded in Durkheim, Spencer, Freud and Weber (and largely ignored Marx). He received a plethora of critiques, especially from the Marxist viewpoint, in particular, from what become known as the ***Frankfurt School***, associated with the critical theory of Max Horkheimer, Theodor Adorno (1903–1969), Herbert Marcuse (1898–1979) and Jürgen Habermas (1929). Parsons also received a lot of attention from feminists, who challenged his work on the nuclear family and its role in socializing us into gender and class roles.

Frankfurt School

THE MICRO

Functionalism

Chicago School

Concurrently, there were also significant developments in theorizing from a micro perspective (looking at the interactions between individuals). The work of symbolic interactionists, partly in response to the limitations of ***functionalism***, focused on the interpretive work of the self. In social interaction, according to this approach, the self is not given but emerges out of social interaction. This perspective builds on the work of Weber and George Herbert Mead (1863–1931), though was coined as a phrase by Herbert Blumer (1900–1987). Much came from the pioneering 'Chicago School' of sociology (Robert Park and Howard Becker were part of this), blending the work of Ferdinand Tönnies, Durkheim and Simmel, to develop theories of the city. It also includes the theory of dramaturgy by Erving Goffman (1922–1982), which emphasizes how much of social life is a performance.

THE INTERRELATION OF STRUCTURE AND AGENCY

Poststructuralism, postmodernity and cosmopolitanism

Many theories or approaches span these macro/micro levels, for example theories of ***poststructuralism*** (Judith Butler, Michel Foucault, Jacques Derrida), ***postmodernity*** (Zygmunt Bauman, Luce Irigaray, Jean-François Lyotard) and ***cosmopolitanism*** (Ulrich Beck, Jürgen Habermas, Anthony Appiah). A key feature of contemporary society has been the inclusion of those on the margins, though arguably they are still more marginal than others. Post-colonial (Gurminder Bhambra, Edward Said, Gayatri Spivak),

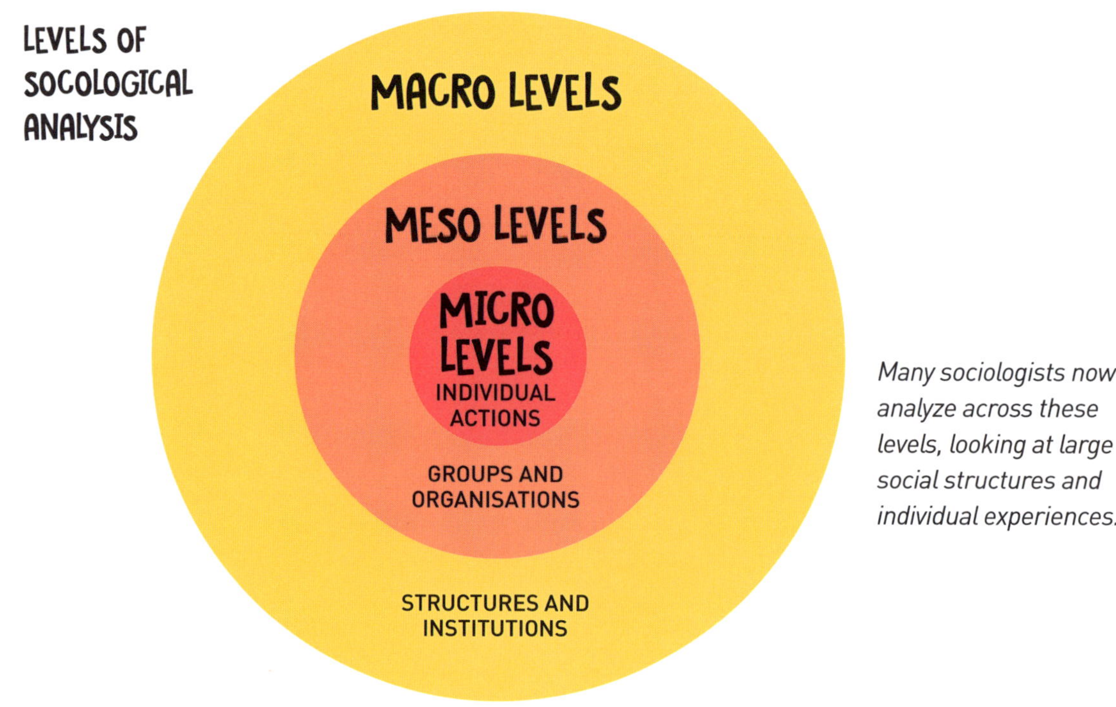

Many sociologists now analyze across these levels, looking at large social structures and individual experiences.

feminist (Sylvia Walby, Anne Oakley, Iris Marion Young), queer (Steven Seidman, Judith Butler, Eve Kosofsky-Sedgwick) and intersectional perspectives (Kimberlé Crenshaw, Audre Lorde, Patricia Hill Collins) have had a strong impact on how sociology is 'done'. Integrative thinkers such as Anthony Giddens, Manuel Castells and Pierre Bourdieu work across divides, looking at, among other things, the incursion of media into society and the effects and drivers of globalization. Giddens' structuration theory consciously seeks to work across the structure/agency, or macro/micro, divide.

Structuration theory

DEBATES, DISPUTES AND NEW DIRECTIONS

Whereas early sociological work looked primarily at social class, key social institutions in society such as religion, and also the economy, as the 20th century developed, we have seen that approaches evolved and scholarship broadened, to include such things as a focus on gender, ethnicity and global perspectives. It's important to note, however, that many of those foundational theorists who are less often referenced were already looking at gender or ethnicity; these aren't solely concerns of the later 20th century and 21st century. Feminist thinking – perhaps most commonly associated with work from the 1970s onwards, particularly in the UK and US – can be seen in the work of Mary Wollstonecraft (1759–1797), or even earlier with thinkers such as Christine de Pizan (1364–1431). The ideas themselves are not necessarily new but the collection of ideas develop to form new perspectives, or a movement of thought.

Feminist theory

We will explore many of these, and more, in detail as we move though the book. The focus on classical theory here will enable you to see the continuities and changes in theory, as you explore how it has been applied to a range of issues. While some have seen the broadening of sociology, and the debates within, as indicative of a fragmenting discipline, the truth, it could be argued, is the opposite. Theory is not static but responds to change; critique and disciplinary ***reflexivity*** are necessary to keep sociology vital and healthy. The arrival of the repressed – via feminist, Black, queer theories – might be perceived as threatening the traditional territory of the 'stale, male and pale' academic, which perhaps explains fears from more traditional corners that the subject is in crisis (see Joseph Lopreato and Timothy Crippen, 2017). Liz Stanley (2005) argued that the 'character of sociology as a discipline is "by art" if not "by nature", plastic and subject to continual intellectual change' – this is what makes sociology exciting and fresh. Sociology has tasked itself with the need to foster a more inclusive social theory, to broaden the restricted perspectives of predominantly white, male, liberal intelligentsia of the Global North. In doing so, it can be concerned with not just how we live but how we *should* live, what Giddens (1987) calls the 'project of modernity'.

Reflexivity

Sociological theory provides the tools for understanding the complexities of social life. As C. Wright Mills (1959) emphasized, the sociological imagination allows us to connect personal troubles with public issues. By engaging with these theories, you'll develop critical thinking skills essential for analyzing social phenomena. Your challenge, as a budding sociologist, is not just to learn these theories but to critically engage with them, apply them to contemporary issues, and potentially contribute to their evolution.

Chapter Three

DOING SOCIOLOGY

Philosophical foundations of research – Epistemology – Ontology – How to ask a question – Inductive and deductive methods – The quantitative-qualitative debate – The rise of mixed methods – Sampling – Primary or secondary – Analyzing data – Research ethics – Feminist theory and research practices

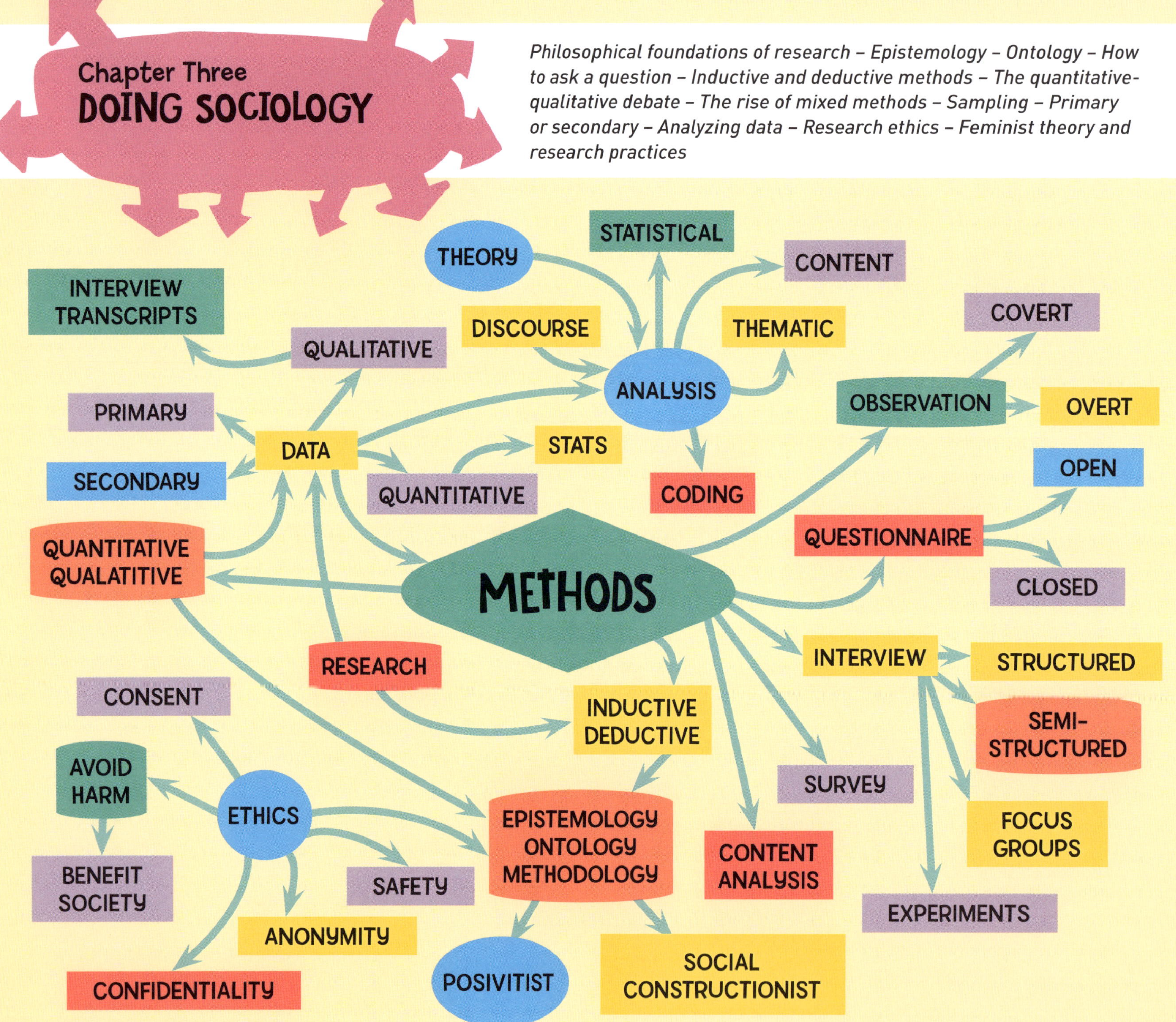

For many, sociology is an empirical subject – one which explores and understands the world by generating, and analyzing, new data. As the discipline has evolved, so too have the methods by which the social world is observed and research conducted. Howard Becker (1998) called these 'the tricks of the trade'. Indeed, sociologists are often thought of as people who conduct interviews, design questionnaires, and study groups. In fact, lots of subjects do this; what makes sociology distinctive is the particular critical approach taken. Research methods is a huge area – this chapter is not going to be a 'how-to' guide, which takes you through the minutiae, or tells you which methods to use to answer specific questions. Instead, it will start to explain the complexities, ideas and decisions involved in designing research. Thus, it is as much about ***methodology*** – the principles guiding the choice of tools (or methods) – as it is about methods. It's also important to note that the research process is an iterative one, in other words it's cyclical rather than linear – unlike a book chapter. Each aspect informs the other elements of research – the analysis of data will be thought about at an early stage, for instance.

There are many stages to research, they inform each other and mean that good research is reflexive.

PHILOSOPHICAL FOUNDATIONS OF RESEARCH: THE 'OLOGIES'

Questions about what is knowable about the social world are interwoven with questions of methodology (the theory of methods). Research emerges as part of the knowledge-making process. Before delving into specific research methods, it's useful to understand the philosophical underpinnings that frequently guide sociological enquiry. Two key concepts in this regard are ***epistemology*** and ***ontology***.

EPISTEMOLOGY IN SOCIOLOGICAL RESEARCH

Epistemology, or the theory of knowledge, is concerned with the nature of knowledge and how we can acquire it. In the context of sociological research, epistemology addresses questions such as: How can we know about social reality? What counts as valid knowledge in sociology?

Different epistemological positions lead to different approaches to research:

1. **Positivism:** This approach, associated with Auguste Comte, argues that social phenomena can be studied objectively, as with natural phenomena. Positivists believe in the existence of universal laws governing social behaviour that can be discovered through empirical observation and measurement. For example, Durkheim's (1897) study of suicide rates across different social groups exemplifies a positivist approach, seeking to identify social laws that explain variations in suicide rates.

NAMES TO KNOW

Karl Popper *(1902–1994)*

Barney Glaser *(1930–2022)*

Anselm Strauss *(1916–1996)*

Liz Stanley *(1978–)*

Ann Oakley *(1944–)*

Ken Plummer *(1946–2022)*

2. Interpretivism: This perspective, influenced by Max Weber, emphasizes understanding the subjective meanings that people attribute to their actions and social world. Interpretivists argue that social reality is constructed through human interaction and cannot be studied purely objectively. Clifford Geertz's (1973) '***thick description***' approach to studying Balinese cockfights illustrates an interpretivist stance, focusing on the cultural meanings and symbolism of social practices.

3. Critical theory: This approach, associated with the Frankfurt School, argues that research should not only seek to understand society but also critique and change it. Critical theorists highlight the role of power relations in shaping social reality. Feminist ***standpoint theory***, as developed by scholars like Dorothy Smith (1987), exemplifies a critical approach, arguing that knowledge is always situated and that research should start from the perspectives of marginalized groups.

KEY EPISTEMOLOGICAL QUESTIONS IN SOCIOLOGY

- What can we know about social reality?
- How can we acquire valid sociological knowledge?
- What is the relationship between the researcher and the researched?

How we come to know what we know is a profound sociological question.

ONTOLOGY IN SOCIOLOGICAL RESEARCH

Ontology, the study of 'being', deals with the nature of reality and what exists. In sociology, ontological questions concern the nature of social reality: is there an objective social world that exists independently of our perceptions, or is social reality constructed through human interaction and interpretation?

Two main ontological positions in sociology are:

1. Realism: This view holds that social structures and phenomena have an existence independent of our awareness or understanding of them. Realists argue that these structures can be studied objectively. Some argue that Marxist theory adopts a realist ontology, viewing social class structures as objective realities that shape individual experiences and social outcomes.

2. Constructionism: This perspective argues that social reality is continuously constructed and reconstructed through human interaction and interpretation. Social constructionists (sometimes referred to as constructivists) stress the role of language, culture and social processes in shaping our understanding of reality. Berger and Luckmann's *The Social Construction of Reality* (Anchor Books, 1966) exemplifies this approach, exploring how social institutions and knowledge are created, maintained and transmitted through social interactions.

Understanding these philosophical foundations is crucial for researchers, as they inform the choice of research questions, methods and interpretations of findings. There is an interesting debate to be had about whether 'social facts' exist in the same way as 'facts' in the natural world. Different epistemological and ontological positions often align with particular research methods, although the relationship is not always straightforward.

HOW TO ASK A QUESTION?

A central aspect of sociological research is the question. This is the element that drives, and even decides, how the research is going be shaped. Most often these are questions related to a problem or social issue that needs to be solved or improved – in other words, is the topic relevant? The question needs to be 'doable' too; this might be in terms of whether it is answerable and data can be collected, or the researcher can feasibly do this under time and budget constraints. It also helps if the topic is of interest to the researcher. Ideally, the research will be addressing a gap in knowledge, rather than redoing something that has been done before. Thus, a literature review is often conducted early on, to assess the field of knowledge. The size of gap will determine the focus of the question – if a lot is known relatively, the question can afford to be very focused and narrow; if less is known, the question is likely to be broader. It will also inform the type of question being asked.

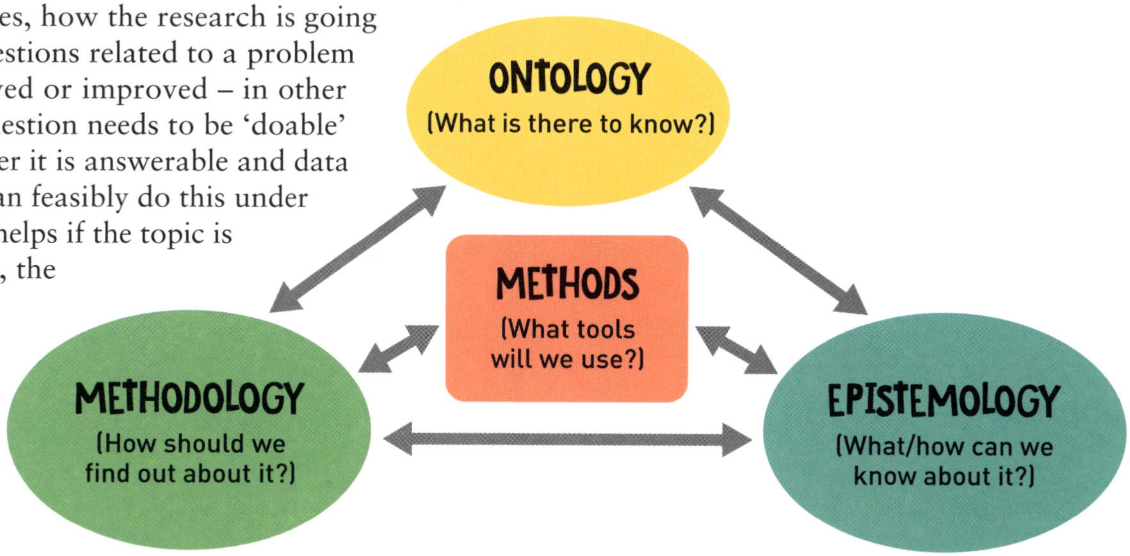

Ontology, epistemology and methodology together help to frame your reserach and help decide on your methods.

BOTTOM(S) UP?: INDUCTIVE AND DEDUCTIVE METHODS

Connected to the philosophical approach to sociology, research can be inductive or deductive. These are often posed as being opposites, but they can complement one another, and some studies combine both. Deductive research begins with a theory, or hypothesis, which the researcher then tests by gathering and analyzing data – the ideas in it are measurable. Thus, the theory drives the collection of data, which is often numerical or statistical. Inductive research might begin with the data, or a very broad research question, which is then analyzed and a theory, or theories, to explain the data may result from that. This sort of research tends to be more open-ended and will often use data that relates to experiences or observations. Arguably, of course, even a very inductive piece of research probably begins with at least a vague assumption or hypothesis and knowledge of existing theory and research. Grounded theory, associated with Barney Glaser and Anselm Strauss (1967), is an example of a 'very' inductive approach. These differences might align to a positivist approach (deductive) or a social constructionist perspective (inductive). Indeed, Karl Popper (1959) argued that most sociological research wasn't 'scientific' because it tended to be inductive in nature. Both approaches have their uses and perhaps have more similarities than is often acknowledged. Deductive research and reasoning works well when we already know quite a bit about an issue; inductive research is great when relatively little is known.

U.S SOCIAL MEDIA RETAIL SPENDING
(IN BILLIONS)

2021	2022	2023	2024*	2025*	2026*	2027*	2028*	2029*	2030*
$33.7	$54.7	$75.6	$90.6	$105.6	$117.5	$129.5	$141.4	$151.4	$167.5

*projection

Logitudinal studies, such as this on spending habits, let us see changes over time.

TIMING IS EVERYTHING...

The question will also prompt the researcher to consider the length of time needed to answer it. A longitudinal study is one that might gather information from a population at various points over a set time frame, such as two periods in a year – or over several decades, such as the Grant Study, which began in 1938 and is following Harvard-educated men to assess what makes for happy and healthy ageing. If information is only needed from one moment, then a cross-sectional study would be conducted. A comparative study might be useful to trace similarities or differences in social processes between historical periods or different countries.

The Census at Bethlehem *by Pieter Bruegel the Elder (1566) depicts large-scale data collection.*

THE QUANTITATIVE-QUALITATIVE DEBATE

Traditionally, sociological research methods have often been categorized into two main camps: quantitative and qualitative. The main difference is the kinds of data they analyze but the division has sometimes been characterized as a paradigm war, with proponents of each approach arguing for the superiority of their methods.

QUANTITATIVE METHODS

One way of understanding quantitative methods is their focus on collecting and analyzing data that can be converted to numbers. They are particularly useful for identifying patterns in social life, testing hypotheses and making generalizations about large populations.

Surveys

Surveys are one of the most common quantitative methods used in sociology. They involve collecting data from a large number of respondents through standardized questionnaires.

For instance, the General Social Survey (GSS) is a long-running survey conducted in the United States since 1972. It collects data on a wide range of social issues, including attitudes towards work, family and politics (Smith *et al.*, 2018).

EXPERIMENTS

Experiments involve manipulating one or more variables to observe their effect on a dependent variable. While less common in sociology than in other sciences, experiments can be valuable for establishing causal relationships. In order to conduct an experiment, sociologists will often create an artificial environment. There are many classic examples that come from social psychology – the Stanford prison experiment (1971) and Stanley Milgram's (1963) 'obedience to authority' experiment – included here because they are about how we conform to social roles. Another example is David Rosenhan's (1973) 'On Being Sane in Insane Places' study, where healthy participants pretended to have auditory hallucinations to gain admission to psychiatric hospitals. Devah Pager's (2003) field experiment on racial discrimination in the labour market, where she sent matched pairs of applicants with identical résumés but different ethnicities to apply for real job openings, revealed significant discrimination against Black applicants.

Experiments using data such as CVs, have revealed bias, for instance institutional racism and sexism.

QUALITATIVE METHODS

Qualitative methods focus on collecting and analyzing non-numerical data, such as words, images, experience or behaviours. They are particularly useful for exploring complex social phenomena in depth and understanding subjective experiences, helping researchers to get close to the meanings that people form and that inform their actions. They tend to involve a smaller number of participants and can be especially valuable for learning about something that hasn't been studied much before. There are multiple ways this is done – too many to mention here – though various examples will be explored later in the book. For now, we will look at a few of the more popular examples.

KEY ELEMENTS OF EXPERIMENTAL DESIGN

- Independent variable(s)
- Dependent variable(s)
- Control group
- Random assignment

In-depth interviews

In-depth interviews are often considered the 'gold standard' in sociological research and might be one of the most popular forms of research, though researchers are now embracing more varied forms of exploration. They typically involve conducting detailed, open-ended conversations with participants to explore their experiences, perspectives and meanings. Interviews formed a significant aspect of Allison Gayapersad *et al.*'s (2003) study of stigma and discrimination against street

QUANTITATIVE AND QUALITIVE RESEARCH

In part, the perceived conceptual differences are rooted in the different philosophical and methodological assumptions introduced above, and are frequently presented thus:

Quantitative research

- Often associated with positivist epistemology
- Focuses on measurement, causality, generalization and replication
- Emphasizes standardized data collection and statistical analysis
- Aims for objectivity and value-neutrality

Qualitative research

- Often aligned with interpretivist or constructionist approaches
- Focuses on meaning, context and process
- Emphasizes rich, detailed data and interpretive analysis
- Acknowledges the role of subjectivity and values in research

While this divide has been influential, many scholars argue that it oversimplifies the complexity of social research and can be limiting.

children in western Kenya. Arlie Hochschild's (1989) study 'The Second Shift' used in-depth interviews to explore the division of household labour in dual-earner, heterosexual couples. Strengths of this approach are that researchers can be flexible, in order to respond to participants.

Focus groups

Focus groups involve facilitating discussions among small groups of participants to explore their collective views on a particular topic. The researcher tends to take more of a back seat, to allow the group's opinions to flow. Alice Yick and Rashmi Gupta (2002) used this method to explore the attitudes and practices around death and bereavement of Chinese immigrants. Focus groups were also used by Amy Slater and Marika Tiggemann (2010) in their study 'Uncool to Do Sport', to understand why some teenage girls were not engaging in physical activity. A bonus of this type of research is you get to observe participants interacting with one another, and potentially to observe body language. They also gauge the opinion of several people at the same time, thus possibly saving time that might be spent conducting several one-to-one interviews. They do require careful planning and moderation, as there is the risk that conversation might be dominated by one or two people, effectively silencing the others. Like interviews, they can yield very rich, detailed data but this can take a long time to transcribe (if recorded) and it might be tricky to discern the different voices – this is where note-taking comes to the fore.

Ethnography

Ethnography, also referred to as participant observation or field research, involves immersing oneself in a particular social setting to observe and, sometimes, participate in the daily lives of the people being studied. It varies a great deal, not just in terms of the extent to which researchers observe and participate, but also whether participants are aware they are being observed, which, as we discuss later, has many ethical implications. This sort of research is great for answering 'how' questions – how events unfold, how people spend their time, and so on. In Alice Goffman's *On the Run* (2014) ethnography, she spent six years living in a disadvantaged neighbourhood in Philadelphia to study the impact of mass incarceration and policing on the daily lives of residents. Hochschild's study supplemented the interviews mentioned above, with observation of some of the couples in their homes. She found that the division of labour wasn't as equitable as many had professed – you can probably guess who ended up doing the lion's share!

The Potato Eaters *by Vincent van Gogh (1885) reflects van Gogh's direct observation of peasant families – a form of ethnography.*

MIXING IT UP: THE RISE OF MIXED METHODS

Mixed methods research

In recent decades, there has been growing recognition of the value of combining quantitative and qualitative approaches, leading to the development of mixed methods research. This approach is based on the premise that combining these methods can provide a more comprehensive understanding of social phenomena than either approach alone. It also recognizes that there are overlaps in principles, procedures and methods.

Ethnography

Advantages of mixed methods:

- **Complementarity**: different methods can address different aspects of a research question, providing a more complete picture.
- **Triangulation**: using multiple methods can enhance the ***validity*** and ***reliability*** of findings.
- **Development**: results from one method can inform the design or implementation of another.
- **Expansion**: different methods can extend the breadth and range of inquiry.

For instance, a study on the impact of social media on political engagement might use surveys to measure overall trends (quantitative), followed by in-depth interviews to explore the meanings behind these trends (qualitative) and social network analysis to map patterns of political communication (mixed).

Despite the growing popularity of mixed methods, some researchers still insist on the primacy of either quantitative or qualitative approaches. Critics of mixed methods argue that:

- the philosophical assumptions underlying quantitative and qualitative research are incompatible
- researchers may lack the skills to competently implement both approaches
- mixed methods projects can be more time-consuming and resource-intensive (a particular issue if funding is scarce)

Choice of method

However, proponents argue that these challenges can be overcome and that the benefits of mixed methods often outweigh the drawbacks. Arguably, the choice of method should be driven by the research question rather than allegiance to a particular methodological camp.

As the field of sociology continues to evolve, it's likely that we'll see further integration of quantitative and qualitative approaches, as well as the development of new methodologies that transcend this traditional divide.

Qualitative / mixed / quantitative

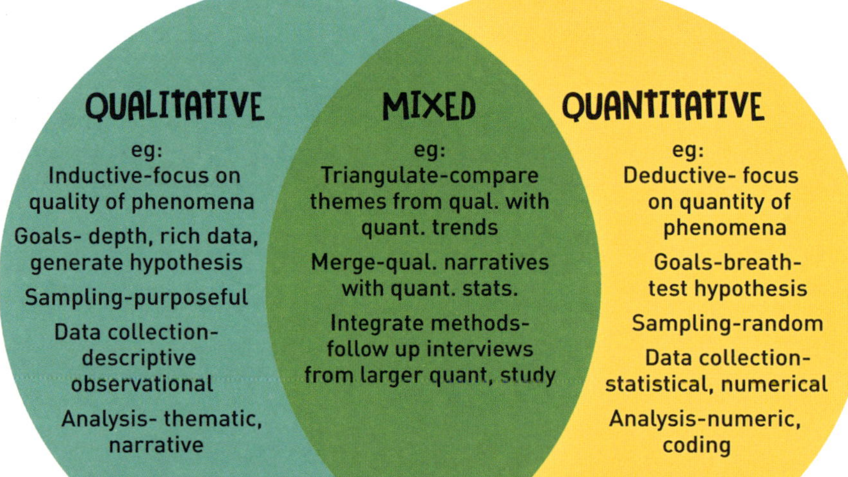

The methods used should emerge from the questions asked.

SAMPLING

Choice of sample

Many of the methods outlined will require a sample from a particular population. Various factors drive the sampling approach, or frame, chosen, such as theoretical perspective, ethical issues and practical ones too. Time and budget restrictions, for instance, would mean it is not possible to include everyone in a given city or country, especially in qualitative research, and transcribing qualitative data, for instance, is very time-consuming.

How many people need to be included is a big question, the answer to which depends on your research question and the moment you arrive at data saturation (the point where data is not giving anything new). Thus, researchers also need to decide on how they will sample the population:

- **Random sampling** is a method used to minimize bias and to make the sample as representative of the general population as possible – everyone has an equal probability of getting chosen and it can be done, with ease, via a computer.
- If particular characteristics are being studied, **stratified sampling** can ensure people are selected from groups according to gender, ethnicity or social class for example.
- **Purposive sampling** is one based on a particular population, as well as the purpose of the study.
- **Snowball sampling** is a process whereby a participant is asked to suggest other participants through their own network.

PRIMARY OR SECONDARY

The forms of research mentioned thus far generate new data and so are referred to as primary research (and primary data). However, increasingly, sociologists make use of existing, or secondary data, both quantitative and qualitative. This might include emails, diaries and social media posts or government statistics, exam results and census data. Durkheim's suicide study is one famous, early example of this type of secondary research. We live in a world where data is 'king', surrounded by ***big data*** collected by companies, institutions and governments about our shopping habits, love lives and much more! Sociologists are accessing this to understand our social lives and they are also analyzing the role the data plays more generally in power relationships.

The Bookworm *by Carl Spitzweg (1850) depicts a detailed examination of archival secondary research sources.*

ANALYZING DATA

You've collected loads of data – now you have to do something with it... The process of analyzing and making sense of the material you've generated varies depending on the type of data produced and, of course, the research questions being addressed. For any, an early stage of this involves assessing the quality of your data. Reliability, generalizability and validity are frequently used terms here, though there is debate about their importance – are they 'valid' positivist terms, for instance? In quantitative analysis, there are various tests a researcher can conduct to check reliability and validity. In qualitative analysis, this might be ensured through processes of transparency (so that a study could be replicated).

Generalizing data

QUANTITATIVE DATA ANALYSIS

Quantitative data analysis might be as simple as counting stuff but typically involves statistical techniques to identify patterns, test hypotheses and make inferences about populations. There is a range of specialized computer programs, such as SPPS, which can be used for this. **Descriptive statistics** summarize and describe the main features of a dataset (e.g. means, medians, standard deviations). Inferential statistics use sample data to make predictions or inferences about a larger population (e.g. t-tests, regression analysis, analysis of variance/ANOVA). Visual representations of data can be used to aid interpretation and communication of findings (e.g. graphs, charts).

Descriptive and inferential statistics

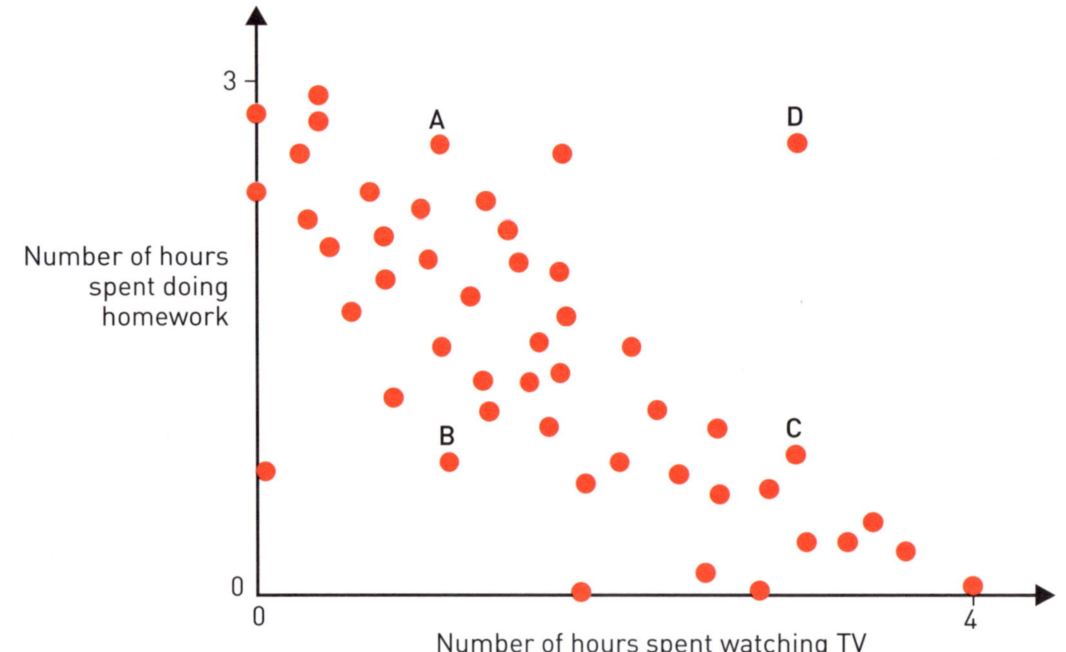

Quantitative data like this helps us to see the impact of one thing on another, in this case homework on TV watching!

QUALITATIVE DATA ANALYSIS

Qualitative data analysis involves interpreting and making sense of non-numerical data. This can be done in a range of ways, depending on preference and size of the data, from a computer program such NVivo, to using coloured pens and scissors. Content analysis is a popular method and can be used to analyze images, text, film and audio recordings. Part of this process often includes coding – identifying and labelling themes or concepts in the data. This might then reveal patterns or themes across the dataset. Examining how language is used to construct social reality is a focus of discourse analysis. This might be done through analyzing conversation, political speeches, the language of institutions such as law, or through studying storytelling or narratives.

STEPS IN QUALITATIVE DATA ANALYSIS

1. Familiarization with the data
2. Generating initial codes
3. Searching for themes
4. Reviewing themes
5. Defining and naming themes
6. Producing the report

RESEARCH ETHICS

Ethical considerations are paramount in sociological research to protect participants, and researchers, and maintain the integrity of the research process. To ensure this, organizations such as universities and funding bodies often have clear and rigorous ethical processes and guidelines. They might include some of the following:

KEY ETHICAL PRINCIPLES

Ethical principles

- **Informed consent:** participants must be fully informed about the nature of the research and voluntarily agree to participate.
- **Confidentiality and anonymity:** protecting the identity and personal information of research participants.
- **Avoiding harm:** ensuring that research does not cause physical, psychological or social harm to participants.
- **Respect for autonomy:** recognizing participants' right to make their own decisions about participation.
- **Justice:** ensuring fair selection of participants and equitable distribution of research benefits and burdens.

ETHICAL CHALLENGES IN SOCIOLOGICAL RESEARCH

Ethical challenges

This means that sociologists often face complex ethical dilemmas in their research. For example:

- **Covert research:** when is it justifiable to conduct research without participants' knowledge?
- **Research with vulnerable populations:** how can we protect vulnerable groups while ensuring their voices are heard?
- **Dual relationships:** how should researchers navigate relationships with participants that extend beyond the research context?

Do the ends justify the means?

Perhaps one of the most infamous studies, which raised many of these questions, was Laud Humphreys' (1970) 'Tearoom Trade'. This study on casual sexual encounters between men in public toilets raised significant ethical concerns about privacy and informed consent. Humphreys suspected that the police and the public held stereotypical and ***prejudiced*** beliefs about men who have sex with men in public spaces, a behaviour that was (and still is in places) illegal and heavily policed. In order to dispel some of those ideas and gain a more nuanced understanding of them and their motivations, he conducted participant observation and interviews (another example of a mixed methods study). He took the role of 'watchqueen' in 'tearooms' (toilets where men meet for sex – known as 'cottages' in the UK) and someone who alerts the others when the police are nearby. He got to know some people quite well, and he revealed to them that he was a researcher, which enabled him to talk to them about their motivations. But in many instances, his role was an undercover one; this was covert observation. With these men, he sometimes followed them, took their car registration details, and with the help of a friend in a local police department, got their names and addresses. A year later, in disguise, he interviewed them in their homes, pretending to be conducting a medical survey. The results of his study were interesting – some men were gay or bisexual; many were straight, married men, using the sex to release stress. The results were important in changing police attitudes, reducing their fervour in criminalizing this behaviour. However, there was much potential for harm – both to the participants with Humphreys' behaviour arguably jeopardizing their marriages and jobs, and to Humphreys himself.

As a result of the controversy caused by the study, covert observations fell out of favour for a long time. Despite such reservations, David Calvey (2018), through his research as a bouncer in the night-time economy, calls for the 'rehabilitation' of covert ethnography in sociology – without it, he states, the sociological imagination is stifled. Marieke Hopman (2021), who used covert research to look at the

Participant observation without consent (covert) can be controversial.

Covert observation has revealed interesting information about behaviour in the night-time economy.

The Gross Clinic (1875) by Thomas Eakins raises questions about consent and observation as well as power dynamics in research.

rights of children living under Moroccan control in western Sahara, argues it's an essential, and ethical, tool to study human rights in authoritarian regimes.

Avoiding prejudice

THE INFLUENCE OF FEMINIST THEORY AND RESEARCH PRACTICES

Feminist theory and research practices have had a profound impact on sociological research methods, challenging traditional approaches and introducing new perspectives on knowledge production. Part of the feminist 'project' of the 1970s and 80s was in critiquing the limited scope of knowledge (which had often left unaddressed the lives of people on the margins of society). This inevitably led to a focus on the capabilities of earlier explanations and the methods by which they arose. This influence extends beyond research specifically focused on gender, affecting

ETHICAL GUIDELINES FOR SOCIOLOGICAL RESEARCH ONE OF E.G.

American Sociological Association (ASA) Code of Ethics

South African Sociological Association (SASA)

Indian Sociological Society (ISS) Code of Ethics

British Sociological Association (BSA) Statement of Ethical Practice

International Sociological Association (ISA) Code of Ethics]

methodological approaches across various social science disciplines. Sociology's embracing of many qualitative research methods, such as the interview, and broader concerns with ethics, which have been discussed above, owe much to the feminist insight of scholars such as Liz Stanley, Liz Kelly, Louise Alcoff and Ann Oakley. Broadly speaking, they have impacted on quantitative methods by critiquing gender bias in measurement and sampling, developing new measures to capture gendered experiences, and encouraging disaggregation of data by gender and other social categories. For instance, the Gender Development Index (GDI) and Gender Empowerment Measure (GEM), developed by the United Nations Development Programme, reflect feminist influence in creating gender-sensitive quantitative measures. In relation to qualitative methods, they have emphasized the importance of listening and giving voice to participants, developing methods like memory work and feminist oral history, and encouraging more collaborative and less hierarchical research relationships. Ann Oakley's (1981) critique of traditional interviewing techniques, for instance, led to the development of more reciprocal and dialogic approaches to in-depth interviewing.

Feminist influence

As a result of critiquing traditional forms of research for its harms to participants (in part through silencing and stereotyping some groups in society), ethics has been central to much feminist research, such as a heightened attention to the power dynamics in research relationships and potential impacts on participants. Interdisciplinarity, now the buzzword of many universities, is something that feminism championed, by encouragement of crossing disciplinary boundaries to fully understand complex social phenomena. Feminist researchers have often been at the forefront of combining quantitative and qualitative methods to gain a more comprehensive understanding. There has also been an emphasis on conducting research that can inform policy and practice to address social inequalities. For instance, the World Health Organization's (2001)

Interdisciplinarity

KEY PRINCIPLES OF FEMINIST RESEARCH METHODS

- ***Challenging objectivity and value-neutrality***: many feminist researchers have critiqued the notion of complete objectivity in social research, arguing that all knowledge is situated and influenced by the researcher's social position.
- ***Emphasizing reflexivity***: feminist approaches have highlighted the importance of researcher reflexivity – the practice of critically examining one's own role in the research process.
- ***Centring marginalized voices***: feminist research often aims to centre the experiences and perspectives of marginalized groups, challenging power dynamics in knowledge production.
- ***Challenging power dynamics in research relationships***: researchers try to minimize the power over those they are working with.
- ***Valuing lived experiences as a source of knowledge:*** personal experience is as valuable as generating statistical data.
- ***Commitment to social change and empowerment:*** rather than doing research for research's sake, feminist researchers are committed to improving the lives of people.

guidelines on researching violence against women and girls draw heavily on feminist research principles, emphasizing safety, confidentiality and respect for participants.

Intersectionality in research design

The influence of intersectionality

Feminist theory, particularly intersectional feminism, has encouraged researchers to consider how multiple social categories (e.g. gender, race, class) interact to shape experiences and outcomes. Kimberlé Crenshaw's (1991) work on intersectionality has influenced how researchers design studies to capture the complexities of social identities and inequalities. Sociologists like Patricia Hill Collins see methodological techniques as a means to intersectional theorizing and acting as a framework for shaping the research itself. Recognizing oppression and one's location within the 'matrix of domination' is one task of the researcher, as well as needing to recognize the complex nature of intersectional identities. Miliann Kang's *The Managed Hand* (2010), looking at nail salons in New York owned by Asian, particularly Korean, immigrants, explores the intersections of 'race' with gender, the body and immigration status. Face-to-face interactions between manicurists and their clients reveal powerful and persistent social divisions.

CHALLENGES AND DEBATES

Keeping a critical eye

While feminist research methods have made significant contributions, they have also faced challenges. Some critics argue that explicitly political or value-laden research compromises scientific objectivity. Of course, it could be argued that no research is value-free and perhaps it is better to be open about one's position and leave it to others to judge your research, based on that. Others are of the opinion that the focus on specific, contextualized experiences limits the generalizability of findings. While widely accepted in theory, operationalizing intersectionality in research design and analysis remains challenging and can become a mere tick-box exercise if not carefully thought through.

Despite these challenges, the influence of feminist research methods continues to grow, encouraging all sociologists to reflect critically on their research practices and the politics of knowledge production.

CONCLUSION

Sociological research methods provide the tools for systematic enquiry into social phenomena. By understanding and applying these methods, sociologists can contribute to our knowledge of society and inform policy and practice. As you continue your studies, you'll have the opportunity to explore these methods in more depth and perhaps even apply them in your own research projects.

We have seen that there is more than one way to conduct research; the approach you take will involve several considerations. Make sure the research tools you select are the most appropriate for what you want to study – the research question(s) is supreme. Keep assessing how things are going – are you generating the kind of information you need, and if not, how can you adapt what you're doing? The important thing is to be flexible, to recognize that your assumptions may be challenged by the data and that is a good thing!

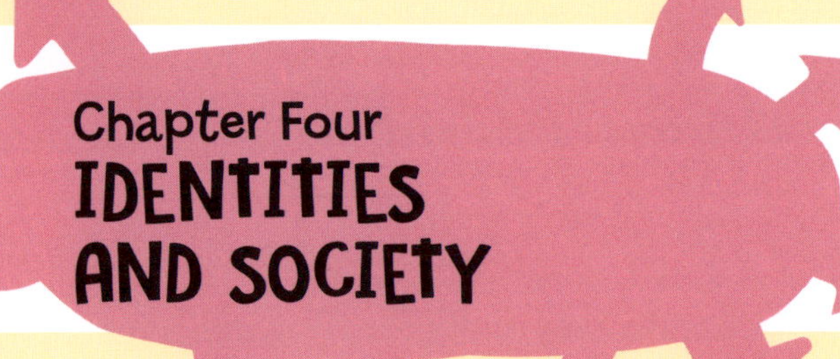

Chapter Four IDENTITIES AND SOCIETY

Sociological understandings of identity – The rules of engagement – Civil inattention and social distance – Territory of the self – Devices and desires: digital co-presence – The ultimate private-public space – The civilizing process and identity – Identity, difference and deviance – Modern friendship

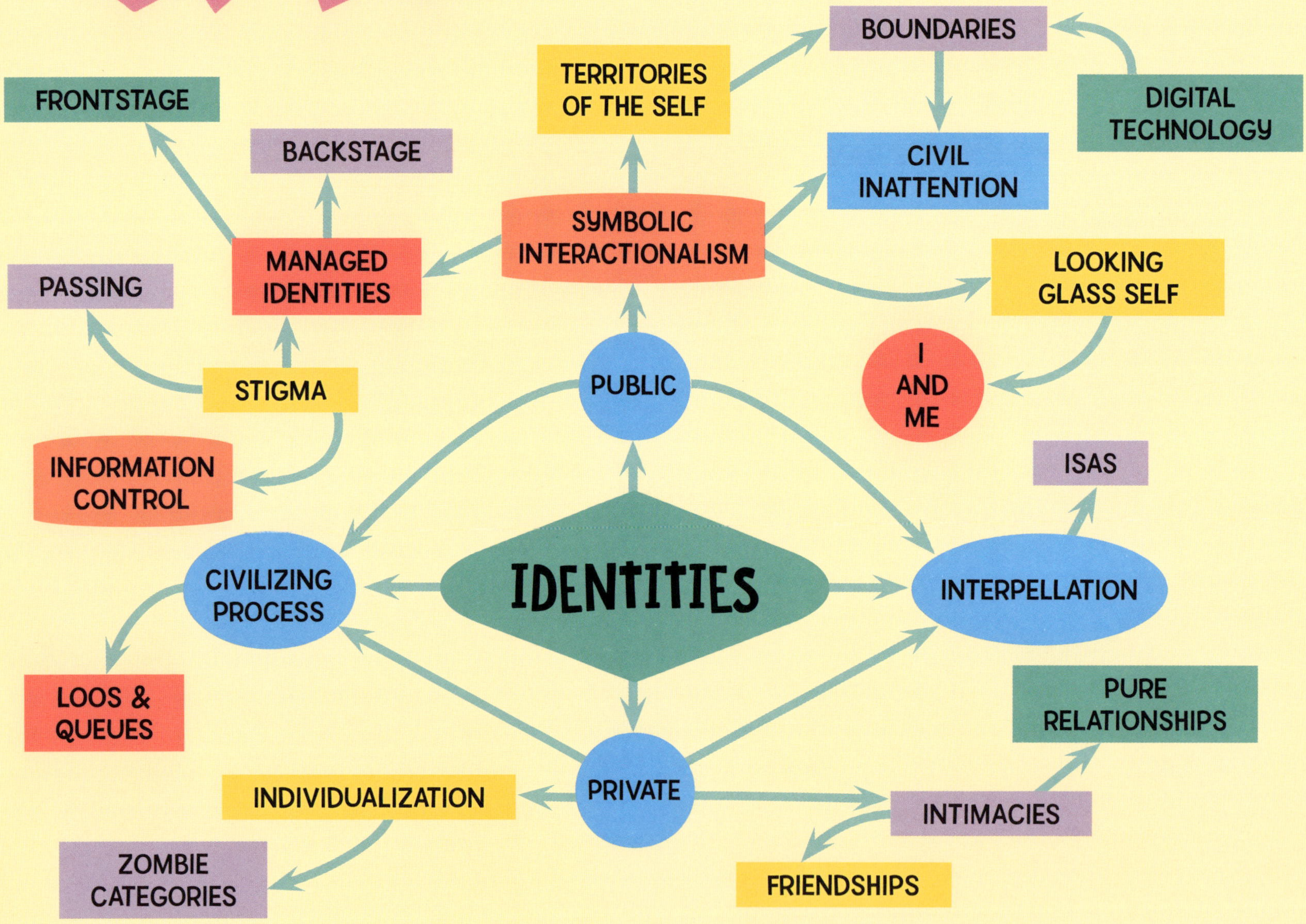

'Who am I?' is a question many of us ask ourselves in the small hours of the morning (or perhaps that's just me). It might be comforting, particularly for those of us who are a little antisocial, to think of ourselves as very much independent from the world around us – unique, autonomous beings with agency – and a subject seemingly outside of sociology's remit. But sociology can unpick the ways in which the self is very much a social being, like it or not. Thinking about some of the personal aspects of our lives, such as the rules and rituals around urinating in a public space, might seem off-topic for a subject more often associated with analyzing the bigger picture. Using our sociological imaginations, however, we can begin to connect the personal with the public in the ways Charles Wright Mills (1959) suggested, connecting the ways in which shame and disgust operate to change behaviour, for example. By looking at our identities, we can start to understand, not just ourselves a little better but also the social processes and institutions around us, which help forge us, as we, in turn, shape them.

A social being

SOCIOLOGICAL UNDERSTANDINGS OF IDENTITY

Sociologists have long been concerned with ***social action*** – in terms of the self, this is the way in which our behaviours and choices are influenced, though not determined, by society. Identity is something beyond the idea of a personality: it involves a degree of active engagement, identifying with a particular group or identity. Indeed, the root of 'identity' is the Latin term *idem* meaning 'same'; 'identical' also comes from this root. We might, for instance be passionate about a football team and wear a shirt or scarf to align ourselves with that team and the others who identify with it. These kinds of symbols can also act to form boundaries and alignments between 'us' and 'them'. Of course, some in society have more choice and fewer constraints than others in relation to forming and performing our identities, which will be examined in more detail later in this book.

It is also useful to think of identity in the plural: we are many things to many people – you may have an identity as a parent and a child, a sibling, an employer or employee, a student, a friend, a lover and so on. Each identity might be expressed slightly differently, depending on context, they might also be sources of tension, being at odds with one another at times. In this sense, we can start to see that identity is very much connected to the social world.

NAMES TO KNOW

George Herbert Mead *(1863–1931)*

Herbert Blumer *(1900–1987)*

Erving Goffman *(1922–1982)*

Norbert Elias *(1897–1990)*

Arlie Hochschild *(1940–)*

Howard Becker *(1928–2023)*

Anthony Giddens *(1938–)*

ME, MYSELF AND I?

The American sociologist Charles Horton Cooley (1864–1929) was among the first to recognize that the ways through which we come to see ourselves as individuals are very much social processes. Our sense of 'self' emerges through the interactions we have with others – their perception, and expectations, of us. This self is understood by sociologists as our ***social identity***; Cooley called it the ***looking-glass self*** (looking glass is an old-fashioned term for mirror). Our identity is forged from

Looking-glass self

how we appear to others, or how we think they respond to us. Depending on how we feel about this perceived 'mirror image', we might adjust our behaviour or attitude. Cooley's theory influenced a colleague of his, George Herbert Mead (1863–1931), who developed the theory of the generalized other – the process whereby we take perceived perceptions of us from others and internalize them. According to Mead, we imitate significant others – parents, siblings etc. – as part of the socialization process, then through games we start to role play imagined figures too, such as superheroes, until we get to the point where we start to imagine how we seem to others. He argues that our sense of self is reflexive, constructed through a dialogue between *I* – our impulsive self – and *me* – the social self; I responds to me. For Mead, reflective (or self) consciousness is what separates humans from other animals (which some might argue is a form of ***speciesism***). Other animals and babies, he argues, only have a pre-reflective consciousness, one aware of the 'bare thereness of the world'.

Las Meninas *(1656), by Diego Velázquez illustrates multiple levels of looking and being looked at and hints at how identity is constructed through others' perceptions.*

SYMBOLIC INTERACTIONISM

Herbert Blumer (1900–1987), a student of Mead's, called this ***symbolic interactionism***. These microsociological approaches provide interesting theories on how we develop as individuals in the social world. Our sense of self is constructed through our social interactions and the social institutions that shape these. Language, and the interpretation of meaning, is central to this formation of self and society – we agree on shared meaning, if only temporarily – thus we are understood as symbolic animals. Society is seen as a social process, rather than a structure, formed through the meanings we make in our everyday social interactions. For instance, William Corsaro's (2017) longitudinal ethnographic studies of children's peer cultures show how children actively participate in their socialization, creating their own unique peer cultures while learning to navigate social rules and develop their sense of self.

ALL THE WORLD'S A STAGE

Building on these interactionist ideas, for Canadian sociologist Erving Goffman (1922–1982), everyday social interaction is like the theatre. Sometimes we are actors and use props, costumes and a script to get us through the act, at other times, we are an audience receiving (and appraising) the performance of others. We might alter our act depending on who the audience is – in other words, in different social situations such as job interviews or first dates, we perform impression management. We have a frontstage: where performances are given, and a backstage: where preparations and rehearsals occur. Backstage might be more relaxed, or less pressured but he didn't mean it was our 'true' self, as he didn't necessarily think there was one, authentic self. For Goffman, our sense of self comes as a result of how others perceive us. This is his famous ***dramaturgical theory***.

Modern technology more generally has created new dimensions of identity management and presentation. For instance, Danah Boyd's (2014) research on teenagers' social media use shows how young people navigate identity presentation across multiple digital platforms while managing different audiences.

LET ME TAKE A SELFIE

Rembrandt's series of self-portraits can be compared with modern selfies.Both are examples of a managed 'self', which might include:

- choice of pose and expression
- use of props and settings
- intended audience
- purpose of self-representation

The stress caused by emotional labour is akin to the psychological disorder portrayed in The Scream *(1893) by Edvard Munch.*

Identity and emotional labour

In *The Managed Heart* (The University of California Press, 1983), Arlie Hochschild expanded this theory to argue that this is particularly the case in commercial settings. Looking at the role of flight attendants, she argued that managing emotions and putting on a particular performance is increasingly an expectation in work. People employed in customer service roles have to perform emotional labour, somehow negotiating their private emotions with the expectations of employers. This might involve surface acting or deep acting. Surface acting is those displays of emotion that might not ring true but are done to please customers; deep acting is when employees draw on emotions they feel are authentic. Being a worker then becomes akin to being a method actor. However, this can cause harm – using Marx's idea of alienation, Hochschild argues that repeatedly having to engage at an inauthentic level can cause distress.

THE RULES OF ENGAGEMENT

CIVIL INATTENTION AND SOCIAL DISTANCE

Erving Goffman's (1963) concept of civil inattention is a useful one for understanding the individual and behaviour in public spaces. This practice is one way in which social order in public spaces is maintained through unwritten principles. It involves acknowledging others' presence while simultaneously demonstrating that they are not objects of

CHAIN REACTION

Randall Collins' (2004) theory of **interaction ritual chains** explains how successful public interactions generate emotional energy and social solidarity. In short, rituals, such as those based around smoking or sex (or perhaps smoking *and* sex) create symbols that can foster group membership. Successful rituals can provide energy, whilst failed ones might drain us. For Randall, they serve to form boundaries, provide a mutual focus of attention and a shared mood. Thinking about these forms of engagement and reflecting on conversations serve to construct our sense of self.

particular attention; rather, we disattend to them. As Goffman observed, people in urban settings typically give one another a brief glance to signal awareness, then look away to indicate respect for privacy; it can also signal that you are not a threat. This is an example of what he refers to as an 'interaction order'. Sometimes people get it wrong, and it makes others uncomfortable. My dad, for instance, when he first left his very rural village for the local city – Norwich – attempted to say hello to everyone he met. Used to everyone knowing each other and stopping to speak, he was dismayed that people either ignored him or gave him some very odd looks; they were letting him know he was being uncivilly attentive! In fact, while we appear to be ignoring one another, when sitting, for instance, on the tube in London, we are, very subtly, interacting with each other. We might also engage in this behaviour to save ourselves, or someone else, from embarrassment. If the person you are speaking to has just eaten something and has some spinach stuck between their teeth, we might purposefully not stare at the spinach, to avoid making them feel self-conscious.

Most people engage in the rules of civil inattention without being aware they know them. When someone else gets it 'wrong' though, we realize very quickly.

TERRITORY OF THE SELF

Concept of personal space

Indeed, public spaces involve constant negotiation of personal space and territory. Goffman's concept of the ***territory of the self*** helps explain how we maintain boundaries in shared spaces. These territories are both symbolic and material and, in part, help produce and maintain our sense of self. He also acknowledges that one's social positioning determines the extent to which a person has control over maintaining their territories. For Goffman, there are eight territories, which include personal space, what he terms 'use space' (the area immediately around or in front of someone), turn space (your position in queues or lines) and possessional territory (your belongings and claimed spaces). Arguably, older people in nursing homes have a relatively small territory of the self. Feminists have pointed out that women also tend to have reduced control over their territories – our, and others', use of space can be one of the ways we become gendered.

RESEARCH SPOTLIGHT

William Whyte's pioneering study of New York's public spaces, *The Social Life of Small Urban Spaces* (Project for Public Spaces, 1980), revealed how physical design influences social behaviour. His research showed that successful public spaces facilitate what he called '***triangulation***' – external stimuli that prompt strangers to interact, in socially approved ways.

In Iris Marion Young's (1980) work 'Throwing Like a Girl' – she argues that to be female, or feminine, is to exist in a smaller space and women often find themselves crowded out on public transport.

The design of urban tube and metro trains allows people to stand in close proximity in a socially approved way.

CASE STUDY: PUBLIC TRANSPORT ETIQUETTE

Public transport provides a fascinating lens for examining contemporary public behaviour and helps us understand how our sense of self evolves as we navigate the rules. Inevitably, we are brought into close proximity to people we don't know. For some, this might mean we have a particular 'travel identity'; others might be less willing to conform to social expectations. Different rules might apply, depending on the form of transport – bus, tube, plane etc. Observe these evolving norms and also consider the ways in which age or gender might alter them slightly:

- ***Traditional etiquette*** (offering seats, volume control, queuing)
- ***Stranger etiquette*** (when and who to sit next to)
- ***Digital etiquette*** (phone conversations, headphone use)
- ***Pandemic-influenced behaviours*** (masking, distancing)

Amy Hanser (2019), in 'The Public Bus as Urban Space', considers these questions and others, such as is it ever appropriate to eat food, or take a nap. Generally, people adhere to these unwritten rules, the result being well-organized collective behaviour.

DEVICES AND DESIRES: DIGITAL CO-PRESENCE

The ubiquity of mobile phones has, arguably, transformed public behaviour and our identities, creating what Richard Ling and Scott Campbell (2009) term digital co-presence. This phenomenon raises new questions about attention, privacy and social obligations. Mobile phones have, effectively, altered our relationship with time, spaces and other people. These forms of communication disrupt traditional boundaries of public and private spaces, for instance.

Impact of technology on the self

'Traditional' phone boxes were examples of enclosed, private spaces within a public space.

Contemporary mobile phone use has dissolved the private boundary of the phone box.

HEGEMONIC MASCULINITY ▶
Developed from Antonio Gramsci's notion of hegemony, meaning dominant, Australian sociologist Raewyn Connell suggests that hegemonic masculinity is the most culturally powerful, or dominant, at any given time.

BINARY OPPOSITIONS ▶
Many sociologists argue that categories like gender are falsely constructed as binary oppositions. In other words, men and women are presented as being polar opposites, when in fact they share many commonalities. Binary systems also don't reflect the reality that many people reject gender labels and are non-binary or gender-fluid.

Richard Ling (2008) has also suggested that digital technology has created new forms of absent presence in public spaces, requiring new forms of interaction rituals. How often have you been out with friends or family for a sociable drink or meal, only to find you are all checking your phones or texting other people, rather than talking to one another? Research by Keith Hampton and Neeti Gupta (2008) identifies two types of public space phone (and other devices) users. True mobiles are people who move while using devices or create portable shields when in a public space such as a coffee shop, signalling that though they are choosing to be surrounded by people, they don't want to encourage any social interaction – a form of 'public privatism'. Often, they use Goffman's forms of civil inattention to indicate their desire to be left alone. In contrast, 'placemakers' are those who might appear to claim territory and create private spheres in public as true mobiles do, however, they want to be seen and heard and will encourage interaction with others. For them, wireless technology enables them to make connections in public spaces.

PUBLIC TOILETS: THE ULTIMATE PRIVATE-PUBLIC SPACE

Public toilets represent a unique intersection of private activities in public spaces and are great places to observe rituals of the self and others – though you need to be careful when doing this! They are spaces where, through emotions such as shame, embarrassment or anxiety, our identity is perhaps tested. They might also be places of safety, belonging and kinship. Ruth Barcan's (2005) research reveals the ways in which gender is performed in public lavatories, looking at the ways they become spaces for reinforcing ***hegemonic masculinity*** (Raewyn Connell, 2005). These are spaces which are often highly gendered, where you are forced to choose between just two binary gender identities. Barcan (2010) also investigates the complex social choreography involved in maintaining privacy and dignity while sharing intimate spaces.

ALL HAIL YOU!

Interpellation

Another way in which identity is forged, or constituted, through society, is via what Louis Althusser (1971) calls 'interpellation' or hailing. In other words, we come to recognize ourselves when particular texts, or ideologies ('the imaginary relationship of individuals to their real conditions of existence') call out to us. For instance, an advertisement for an aftershave might present the wearer as sociable, sporty and suave and we might think, *That's me!* This can be a conscious or unconscious recognition but it might recruit us to particular roles or positions in society that will have a certain set of rules. Althusser presents a more structuralist (believing the State serves the bourgeoisie), Marxist understanding of identity formation. While it might seem like we are making considered, individual decisions, actually we are subtly being

Design elements – cubicles or urinal, gender-neutral or segregated loos, free or charged

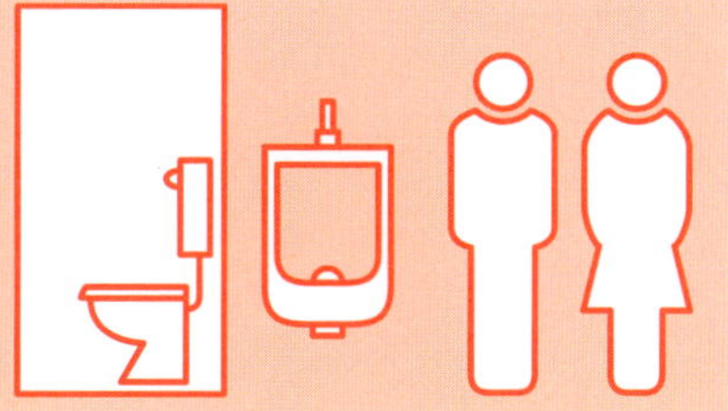

Behavioural norms – no eye contact or conversation at urinals, leaving a space

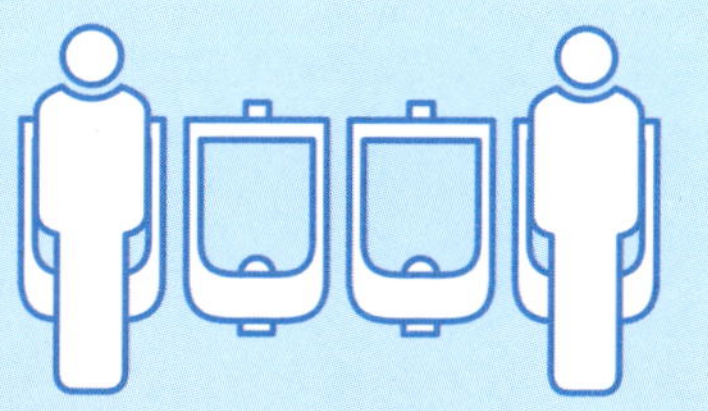

Gender differences – group chats or no chat, when to use the cubicle

Cultural variations – bidets, holes in the ground, individual stalls, etc.

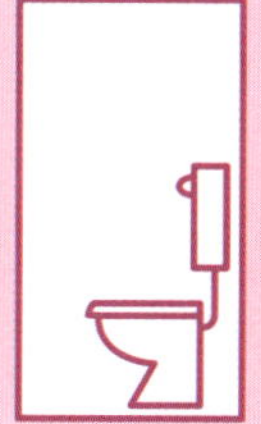

Behaviour in public toilets reveals a lot about any given culture and is a factor in shaping our identity.

WAITING YOUR TURN: QUEUING AND NATIONAL IDENTITY

The act of queuing represents a fascinating example of social order emerging from shared cultural expectations. As Leon Mann's (1969) classic study showed, queue jumping triggers strong responses because it violates both fairness principles and territorial claims. We can see queues as living, breathing social systems that reflect the norms and values of its culture. Once in the queue, the collective group share an identity and might respond together to changes in the queue, such as speed, or length. There might be rules around letting people in or asking them to save your space.

Different queuing cultures around the world:

- **British:** single-file emphasis
- **Chinese:** more fluid, clustered approach
- **Japanese:** multiple organized lines
- **Israeli:** more assertive, less formal

How do you queue? Do you feel awkward holding someone's place or letting friends in? Do queue jumpers make you feel angry? You might consider where these 'rules' come from.

INTERPELLATION ▶ ***Althusser argues that when we recognize ourselves in something like an advert, or government speech, we are interpellated. The text calls to us or hails us and thus, in part, shapes our identity.***

PROTECT YOUR REPUTATION!
Developing the work of Elias Cas Wouters (2007) research on manners shows how informal standards of behaviour have evolved while maintaining complex forms of self-regulation. Many of his books were about 'the lust balance', where the desire for sexual gratification was balanced with a wish for an enduring relationship. Thus, many manners books guided young men and women on 'not going too far' or damaging 'reputations'.

compelled to behave in particular ways to suit the ideology. For instance, we might repeatedly watch a soap opera that has family dynamics we recognize and perhaps identify with, where men are breadwinners and women work in the home caring for everyone, and this then normalizes that behaviour for us. We come into being when we are interpellated and this shapes our ideas of gender, ethnicity, ***nationality***, (dis) ability, sexuality, age and so on. Key institutions in society, such as the media, the education system or the family – what Althusser calls ***Ideological State Apparatuses*** (ISAs) – function by ideology and reinforce the hegemony of the dominant classes by constantly reproducing it.

THE CIVILIZING PROCESS AND IDENTITY

Norbert Elias's (1939) work on the ***civilizing process*** provides an historical perspective on how standards of behaviour and self-control have evolved over time. In part, this process has given rise to the false belief that we have a true, inner self, a pre-existing core unaffected by society. What seems to be 'inside' is very firmly 'outside' for Elias. Manners make the modern person – controls and rules over our impulses, actions, bodies and emotions are an important aspect of this. He is not arguing that society has become progressively more 'civilized', rather that we have become increasingly controlled, monitored and individualized in some ways. This can lead to the belief that we stand, as individuals, outside of society.

A private function

If we go back to toilets for a moment, Elias uses this as just one example of the ways in which we have come to associate urination and defecation as something shameful and private. He traces the history of this from when we might have shared a communal pot and thrown the contents into the road, to having an outside privy that served a street, culminating in expectations of having not only an indoor toilet but possibly several. Lavatories function to denote class, wealth and self-control. In part, this was guided by court behaviours – people followed the fashion of the wealthy aristocracy and royal court life. Rules might initially be formalized in books of etiquette but gradually are internalized and no longer need to be written down. For instance, early etiquette books for 'gentlemen' suggested they shouldn't break wind in front of women or point out faeces to their companions. Changes in bathing and eating habits also reflect this increased expectation around bodily and emotional self-control, and a move away from communal behaviours to increased individualization. This is not always linear and we might think of examples of 'de-civilizing' processes, such as public urination on urban streets when pubs and clubs close, activities that perhaps reunite us with communal behaviours.

Through the civilizing process we see a shift from:

1 *Communal pots emptied in the street, to:*

2 *Enclosed holes which evacuate straight outside, to:*

3 *Privatized, enclosed, modern lavatories.*

IDENTITY, DIFFERENCE AND DEVIANCE

Labelling others

As we have already seen, part of the process of shaping identity is drawing boundaries between groups. Edward Said (1978) has shown how some groups are marked as 'other' in society, via processes of power and inequality such as racism, sexism, ableism and homophobia, whereby difference might come to represent 'deviant'. There are several theories that attempt to explain why some groups are more likely to become labelled as deviant, Howard Becker's (1963) labelling theory perhaps being among the most famous. He explains that what is considered deviant is very much dependent on context (time and location) and who is doing the perceived dirty deed. A barrister or judge caught speeding because of an emergency might be able to navigate the system and get away it with it, compared to a young working-class man, who might be labelled a 'boy racer'. An act in and of itself is not deviant; certain groups have the power to label particular people (who are usually more likely to be under surveillance) as being

Young people, according to Becker, are more likely to be labelled as deviant and outsiders. This still from Reefer Madness *(1938) shows how certain behaviours (e.g. smoking cannabis) are constructed as deviant.*

deviant. Labels, however, even though socially constructed are very sticky – once labelled, it becomes very difficult to shake off and it may well become part of a person's identity. We might start to actively embrace the role of being an 'outsider'. Robert Merton (1948) called this a ***self-fulfilling prophecy***.

STIGMATIZED IDENTITIES

Whereas some might embrace their label of being different, not everyone finds this desirable. Goffman's (1963) work on ***stigma*** remains crucial for understanding how people manage 'spoiled' identities. To have a spoiled, or stigmatized, identity is to be viewed by society as 'not quite human', according to this theory. Such discrimination can impact severely on people's life chances – educational attainment, job security, personal relationships and health. The language of Goffman's theory sounds dated now but he suggested there were different types of stigma, including 'physical deformities', 'character blemishes' – such as being gay, a criminal or an addict – and 'tribal stigma' (ethnicity, nation, religion). The views of others – ascribed identity – interact, often in a negative way with self-identity, leading some to attempt to minimize their perceived stigma, or hide it. Joseph Schneider and Peter Conrad's (1980) study of epilepsy sufferers, a condition and identity that at the time was more stigmatized than today, reveals strategies people used for managing their identity. This included 'information control' or being careful about who they told, and '***passing***' – attempting to present as not having epilepsy. In short, they drew parallels with ***LGBTQ+*** people's experiences of being in the closet and coming out.

Classifying kinds of stigma

INTIMATE IDENTITIES

Contemporary understandings of friendship and intimate relationships are another way we can understand the self. These have undergone significant changes, as analyzed by theorists like Anthony Giddens and Ray Pahl.

MODERN FRIENDSHIP

Pahl's (2000) work on friendship shows how:

- friends have become increasingly important in modern society
- friendship networks often replace traditional family support
- the boundaries between friendship and family have become blurred

Making support networks

For Pahl and many others, friends influence our beliefs and behaviours, offering an important aspect to identity formation. Lynn Jamieson (1999) has argued that, as the 'least structured of intimate relationships' they can do many things. Sometimes friends are an Aristotelian 'other self' or a mirror of ourselves, while at other times they might challenge us. Spencer and Pahl's (2006) research on personal communities reveals how individuals create support networks combining both family and friends in unique ways. In societies with more solitary living patterns and a lessening of family ties, friends become our 'comforters, confidantes and soulmates'. Friends may well become 'families of choice', a concept popularized by Kath Weston (1991) and often associated with the bonds forged by LGBTQ people.

Friendships, whatever their type, plan an important part in forging 'identity'.

THE PURE RELATIONSHIP

Giddens' (1992) concept of the **pure relationship** characterizes an optimistic take on modern intimate relationships. He claims our personal, intimate relationships have transformed under late modernity and are:

- based on emotional and sexual equality
- maintained for their own sake
- continuing only as long as both parties derive satisfaction

Religion, laws and social norms, he argues, have less sway over our relationships – choice and equality are the governing principles. This democratizing of ***intimacy***, he argues, has huge consequences for the gender order, meaning less oppressive roles for women. Arguably, this is an overly optimistic view – the continued presence of abuse in intimate relationships, for instance, might suggest otherwise. These relationships, for Giddens, are just one of the many ways we can work on the project of the self.

Zombie identities

Ulrich Beck and Elisabeth Beck-Gernsheim (2001) argue that such apparent choices and freedoms have led to 'compulsory' individualization (acting and defining ourselves as individuals). Our identity is formed based on individual experiences, rather than our relationships with others. Entities such as class, family, gender or neighbourhoods become ***zombie categories***: the ideas live on despite having less meaning in people's lives. This is a contradictory state where it feels like we are liberated – for instance, women are told they are free from patriarchy – but when it fails, the individual is blamed and punished and the real reason, or system, behind this is left uncritiqued. The 'self', in this state, becomes central in our lives.

WHO DO YOU THINK YOU ARE?

Modernity, for Zygmunt Bauman (2004), with its collapse of stable or fixed identities around gender or class, for instance, has led to identity insecurity or disease. Though he doesn't think identity ever was stable, the difference now is that its fragility has become more apparent. The impact of technologies such as mobile phones, and the plethora of choices available to (some of) us, have led to starker concerns around the question of 'Who am I?'.

The instability of indentity

The extent to which all identities are fluid is, of course, up for debate – some seem resolutely fixed. There is no 'normal' or 'abnormal' identity; they are all social constructions and products of social relations and processes. What gets to count as normal, however, tells us a lot about the rules and norms of a particular time or culture and is subject to change, just as our own identities are. Many of the assumptions about normality are based on key forms of ***social stratification*** – such as social class, ethnicity, gender, sexuality – and that is what the next few chapters are concerned with.

Chapter Five

SOCIAL CLASS, POVERTY AND INEQUALITY

Identifying class – Framing class – Traditional class analysis – Contemporary models – The cultural turn in class analysis – Mechanisms of class formation – Contemporary class experiences and identity – Understanding poverty – The deserving and undeserving poor – Contemporary class experiences – Global inequalities

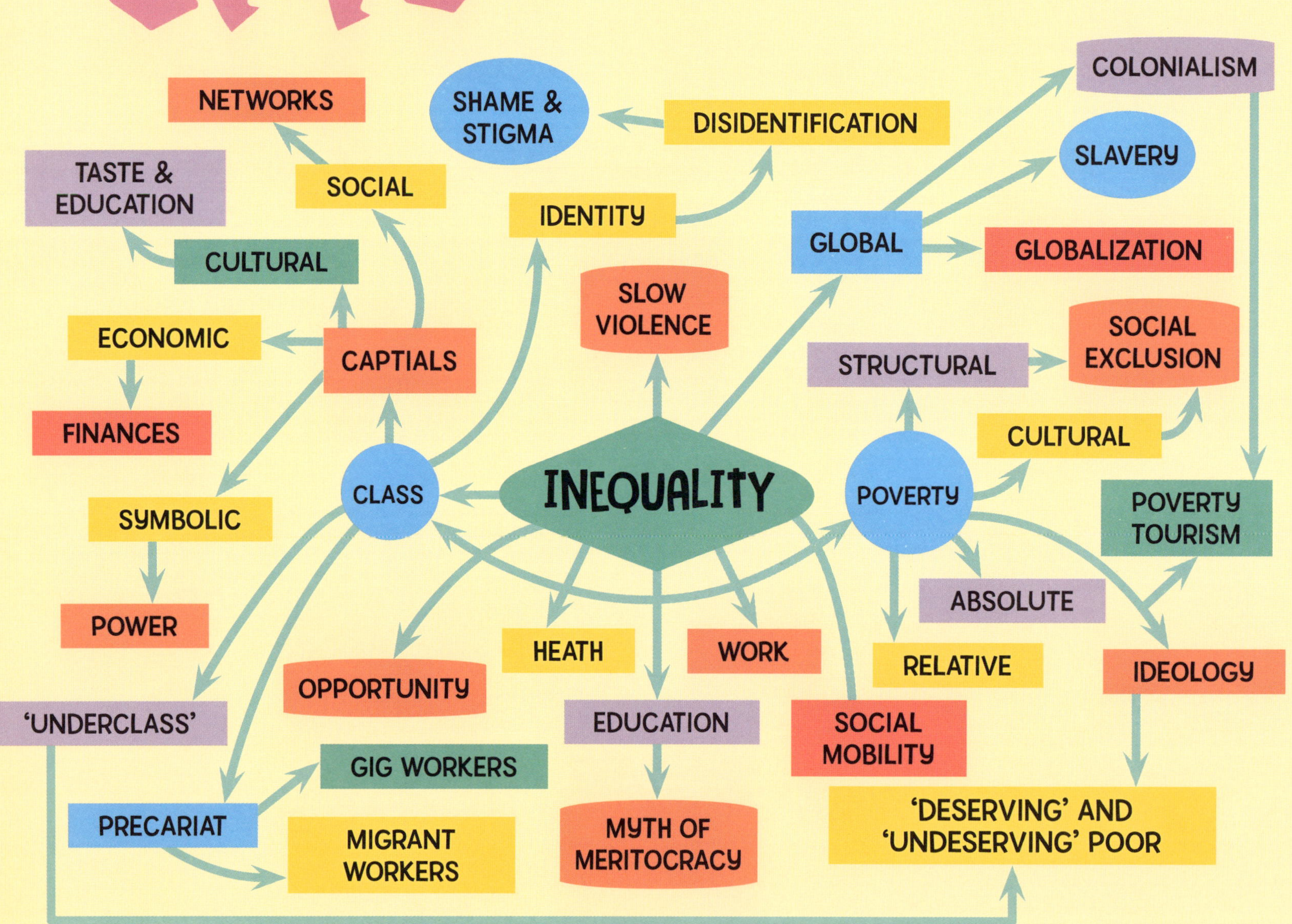

We might spend a large portion of our lives comparing ourselves to others – on popularity, attractiveness, wealth and so on. Sociologists understand inequality in a similar way – societies that are organized into groups such as gender, ethnicity or, as we focus on here, social class (known as ***social stratification***), tend to be hierarchical, meaning that some groups have more access to resources than others. This might be in terms of salary, ownership of property, cultural assets and power. These kinds of attributes are significant in that they give the owner a degree of control over the dynamics that impact on us all, such as education, health, lifestyle and even death. The inequalities related to this distribution are persistent, continuing over lifetimes and generations.

Impact of social stratification

You might have questioned why it is that some of the richest countries in the world (by GDP) like the US (No. 1) and the UK (No. 6) have so many people living in poverty. Within the UK, the Office for National Statistics (ONS) calculated in 2020 that the richest 10 per cent households had 43 per cent of all the wealth, whereas the bottom 50 per cent of households owned only 9 per cent. A popular measure, the Gini coefficient, which calculates using income before housing costs are deducted, has shown rising levels of such inequality since 1979. There have also been growing numbers of deaths involving malnutrition – in 2022 there were 436 such deaths in England and Wales. Despite rising temperatures year on year this century (discussed more in Chapter 12), poverty means that more people are dying from living in inadequately heated homes in the UK. During winter 2022/23, 4,950 excess winter deaths were caused by living in cold homes (End Fuel Poverty Coalition). The closely related concepts of poverty and class have been used to help explain such problems.

Rising levels of inequality

Such inequalities exist on a global scale, meaning as well as inequality within countries, there is a pattern of inequality between countries (in crude terms, the Global North has more resources than the Global South). This has a history in colonialism, the impact of which is ongoing. Globally, the richest one per cent have more wealth than the bottom 95 per cent of the world's population put together (Oxfam 2024). Thus, we can see how poverty and class inequalities positively thrived as (some) societies became more affluent; capitalism, many argue, is the driving force behind this.

North vs South

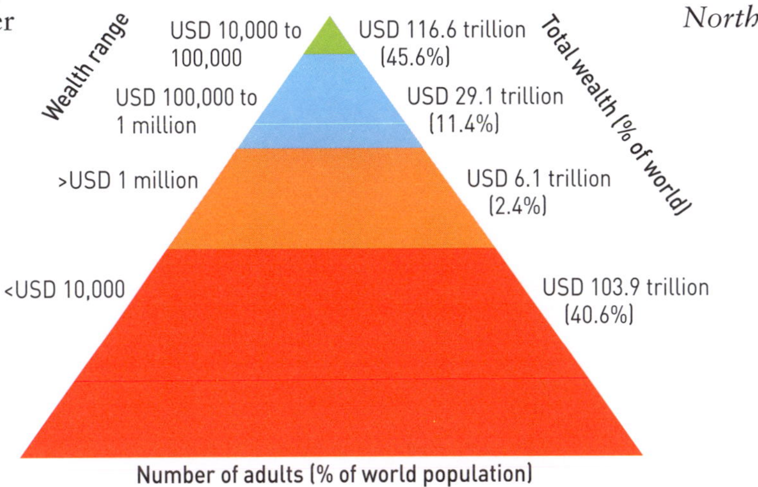

Data such as this shows clearly that a minority of the world's population owns the majority of the wealth.

KNOW YOUR PLACE! IDENTIFYING CLASS

Though we might not always like to talk about class, sociologists argue that most of us have a very clear idea of our own social class position. Indeed, in the previous chapter we talked about identity formation, and social class is often a key aspect of people's identity. Even before starting school, children are aware of differences between rich and poor and once at school, many can identify people and jobs that have more status or prestige.

Understanding social class

In recent decades, social class has re-emerged as a crucial lens for understanding contemporary inequalities. Despite predictions of its declining relevance in late modernity, class continues to shape life chances, cultural preferences and social identities in profound ways.

FRAMING CLASS

Think about the last time you went to a coffee shop. The person making your oat latte, the owner of the shop, and the CEO of the coffee chain all play different roles in the same economic story. But how do sociologists make sense of these different positions in society? This is where class analysis comes in.

TRADITIONAL CLASS ANALYSIS: THE FOUNDATIONS OF CLASS THEORY

Class analysis, as we saw in Chapters 1 and 2, emerged during one of history's most dramatic social transformations: the Industrial Revolution. As society shifted from agricultural to industrial production, social theorists noticed stark new divisions emerging between those who owned factories and those who worked in them.

Karl Marx was of the opinion that, in effect, the bourgeoisie controlled, or pulled the strings of, the proletariat.

Marx's binary class model

Karl Marx saw society as fundamentally split between two main classes, locked in an ongoing struggle:

- The bourgeoisie (capitalist class), who own the means of production (factories, resources, technology). They employ others to work for them, profiting from the surplus value of workers' labour
- The proletariat (working class), who sell their labour power to survive. They do not own means of production, so must work for others to make a living.

He did recognize other class groupings such as the petty bourgeoise (shop owners for example) and the lumpenproletariat (the lowest social grouping, devoid of class consciousness and thus dangerous) but for him, they had less significance in the class war.

Weber's multi-dimensional approach

Max Weber expanded this view. Like Marx, he thought class was based on economics and a person's position in the market and whether they owned property. However, he also thought class was about status – the degree of prestige someone has – and also their political power or ability to influence society.

Weber's model helps explain why a university lecturer might have reasonably high status but moderate wealth, while a successful plumber might have a high income but moderate status.

Functionalist approaches

Émile Durkheim saw society as divided into different functions; differentiated roles were a useful aspect of society, but he didn't think significant material inequality was beneficial. Functionalists, who often drew from Durkheim's work, typically paid less explicit attention to class than Marx or Weber did. Talcott Parsons referred to class on occasion, using a similar approach to Weber. Other US sociologists, such as Kingsley Davis and Wilbert Moore (1945), saw social stratification as the ranking of individuals based on their value to society. Such ***hierarchy***, they argued, is necessary and an advantage – those jobs that benefit society the most should have the better rewards in terms of finance and prestige. The problem is, who gets to decide which is more rewarding – thus a Marxist would argue that middle-class ideology plays a big role in shaping these attitudes.

Care workers typically earn a very low wage relative to those working in areas such as marketing. Does this mean their work is less valuable?

CONTEMPORARY MODELS OF CLASS

Marxist and Weberian approaches to class still have a strong, and relevant, influence on understandings of class and inequality. Functionalist ideas on class (and on many other things) have much less authority, with many having a strong antipathy to their inherently conservative argument.

Though much has changed in society since Marx and Weber were making their observations, what endures is the idea that class can, and should, be defined and measured. The ways in which that definition and measurement have occurred, however, have differed greatly, in part reflecting changing social dynamics and attitudes. Indeed, though many in the UK may be quick to place the people they meet into one of three presumed classes – working class, middle class or upper class – depending on their accent, job or attitude, office measurements have recognized many more classes. From 1911 until the 1980s

In the UK, despite social shifts meaning there are several social classes, many people recognize three main classes: upper, middle and working.

in the UK, the Registrar General's (RGSC) measurement of class was based on the occupation of the 'head of a household' (male) and social standing (very Weberian), which identified five basic classes. This is an example of what Pamela Abbott and Claire Wallace (1997) termed a 'malestream' approach, with women and children assumed to be the same class as the 'man of the house'. In 1990, the Standard Occupational Classification (SOC) still used occupation, but also the degree of skill required for each job, and created seven classes. Some, like John Goldthorpe, thought socioeconomic groups (SEGs) were a better measure than social class for social scientific purposes. He proposed 17 groups.

Changing measures of class

CASE STUDY: THE AFFLUENT WORKER STUDIES

John Goldthorpe's influential research in 1960s Luton, UK, challenged assumptions about working-class ***embourgeoisement*** (a supposed growth of the middle classes). Despite rising prosperity, distinct class-based attitudes and social networks persisted.

The rise of the leisure class? Some have argued that many people have more time and money to engage in leisure pursuits.

THE DECLINE AND RE-EMERGENCE OF CLASS ANALYSIS

The period after the Second World War saw unprecedented ***social mobility*** and the rise of mass consumption, particularly in the US but also across Europe, leading some sociologists to question the continued relevance of class. This 'death of class' thesis was seen to be supported by rising living standards across society, an expansion of white-collar employment, the growth of mass education and increasing individualization of society.

However, many academics showed clearly that class-based inequality and poverty had never gone away and was still a major cause of social division.

THE GREAT BRITISH CLASS SURVEY

Recent theoretical developments have moved beyond purely economic definitions of class to examine how inequality operates through cultural and social mechanisms. The largest study of class in British history, Mike Savage *et al.*'s (2011) Great British Class Survey (161,000 respondents) revealed seven distinct social classes, demonstrating the complexity of modern class structures:

1. Elite
2. Established middle class
3. Technical middle class
4. New affluent workers
5. Traditional working class
6. Emerging service workers
7. Precariat

This survey took into account the types of school people attended, the music they listen to, who their social groups are, as well as earnings and occupation. But this doesn't fully explain why people are in these categories; for this we need to grapple with ideas of exploitation, representation and power. In other words, we need to understand why some cultures are valued and others are not.

THE CULTURAL TURN IN CLASS ANALYSIS

Pierre Bourdieu's work, influenced by Marx and Weber, revolutionized class analysis, adding to a focus on economics by introducing a variety of concepts. His work on capitals (or resources) is perhaps the best known.

- ***Economic capital***: financial resources and assets
- ***Cultural capital***: educational qualifications, cultural knowledge
- ***Social capital***: networks and connections
- ***Habitus***: our dispositions, our tastes, our experience of our bodies
- ***Fields***: social 'games'; there are educational, political, cultural, economic etc. fields
- ***Symbolic capital or power***: prestige and honour – legitimation in the eyes of others, converts to power and which enables us (or not) to 'play the field'

The foods we typically eat are a strong indicator of the class to which we belong.

His approach showed how class distinctions are reproduced through subtle cultural mechanisms, from taste in art, food and music to bodily dispositions and linguistic styles. The resources (capitals) we have, determine our tastes (habitus) and behaviour in various social contexts (fields). Thus, his ideas provide crucial tools for analyzing how class privilege is maintained across generations.

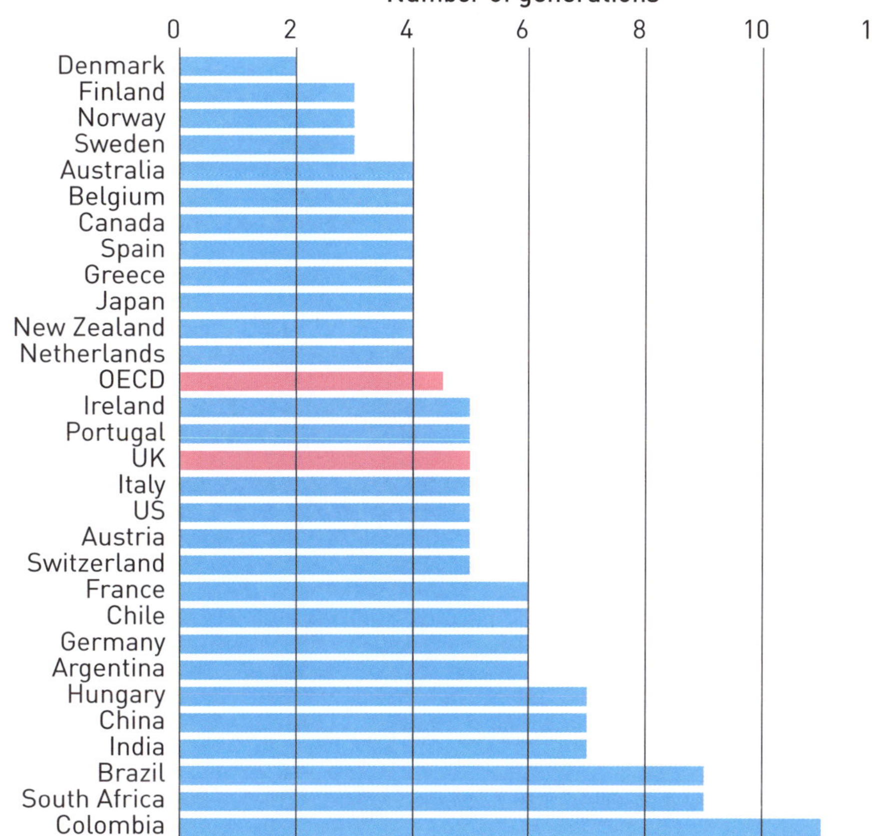

This graph shows rates of intergenerational income mobility. The UK and US don't fare that well.

MECHANISMS OF CLASS FORMATION

Education and social mobility

Bourdieu was particularly interested in the role that education played in perpetuating ideas about class. Contemporary research reveals persistent class inequalities in educational outcomes:

- Only 6 per cent of doctors and 7 per cent of barristers come from working-class backgrounds (UK Government, 2023).

- Children from privileged backgrounds are 80 per cent more likely to attend elite universities such as Oxford and Cambridge.

There is little evidence to suggest that trickle-down economics or crumbs from the table – happens!

The myth of meritocracy

One argument against class being a barrier in education or employment has been a suggestion that neoliberal societies are meritocratic. In other words, some argue that people's success or failure is determined by their ability because there is equality of opportunity. To support such an argument, they will often find examples of a working-class person who has 'made it', rising through the social and cultural ranks. However, many recent (and older) studies challenge the notion that we live in a true ***meritocracy***.

Bourdieu showed that education is important for dominant groups in society because it reproduces power inequalities. Success at things like exams requires cultural capital, not just the right knowledge but also the language to respond in the expected/required way. Cultural capital obscures the inequalities at play, focusing on the few working-class children who succeed, and the myth of meritocracy is perpetuated. Meritocracy, as Daniel Markovits (2019) argues, favours the rich even when everyone is playing by the same rules.

Sam Friedman's *The Class Ceiling* (2019) reveals how privileged backgrounds continue to advantage people even after entering elite professions. Research by Mike Savage *et al.* (2015) shows how 'merit' itself is often defined in class-specific ways. Their work clearly shows the role of inherited capitals in perpetuating inequality and the structural barriers to social mobility (the ability to move 'up' the class system).

Trickle down economics?

Many who purport meritocracy also argue for so called 'trickle-down' economics theory – that the super-rich (or 'over-rich' as Mike Berners-Lee prefers) will invest etc. and as a result, bring everyone up. As we shall see, there is not much evidence for that happening.

CONTEMPORARY CLASS EXPERIENCES AND IDENTITY

CLASS, SHAME AND (DIS)IDENTIFICATION

As we shall see, understandings of class often invoke moral judgements. Charles Booth's poverty maps (described below) remain very important but they were not without their problems; his colour-coding of the most poverty-stricken areas of London came with the moralistic description of 'Lowest class. Vicious, semi-criminal'. More recently, Imogen Tyler has shown how labels such as 'chav' (UK) or 'white trash' (US), along with many other terms like 'pramface', repeatedly depict the working classes as 'revolting subjects', which further marginalize them. Using the work of British sociologists Beverley Skeggs (1997) and Steph Lawler (2005), we can start to understand the ways in which people negotiate class identities, and associations of disgust and shame, in often very complex ways.

How words marginalize people

The politics of respectability

What is 'respectable'?

Skeggs argues that class is not just an economic position but is produced through cultural representations and, crucially, is marked through moral evaluations and inscribed or written on bodies. The media is an institution able to legitimize the ***symbolic power*** of the middle classes and denigrate the working classes, an act of ***symbolic violence*** for Bourdieu and an example of the reproduction of inequality. Representations of working-class people effectively prevent the power to convert cultural capital to symbolic capital; it devalues and denigrates their meagre capitals. Reality television, for instance, often presents the working class, especially women, as 'doing things wrong' – being 'bad' parents, consuming too much of the wrong food, alcohol, cigarettes and so on. Her research demonstrates that these judgements are so powerful, they impact how many working-class women see themselves.

Ideas of ***respectability*** were woven into the emergence of class, which is a process of differentiation: the middle-classes were able to define themselves as respectable and by turns, working-class subjectivity became its opposite, associated with hatred, fear and anxiety, a threat to middle-class values. The women Skeggs observed invest in respectability as a form of cultural capital. They distance themselves from pathologized representations of working-class identity, an identity given little or no value in society, creating alternative value systems outside middle-class norms

The portrayal of Vicky Pollard in Little Britain *is an example of a pathological representation of working class femininity.*

Hidden injuries of class

Lawler's work examines how middle-class identities are constructed through expressions of disgust at working-class tastes. Using Bourdieu's ideas, she argues that presentations of the working class in relation to 'lack' (not of resources but of taste or even humanity) and 'decline' (from a once hard-working class to a class presumed to be work-shy

White stilettos were a middle-class symbol of, or joke about, working-class 'Essex girls'.

THE PAULSGROVE WOMAN

One example of middle-class disgust that Lawler cites comes from a middle-class broadsheet newspaper, describing a protest about child abusers who had been housed on a particular estate:

> *There on TV were the mums (no dads) faces studded, shoulders tattooed, too-small pink singlets worn over shell-suit bottoms, pallid faces under peroxided hair telling tales of a diet of hamburgers, cigarettes and pesticides.*
>
> *And they'd taught their three-year-old kids (on whose behalf all this was supposedly being done) to chant slogans about hanging and killing. Paulsgrove Woman, I felt, was of an alien race to me. No wonder the BBC employed anthropologists with cut-glass accents to interpret these people for the sake of their bemused viewers. Never had the social divide seemed so wide (Aaronovitch, 2000).*

This example, Lawler argues, assumes that most readers will be similarly bemused by, perhaps frightened of, working-class people. We see the power of middle-class representations to produce working-class bodies as other: style choices such as tattoos and piercings that are read as personal expression on middle-class bodies becomes a symbol of 'the mob' on working-class bodies.

Thus, Lawler's work reveals:

- the role of shame in class experience
- how class is read through bodies and appearances
- the power of 'knowing' and 'not knowing' cultural codes

Using ideas from Marx and Bourdieu, research by both Skeggs and Lawler identifies common strategies:

- Distancing from stigmatized identities
- Claims to ordinariness
- Moral boundary drawing

CONSUMPTION AND CLASS

In 1899 the American sociologist and economist Thorstein Veblen coined the phrase 'conspicuous consumption' to refer to the ways in which the emerging wealthy leisure class – those who don't need to work – bought (often unnecessary) goods, jewellery for instance, in order to make a public display of their wealth and, crucially, to distinguish themselves from those less well-off. He argues that those in the lower social class will try to emulate the lifestyle of the one above; as this happens, the leisure class may disregard an item as it becomes more affordable and ubiquitous, and a new product will be used to symbolize wealth and taste.

Elizabeth Currid-Halkett's *The Sum of Small Things* (Princeton University Press, 2017) shows how the new elite distinguish themselves through inconspicuous consumption – spending on education, healthcare and child-rearing rather than luxury goods.

Expensive but useless? A gold-plated lavatory is an example of unneccessary, ostentatious, 'conspicuous' consumption.

'scroungers') is part of a long-standing middle-class tactic of distinguishing itself. The middle classes can claim a 'natural' superiority through processes of cultural gatekeeping and pathologization of, for example, white working-class parenting. As a result, working-classness becomes 'othered' and middle-classness 'normalized'.

Othering and normalization

UNDERSTANDING POVERTY

It is no surprise that social class is closely related to poverty – those with fewer resources and access to 'capitals' are more like to fall into poverty.

One of the earliest studies of poverty was businessman-turned-social reformer Charles Booth's (1886) mapping of London, which took 20 years. The map was colour-coded with each street given a colour, for instance black to signify the poorest and yellow the richest. Through a series of interviews, he concluded that anyone earning less than 21 shillings a week was living in poverty and, he calculated, about 30 per cent of people in London were in poverty. A bit later on, 1891–1901, Seebohm Rowntree (of the British confectionery-producing family), another philanthropist and sociological researcher, studied poverty in York. He concluded there was a 'poverty line'. And like Booth, he estimated this to be anything under than 21 shillings a week. Unemployment

Charles Booth's study of poverty

PHILANTHROPY ▶ *before the welfare state, society relied on rich well-meaning people (philanthropists) to donate money to support the poor. We are fast returning to that need in the UK today.*

Käthe Kollwitz's Poverty *is a stark reminder of the conditions many lived in, and increasingly do again.*

The 'underclass'

Relative and absolute poverty

Below Average Resources measure

THE 'UNDERCLASS' – A POVERTY OF THOUGHT?

A concept rejected by most sociologists, but which is still heard in public discourse, is the 'underclass'. Coined by a journalist but made popular by US New Right political scientist Charles Murray, it referred to a 'type of poverty'. Taking a functionalist and moralistic approach, Murray argued that the ***welfare state*** had encouraged dependency. He believed there were incentives to become a lone parent, and these 'illegitimate' offspring would become a generation of work-shy youth who would turn to crime. While there is no correlation between youth unemployment and crime and the Joseph Rowntree Foundation have shown conclusively there is no evidence for his assumed culture of lazy dependency, his ideas were very popular at the time. In 1989, the *Sunday Times* newspaper invited him to 'study' Britain, and he came as 'a visitor from a plague area, assessing the spread of the disease'. Murray visited then UK Prime Minister Margaret Thatcher and attended Conservative Party conferences, arguably exerting influence on their policies. Like Murray, Thatcher believed the (heterosexual) nuclear family, with the wife at home, was the ideal. Her government began a dismantling of the welfare state that has continued in her wake.

and illness were the main causes of poverty according to both men. Rowntree also distinguished between primary and secondary poverty. Primary poverty is having too little income to meet the most basic needs (food, heating, shelter). Secondary poverty, he believed, was when people might misuse resources on 'wasteful' things like alcohol – this rather moralistic opinion remains a very popular line of argument today.

Rowntree's concept of primary poverty is still used today, though more often the term 'absolute poverty' is used to describe situations where people cannot afford adequate clothing, fuel, accommodation or household goods. 'Relative poverty' is used in relation to the lack of resources necessary to avoid the lifestyle and living conditions customary to a society. Thus, this poverty line is always shifting – 60 years ago, we would not have conceived that a mobile phone might be necessary for a teenager to feel socially included, for instance, or that all households 'need' a washing machine.

In recent years, the main poverty measure in the UK has been the Households Below Average Income (HBAI), which determines the percentage of those living in low-income households in terms of both absolute and relative poverty. The Department for Work and Pensions (DWP) is now developing a new poverty measure named 'Below Average Resources' (BAR), which will provide a little more information on types of income and assets and unavoidable expenses like childcare or disability costs.

POVERTY AND INEQUALITY IN THE 21ST CENTURY

Richard Wilkinson and Kate Pickett's groundbreaking research in *The Spirit Level* (Allen Lane, 2009) demonstrates that more equal societies almost always perform better on key indicators including:

- mental health
- physical health
- educational performance
- social mobility
- trust and community life

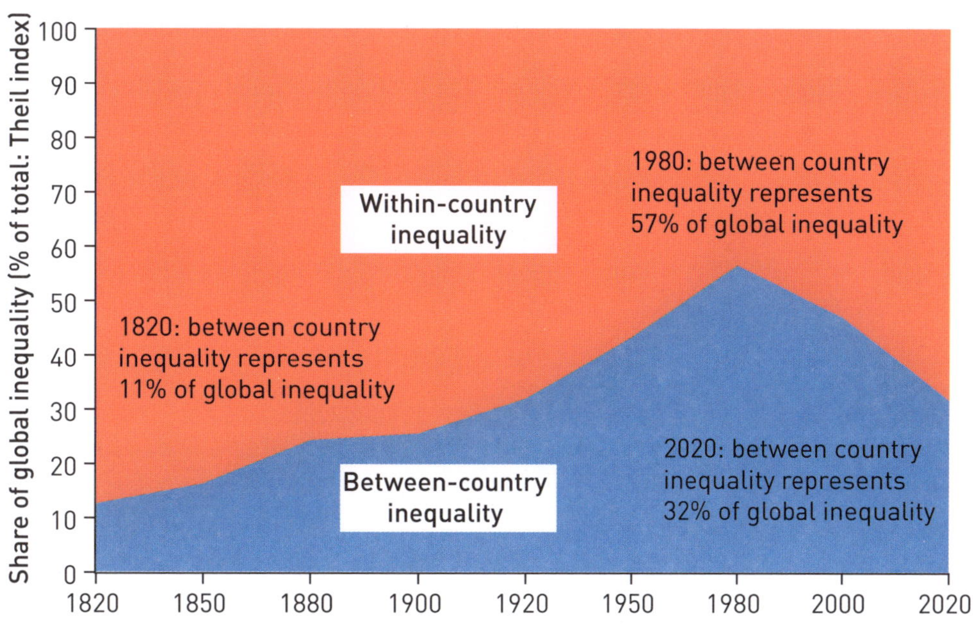

The graph shows relative shifts in between and within country 'inequality'.

CASE STUDY: STRUCTURAL VIOLENCE: POVERTY, INEQUALITY AND HEALTH

The relationship between poverty and health represents one of the most profound examples of social inequality in modern societies. A review led by Professor Michael Marmot (2020) revealed that in the UK, people living in the most deprived areas have life expectancy approximately ten years shorter than those in the least deprived areas. Recent studies highlight concerning trends in infant mortality rates across socioeconomic groups. Data from 2014–2024 shows that infant mortality rates in the most deprived decile are more than twice those in the least deprived areas. This disparity has widened since the 2008 financial crisis, suggesting that ***austerity*** measures have exacerbated health inequalities. The Norwegian sociologist Johan Galtung (1969) introduced the term ***structural violence*** to refer to the ways in which social structures and institutions can limit life in such a way.

Luke Filde's Applicants for Admission to a Casual Ward *was commissioned for a social reform magazine. It shows a queue of homeless people seeking admission to a workhouse.*

Inequality diminishes empathy

In other words, wealthy but unequal societies (with large gaps between the richest and the poorest) such as the UK and the US do badly on these factors. They also showed that the more unequal a society is, the less empathy citizens have for those less fortunate than themselves. Together, they co-founded the charity Equality Trust, which analyzes inequality and lobbies for change.

THE DESERVING AND UNDESERVING POOR: A PERSISTENT DICHOTOMY

Deserving or undeserving

Skeggs, Lawler and many other sociologists allude to the unfortunate persistence of ideas about the 'deserving' and 'undeserving' poor – those deserving of our sympathy and those we are told we should not feel sorry for – when analyzing class, poverty and inequality. The distinction has deep historical roots, including:

- 1601 Elizabethan Poor Law categories
- Victorian workhouse system

- moral judgements about 'idle' vs 'industrious' poor
- Christian ideas of worthy charity recipients
- gender and family status distinctions

Historical literary and artistic depictions reinforced these distinctions, such as in political cartoons, Victorian social novels and campaign materials for charities.

Contemporary manifestations

Modern political rhetoric often reproduces these categories through binaries of 'strivers' vs 'skivers' or 'hard-working families' vs 'benefit scroungers'. These are reinforced through contemporary media representations such as documentaries like *Benefits Street*.

Moral judgement on who deserves benefits

Welfare conditionality serves to underline the moralistic divisions. Modern benefit systems embed deserving/undeserving distinctions through a range of ways. Valerie Walkerdine (2003) has shown how

Increased levels of shame and stigma attached to receiving benefits, mean that fewer people now take up what they need and are entitled to.

STIGMA AND BENEFIT TAKE-UP
The Poverty Alliance (2023), working with the Scottish government, revealed the impact of stigma on benefit take-up rates. Among other things, the study showed the ways in which stigma is built into benefits processes. Many talked about the ways in which stigma around benefits overlapped with other forms of prejudice and discrimination. Common misconceptions that people claiming social security are falsely claiming and committing fraud, or are making a lot of money out of the system, have intensified during the cost-of-living crisis.

THE SEVEN FORMS OF LABOUR SECURITY MISSING FOR THE PRECARIAT
Standing highlighted seven areas of employment security that have been eroded in the recent era:

1. ***Labour market security***: adequate income-earning opportunities
2. ***Employment security***: protection against arbitrary dismissal
3. ***Job security***: ability to retain a niche in employment
4. ***Work security***: protection against accidents and illness at work
5. ***Skill reproduction security***: opportunity to gain skills
6. ***Income security***: assurance of adequate stable income
7. ***Representation security***: having a collective voice in labour markets

the welfare system forces working-class people to tell tales of redemption in order to be given money to live. There might be behavioural conditions, digital surveillance and claimant conditions that reinforce value judgements. Those living in poverty face constant scrutiny of their spending decisions.

We can see these attitudes in relation to the ways different groups receive varying levels of public sympathy and support. For example, pensioners might generally be seen as 'deserving', single parents have historically been under more negative scrutiny, and migrants are frequently excluded from legitimate need.

Internalized shame

These moral categories affect how people seek assistance. Studies have revealed a reluctance to claim entitled benefits, delayed help-seeking, self-blame for circumstances, a distancing from 'undeserving' others and an emphasis on personal responsibility that ignores the social structures causing poverty.

As a result of such stigma, many undergo ongoing and often exhausting strategic presentations of self. For instance, many people feel they must present themselves as 'deserving' by demonstrating constant job search, emphasizing illness/disability and proving 'genuine' need.

Thus, despite centuries of criticism, the deserving/undeserving distinction remains deeply embedded in political discourse, policy design, public attitudes and institutional practices. This persistence reveals how moral judgements about poverty continue to shape responses to economic inequality.

CONTEMPORARY CLASS EXPERIENCES

THE PRECARIAT: A NEW DANGEROUS CLASS?

British economist Guy Standing's (2014) work identifies the precariat, classified in the Great British Class Survey as a distinct social class formed through neoliberal globalization.

Unlike the traditional proletariat, the precariat is characterized by fundamental insecurity across multiple dimensions:

- Job insecurity
- Lack of professional identity
- Limited access to state benefits
- Uncertain future prospects

Portraits of those in the precariat

Ken Loach's 2020 film Sorry We Missed You *highlights the problems of being a gig economy worker by following a fictionalized delivery driver.*

Standing identifies three main groups within the precariat: those falling into the precariat from working-class communities and families; migrants and ethnic minorities; and educated youth and professionals without career paths.

Gig workers

So-called ***gig economy*** workers are an example of the precariat. Instead of having a permanent job, these workers either have short-term contracts or do freelance work and instead of a regular salary, they are

FOCUS: AUSTERITY AND ITS IMPACT
Global austerity policies (across the EU, especially in Greece and the UK), which tend to involve higher taxes and cuts to government spending, as a response to the global financial crisis of 2008, have dramatically affected social inequality. These ongoing measures have seen rising food bank usage, a notable housing crisis, cuts to public services, which impact on many but especially women and minority groups. Thus, they have played a role in reinforcing and expanding class divisions.

More and more people need food banks, such as this one in New York, but sadly, fewer people are donating to them.

paid for each 'gig'. Uber and Lyft drivers, Deliveroo, DoorDash and Instacart couriers have created a large pool of precarious workers – workers not entitled to sick or holiday pay nor the minimum wage.

Using concepts from Marx and Durkheim, Standing argues that the precariat experiences distinctive emotional/psychological effects including anxiety about multiple insecurities, alienation from labour, anomie from lack of meaningful career paths and anger at blocked life chances.

There are also significant political implications according to Standing; drawing on Marx's definition of the lumpenproletariat as a dangerous class, he argues that the precariat represents a 'dangerous class' because it lacks occupational identity. Since it has fundamentally different needs from traditional labour movements and experiences anger without clear political direction, it may be attracted to populist, far-right politics.

Migrant workers

As Panos Theodoropoulos (2025) has shown, migrant workers, both documented and undocumented, often find themselves in highly precarious employment, such as seasonal agricultural labour, and construction and domestic work. Their status means they have a lack of labour protections and are particularly vulnerable to exploitation and abuse. Their precarity increased during the Covid-19 pandemic with, for instance, border closures and economic disruptions exacerbating the insecurity of migrant workers worldwide. Shubhda Arora and Mrinmoy Majumder (2021) argued this was particularly so for women migrant workers. Past, present and future crises because of climate change also contribute to this, making these people casualties of what Rob Nixon (2013) calls ***slow violence***.

GLOBAL INEQUALITIES

Studies on class, poverty and inequality are often focused within one nation state, usually somewhere in the Global North, but what about in a globalized world? Satnam Virdee (2019) argues there has been a 'wilful indifference' to the intersection of class and 'race'; the role of imperialism in producing class relations and inequality is often overlooked. Gurminder Bhambra (2007) points to the ways in which colonialism and the displacement of enslaved people has been central to the growth and 'success' of capitalism and unequal global distribution of resources.

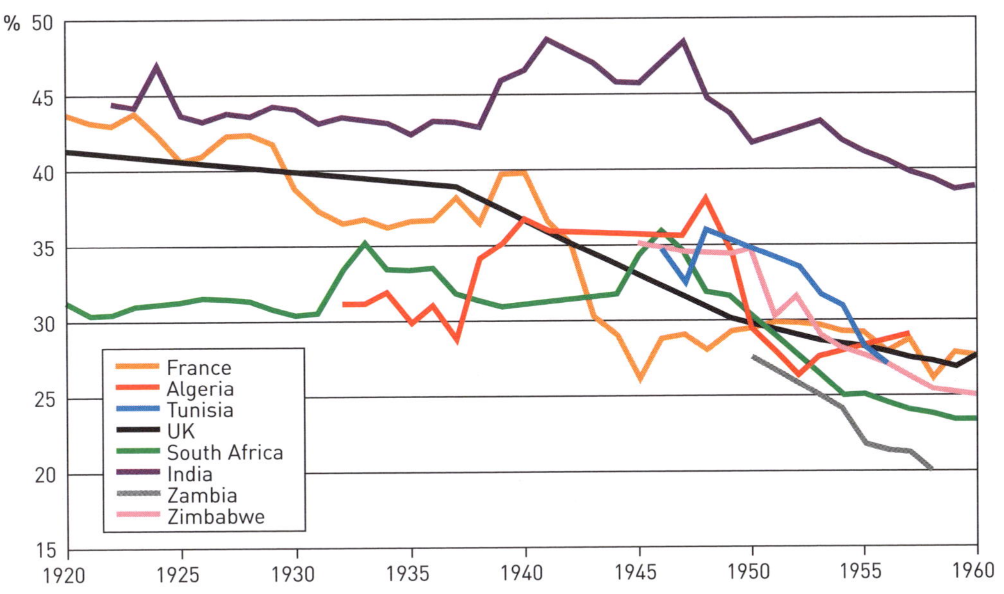

This chart reveals fluctuating yet persistent levels of income inequality.

Global South countries own just 31 per cent of global wealth, despite being home to 79 per cent of the world's population (Oxfam, 2024). Global inequality must be understood through the lens of historical power relations and contemporary economic structures:

The immense wealth gaps we see between nations today have their origins in centuries of colonial exploitation, ***uneven development***, migration and the global expansion of capitalism. These will be discussed further in Chapters 6 and 10 but it is worth reflecting on here.

Uneven levels of development

Case study – garment factories in Bangladesh

Major international high street fashion retailers source clothes from factories in places like Bangladesh where workers are subjected to a range of abuses including violence, harassment, poor ventilation and poverty wages. These companies often pay below the cost of production.

Empire building under colonialism, saw the globe 'carved up' between wealthy nation in the global North.

The colonial legacy

The rise of European colonial empires from the 16th century onwards was predicated on the extraction of resources, the subjugation of local populations and the accumulation of wealth in the imperial centres. This laid the foundations for enduring economic and political imbalances.

Scholars like David Harvey have theorized how capitalism inherently produces 'uneven development' – the concentration of wealth and power in certain regions at the expense of others. This dynamic has persisted in the post-colonial era. Poverty remains concentrated in the Global South, with sub-Saharan Africa and South Asia bearing the brunt of extreme deprivation (in addition, pockets of poverty also persist in wealthy nations, along racial and geographic lines).

The global division of labour

The integration of the Global South into global supply chains and trade networks has often reproduced colonial patterns of resource extraction and low-wage manufacturing. Multinational corporations wield immense power in these asymmetric economic relationships.

Poverty tourism: the commodification of poverty and social inequality

Poverty as entertainment

In many respects, as we have seen, poverty has provided considerable entertainment for the middle-classes, and it has deep roots. Watching the proceedings at the Foundling Hospital, where mothers were forced to take their babies and children if they could not afford to feed them, was possible for those who could afford to pay and watch from the gallery. A child's admittance was on a lottery system. Coloured balls were picked from a bag by the mother – if white, the child was taken in, if black, it was turned away (hence the phrase 'blackballed' to mean not accepted/admitted). 'Slumming' in Victorian Britain and early 20th-century America, a form of urban tourism, was also a popular pastime. The East End of London, being especially poor, was a favoured destination for the rich to visit, curious to witness the assumed 'danger and uncivilized' behaviour of those living in poor areas, or slums. Fabian Frenzel (2015) traces poverty tourism to colonialism and such things as colonial exhibitions and missionary activities.

By the late 1970s, localized slum tours became more popular on a global level. Here, the affluent of the Global North visit the underprivileged of the Global South. Also known as 'slum tourism' or 'poorism', it involves a range of experiences such as organized tours of impoverished areas, educational or charitable visits to poor communities and disaster tourism. Popular sites include:

- Dharavi, Mumbai
- Favelas, Rio de Janeiro
- Townships, South Africa
- Kibera, Nairobi
- Informal settlements, Manila

THEORETICAL PERSPECTIVES

There are a range of sociological frameworks useful for understanding poverty tourism:

- Commodification of poverty (Marx)
- The tourist gaze (Urry)
- Cultural capital (Bourdieu)
- Post-colonial theory

Such theories help us to unpick how poverty becomes spectacle, local people are objectified, ideas of authenticity are constructed, difference is commodified and power relations are reinforced.

Research by Malte Steinbrink (2012) showed annual participation of over 1 million tourists in organized slum tours globally.

Benefits of volunteer tourism?

Volunteer tourism, such as short-term volunteering projects, gap years and 'voluntourism' packages, can, according to Wanda Vrasti (2013), reproduce neo-colonial relationships while providing emotional satisfaction for privileged participants. Frenzel's work supports this, documenting tourist comfort is often prioritized over community benefits. What ostensibly is about alleviating poverty can become an act of exploitation and voyeurism, the reproduction of stereotypes, and the commodification of suffering. It can also serve to bolster the position of the powerful; research by João Afonso Baptista (2017) shows how poverty tourism experiences can be converted into cultural capital on social media, becoming a mark of cosmopolitan awareness.

WE'RE ALL IN THIS TOGETHER?

Social inequality remains one of the most pressing issues of our time, with widening disparities in wealth, income and opportunities affecting societies globally. Despite claims of classlessness, it remains fundamental to understanding contemporary inequality, shaping life chances and intersecting with gender, ethnicity, age etc. in sometimes complicated ways. Events such as the 2008 financial crisis, Covid-19 pandemic and climate change have exacerbated class inequalities, throwing more people into poverty. But this is neither natural nor inevitable – sociologists argue that these differences in outcomes are based on the organization of social institutions such as the education system, law, the media and so on. The divisions are a direct result of social processes, formed through interaction with organizations and groups, and are related to power; some groups have more power than others. In other words, the divisions often exist because those with power benefit from them. In relation to social class, Marx believed power was tied in with the economy; many agree but have expanded his theory to look at this in relation to culture too. Gramsci's 'pessimism of the intellect, optimism of the will' enables hope for change.

Chapter Six
RACE AND ETHNICITY

The historical construction of 'race' – The (not so) enlightenment period – Atlantic slavery and 'scientific' racism – Colonialism and its legacies – Consequences of the myth of 'race' – Systemic racism in the US – The holocaust: a failure or product of modernity? – Distinguishing 'race' and ethnicity – The cultural turn – Structural racism and institutional discrimination – Resisting racism – The persistence of racism?

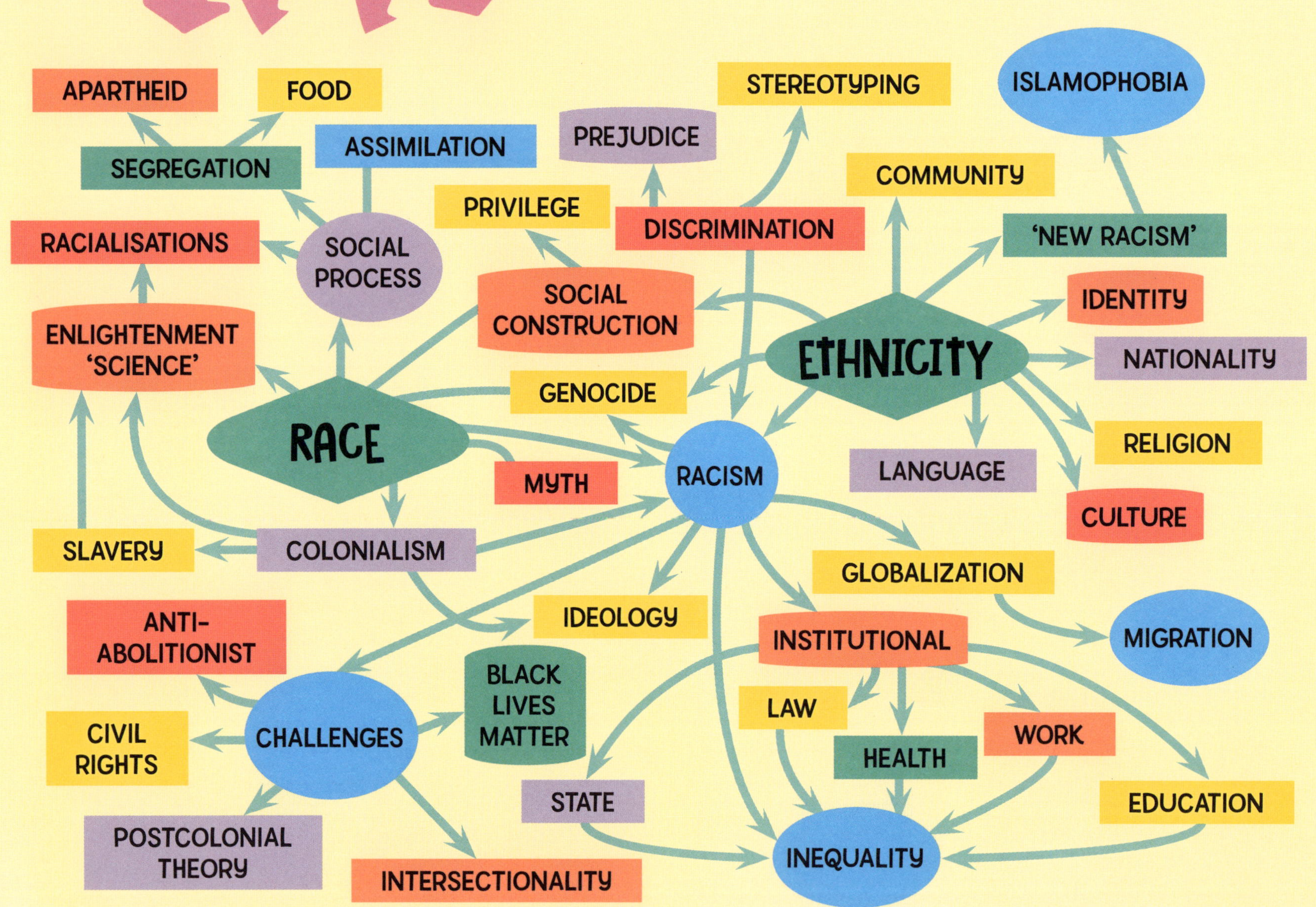

Many people across the globe gathered to protest about racist policing.

STOP AND SEARCH ▶ ***a power given to police, enabling them to stop, and search, anyone they suspect might be a criminal. In* Policing the Crisis*, Stuart Hall (1978) revealed how such powers were used much more on Black people.***

In 2020 the murders of Breonna Taylor and George Floyd, among others, by white police officers in the US, made global news and drew much-needed attention to the issue of systemic racism. This was compounded by a series of events such as when black Olympic sprinters Bianca Williams and Ricardo Dos Santos were pulled over by Met Police Officers in London for a stop and search. The athletes were on their way back from a training session and had their three-year-old son in the back seat of their car, which was followed by the police who claimed they suspected they were linked to gang activity. The officers were sacked (then reinstated) when courts ruled they'd lied about smelling cannabis. Stop and search powers and physical force are much more likely to be used on Black and Minority Ethnic (BAME) people; research consistently shows that there is significant disproportionality in police treatment of BAME people compared to white people. Sociological theories of 'race' and ethnicity help to explain why this is so.

CASE STUDY: SOME LIVES SEEM TO MATTER MORE THAN OTHERS...

Black Lives Matter (BLM) is a global grassroots movement formed in 2013, after the murderer of Trayvon Martin was acquitted. Martin, an unarmed teenager, was shot by George Zimmerman, a neighbourhood watch volunteer. The acquittal of Zimmerman led to a series of protests and BLM was formed on social media with the hashtag #BlackLivesMatter. In the years between 2013 and 2020, many other African Americans were shot, killed in 'choke holds' or died in police custody, though these murders received very little media coverage. It was the murder of George Floyd, an unarmed Black man, however, that galvanized the movement worldwide. A bystander had recorded a police officer kneeling on Floyd's neck, as he repeatedly said he couldn't breathe. The white officer, Derek Chauvin, ignored him and after nearly 10 minutes in this 'hold', Floyd died. When the video circulated, there were nationwide and global demonstrations.

The concepts of 'race' and ethnicity have profoundly shaped society, particularly over the last couple of centuries. Yet 'race' is a concept many sociologists agree doesn't exist. So why, then, focus on it? As we shall see, while 'race' has no biological basis, its social and political impacts have been – and continue to be – devastatingly powerful and real. We will examine how modern ideas about 'race' emerged and evolved, paying particular attention to their social construction and the deep-felt consequences of racist ideologies.

THE HISTORICAL CONSTRUCTION OF 'RACE'

THE (NOT SO) ENLIGHTENMENT PERIOD

Modern conceptions of 'race' emerged during the European Enlightenment, as philosophers and scientists attempted to categorize human diversity within their new systems of knowledge. Scholars like Carl Linnaeus (1707–1778) and Johann Friedrich Blumenbach (1752–1840) developed racial classifications that reflected and reinforced European colonial power.

CASE STUDY: BLUMENBACH'S FIVE 'RACES'

Blumenbach's influential 1795 work established five racial categories: Caucasian, Mongolian, Ethiopian, American Indian and Malayan. While he believed all humans shared a common origin, his hierarchy erroneously placed 'Caucasians' at the centre as the 'original' 'race' (he also displayed a bias, stating that Georgian women were the most beautiful). While he wasn't racist in his attitudes, many of his assumptions were used to reinforce European supremacist ideologies (an idea that a group – often along lines of 'race', religion or gender – is superior and others inferior).

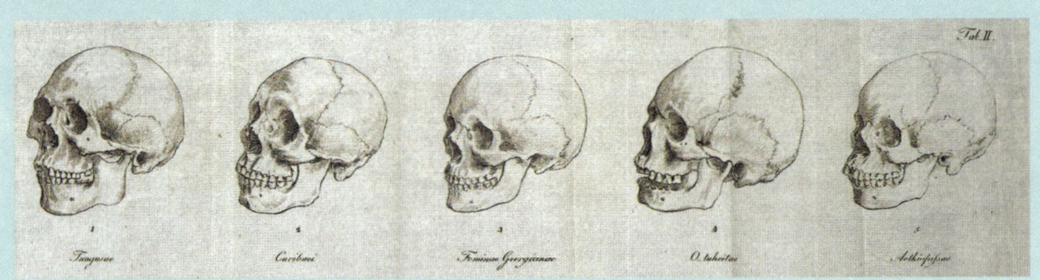

Illustration from Blumenbach's original 1795 work, De generis humani varietate nativa, *showing skulls, with racial categories.*

'RACE' ▶ *an historical classification system that attempts to group people according to surface, visual traits or differences such as colour of skin or hair type. There is no genetic basis for this grouping. The inverted commas around 'race' connote its contested/troubled origins and usage.*

RACIALIZATION ▶ *the process by which different groups in society are put into categories based on ideas of 'race'.*

RACISM ▶ *the prejudice and discrimination based on 'race'*

ETHNICITY ▶ *a broader concept than 'race' that refers to the ways groups are marked, or construct themselves, as 'different' based on shared cultural heritage, including elements like language, religion, nationality and traditions.*

COLONIZATION ▶ *the invasion and taking over of land to exploit it economically*

NATIONALITY ▶ *being recognized as a citizen of a nation, perhaps through birth or marriage.*

ATLANTIC SLAVERY AND 'SCIENTIFIC' RACISM

The transatlantic slave trade created powerful economic incentives to justify racial hierarchies. Plantation owners and colonial authorities increasingly relied on pseudoscientific theories – forms of biological racism – to defend the enslavement of African peoples.

Once Europeans discovered the Americas, such as when Christopher Columbus arrived in the Caribbean in 1492, they very quickly realized the huge economic potential therein. Portugal, Spain and many other countries took control of territories, using violence to force Indigenous people to mine for metals and minerals such as gold, or to farm crops including tobacco. Through the imposition of Christianity, they also attempted to force a rejection of their culture and beliefs. As these (stolen) empires grew, they needed a substantial workforce. Between 1500 and 1800, at least 13 million African people were forced into slavery and trafficked to European colonies and plantations in the Americas, the Caribbean and South Asia. Thousands of journeys were made by the slave ships, packing enslaved people in inhumane conditions – up to two million people died on those journeys due to malnutrition, violent punishments, abuse and poor sanitation. Many British companies, people and ports – like Liverpool, Bristol and London – grew very wealthy as a result of their role in the slave trade.

Plan of lower deck with the stowage of 292 slaves –130 of these being stowed under the shelves.

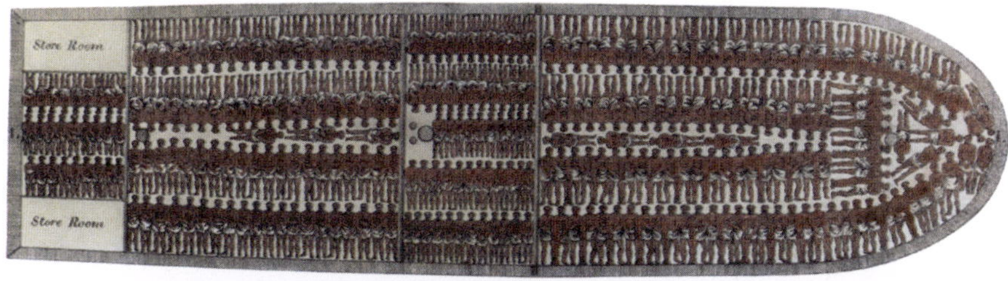

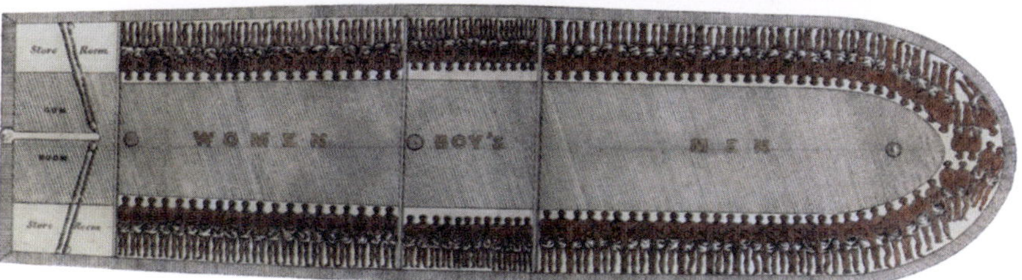

More than 12 million enslaved Africans were transported in horrific conditions, in ships design to crowd as many bodies in as possible.

Philosophers and scientists like David Hume (1711–1776) argued that science 'proved' that some 'races' were inferior to others. Some erroneous yet influential ideas included polygenism, the false theory that different 'races' had separate origins. Thomas Herbert in 1634, for instance, tried to prove that Africans were descended from apes and were a separate and inferior 'race'. Later, pseudoscientific ideas such as ***Social Darwinism*** misapplied Charles Darwin's (1859) evolutionary theory to justify racial inequality. The idea of 'survival of the fittest', which many attribute to Darwin, was in fact coined by the sociologist Herbert Spencer (1820–1903), when describing Darwin's work. He thought societies were evolving, some becoming more superior and that these were linked to 'race'. Phrenology, the pseudoscience of measuring skull shapes to determine characteristics, was used by people like Charles Caldwell (1772–1853), who also happened to be a slave owner. He claimed that certain bumps on the skulls of Africans denoted 'tameableness', going so far as to claim they 'needed' masters.

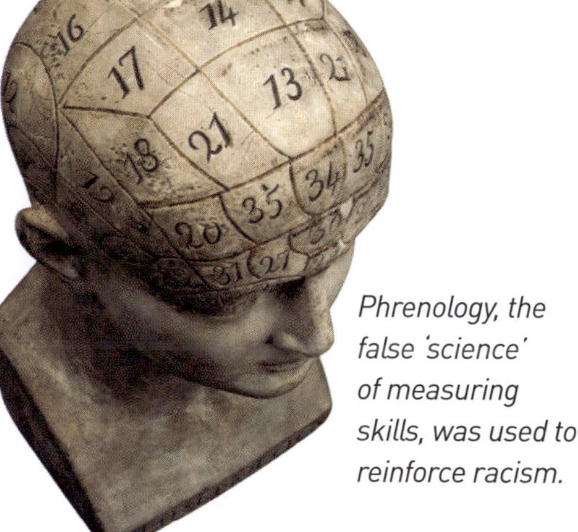

Phrenology, the false 'science' of measuring skills, was used to reinforce racism.

Enslaved people physically carrying the ruling class, a metaphor too, for colonialism and its ongoing impact.

COLONIALISM AND ITS LEGACIES

Frantz Fanon (1952, 1961) examined the psychosocial impacts of colonization and the ways in which colonial systems affect both colonizer and colonized. This oppressive dynamic created what he termed a 'Manichaean world', one divided between the European and the native. Manichaeism was a religion that developed in Persia in the 3rd century CE. It is concerned with a struggle between light (good) and dark (evil). Fanon used this as an analogy to describe the ways in which the colonials represent themselves as a force for the good, with the colonized described as having the potential for evil. The English, for instance, described Africa as the 'Dark Continent', and narratives depicted Africans as lazy, criminal or evil and in need of 'correction' or salvation via white settlers. Fanon's perspective influenced ***postcolonial theory*** and sociological approaches to studying racial dominance.

Colonial systems established racial hierarchies that continue to shape contemporary societies. The millions of displaced, enslaved Africans have resulted in an African diaspora: people across the world who continue to face often violent treatment as a result of continued racist ideologies. Sociologist Julian Go (2016), for instance, analyzes how the colonial practices and ideologies that enabled imperial expansion while creating racialized systems of governance that justified European domination, continue to negatively impact people through such things as the policing practices described at the beginning of this chapter.

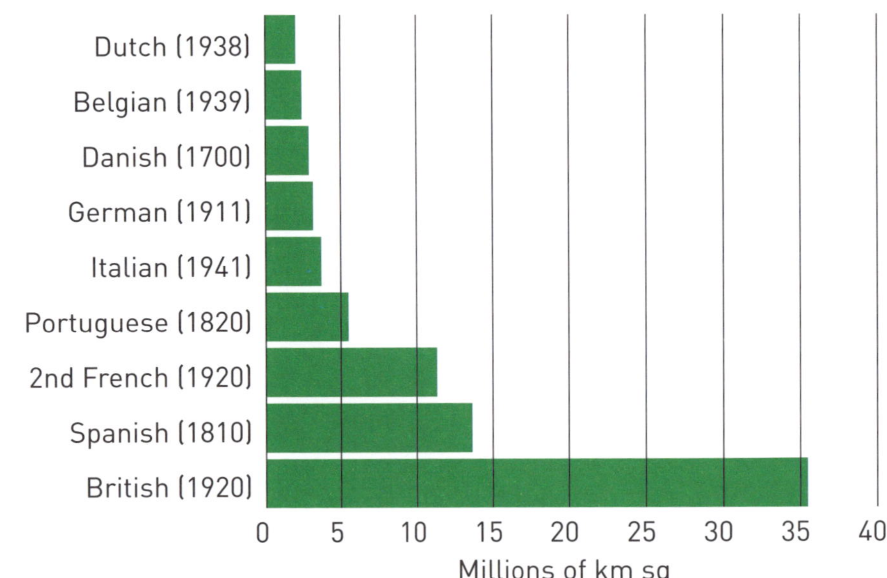

A graph showing the extent of the European colonial empires at their height.

Indeed, sociologist Gurminder K. Bhambra (2007) argues for 'connected sociologies' that acknowledge how colonialism shaped modernity itself, challenging Eurocentric narratives that treat Western (or Global North) development as separate from colonial exploitation. With reference to British conquest and rule in India, Dipankar Gupta (2017) argues that racism in contemporary India is a colonial inheritance.

PROTEST SONGS
Protest songs, such as 'Strange Fruit', made famous by Billie Holiday, drew attention to the racist attacks. More recently, 'Killing in the Name' by Rage Against the Machine drew parallels between the actions of the Ku Klux Klan and police brutality in the 1990s.

CONSEQUENCES OF THE MYTH OF 'RACE'

Modern genetic research has conclusively demonstrated that there is more genetic variation within traditionally defined racial groups than between them. The Human Genome Project and subsequent studies have shown that superficial physical differences account for only a tiny fraction of human genetic variation. Perhaps the most fundamental sociological insight about 'race' is that it is socially constructed. While physical differences between humans exist, the categorization of these differences into discrete 'races' is a social process rather than a biological reality. As sociologists Michael Omi and Howard Winant (2014) argue, 'race' is 'a concept that signifies and symbolizes social conflicts and interests by referring to different types of human bodies'. In other words, racial categories are created, maintained and transformed through, often violent, social and historical processes.

The historical evidence for this social construction is compelling. Racial classifications have varied dramatically across societies and historical periods. For example, the political scientist Melissa Nobles (2001) highlights how the US census has repeatedly changed its racial categories over time, reflecting shifting social understandings rather than biological discoveries. A person classified as 'Black' in the United States might be categorized differently in Brazil, the Dominican Republic or South Africa – not because their biology changes when crossing borders, but because racial classification systems differ between societies.

Nevertheless, the consequences of racist 'scientific' discourse have been devastating. What follows are just a few of the many examples we can take from history, the consequences of which are still felt.

LYNCHING ▶ ***the murder of someone for an alleged crime without an official trial. It is a form of mob rule. These public executions are usually done by hanging but sometimes whipping, burning or tarring-and-feathering. While anyone can be lynched, sociologists have argued that lynching in the Southern states of the US was a form of terrorist control over Black Americans.***

SYSTEMIC RACISM IN THE UNITED STATES

As we have already seen, the Americas played a role in the Atlantic slave trade and one of its legacies is a large African American population in North America. Another legacy is systemic racism. We should also not forget that North America is founded on the ***genocide*** of Native American populations and the taking of their land.

In the late 1800s and early 1900s, lynching of African Americans by white supremacist mobs such as the Ku Klux Klan (KKK), served to marginalize and exclude Black Americans. The KKK were a Protestant, far-right, white supremacist group who emerged in 1865 in protest at the results of the American Civil War and the abolition of slavery. Ida B. Wells (1862–1931), for instance, an American sociologist and early civil rights activist, argued that lynching was 'that last relic of barbarism and slavery'.

Post-slavery segregation in the US

Between 1874 and 1965 in the South, states imposed segregation of Black and white people – they had to attend separate institutions such as schools, churches, hospitals and could not sit together on buses or park benches, and they were not allowed to marry one another. These rulings, known as the 'Jim Crow Laws' (Jim Crow was a travelling minstrel band) were, ostensibly, supposed to ensure 'separate but equal' facilities but the reality was that Black people received inferior treatment and a range of other abuses. W.E.B. Du Bois, another early sociologist to analyze 'race', gave many examples of social, legal and economic discrimination against African Americans. In 1903 he argued that 'the problem of the Twentieth Century is the problem of the colour-line'.

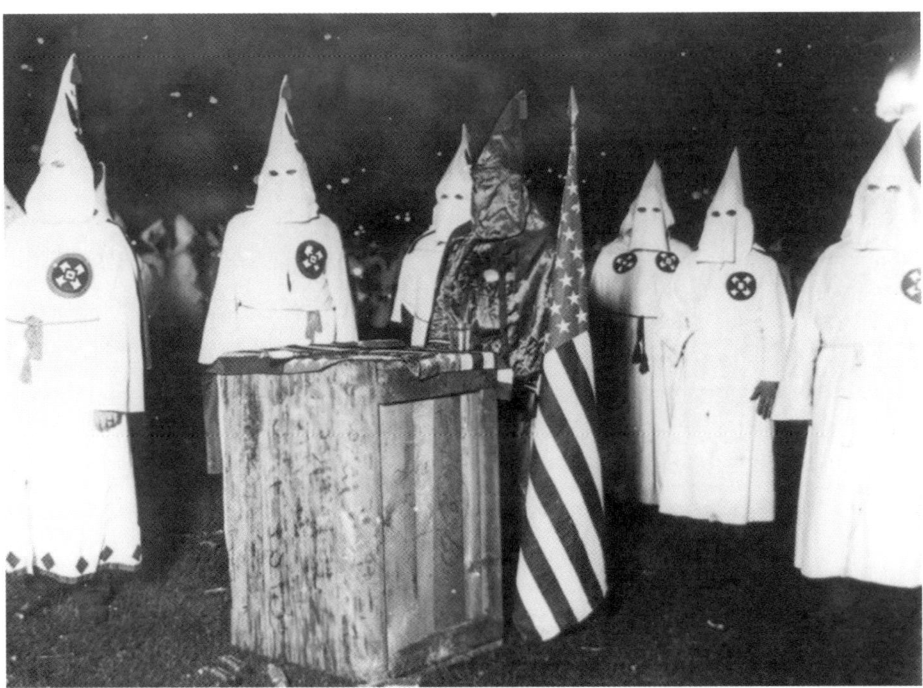

A meeting of the Ku Klux Klan. They wear conical hoods, disguising their faces, along with the white robes embroidered with a cross. All of these symbolize hatred.

Impact of Jim Crow laws

Many US social institutions and key organizations were formed at this time of exclusion and so, as we shall see, are still arguably inherently racist; exclusion is built into their fabric and practices.

THE HOLOCAUST: A FAILURE OR PRODUCT OF MODERNITY?

A deadly racial ideology

The Nazi regime in Germany built upon centuries of European anti-Semitism, combining it with earlier forms of ***scientific racism*** and contemporary eugenics theories to create a deadly racial ideology. History points to the ways in which Jews once more became a convenient scapegoat – a group blamed for things for which they are not responsible – to blame for the economic hardships Germany suffered, this time after the Second World War. German scientists like Eugen Fischer (1874–1967) developed elaborate racial classification systems that were used to justify genocide. Fischer experimented on people in Africa, for instance, sterilizing Herero women against their will. His arguments that interracial marriages should not be allowed meant that by 1912 German colonies did not allow them.

The Nazis and anti-semitism

Even before Hitler came to power, Nazi anti-Semitism was no secret. Jews were constructed as a 'race' by the Nazis, rather than a religious group – the *Untermenschen* (German for 'subhumans') who were constructed as un-German. A range of increasingly discriminatory laws were introduced, and organized anti-Jewish violence forced many people to leave their homes and seek asylum elsewhere. During the ***Holocaust*** itself, six million Jews were murdered. Zygmunt Bauman's controversial book *Modernity and the Holocaust* (Polity Press, 1989) challenged traditional views of the Holocaust as being an aberration in the face of modern ***rationality***. Rather, he argued, it was a product of a modern rational society – the Weberian bureaucracy and efficiency of society enabled the totalitarian control and violence we saw in Nazi Germany.

HOLOCAUST ▶ ***the state-sponsored genocide of six million Jews in Europe. (Roma and Sinti people, gay men, lesbians, disabled people, communists and other prisoners of war take the figure closer to 11 million people.)***

Millions of people were deported by Nazi Germany to killing centres via the European train networks, in shocking, crowded conditions.

Nelson Mandela, leader of the African National Congress (ANC), a group who lobbied for the end of apartheid. Mandela (1918–2013) was imprisoned for 27 years. On his release in 1994, he was elected as the first Black President of South Africa and apartheid formally ended.

Often on the periphery of towns and cities, townships commonly have few resources and poor infrastructure. This picture shows Tulbagh, Western Cape.

APARTHEID SOUTH AFRICA

Apartheid is a term that emerged in South Africa. In Afrikaans – the language of the descendants of the Dutch white colonists of the 17th century – it means 'apartness' or 'separateness', and it is institutionalized segregation along lines of 'race'. After the Second World War, the National Party, with their racist white supremacist ideology, came to power. In order to maintain white minority rule, from 1948 a series of laws enforced segregation, which oppressed the Black majority. These included denying Black employees access to jobs of status and good pay and separate education with schools for Black children having few resources. Another significant law enforced the removal of Black communities from their land and forced them into segregated areas known as townships.

Although legislated apartheid ended in 1994, its impacts remain, with stark divisions in terms of access to social and economic resources.

AUSTRALIAN GENOCIDE

As British colonisers 'settled' in Australia from the late 1700s, there were many massacres of its Indigenous Peoples. Once the whites were established in power, they had a series of policies that enforced 'assimilation'. The intention was that Blackness would 'die out'. One tactic, from 1910 to 1970, was to remove children from their families and place them with white families or in boarding schools. There, many of these children experienced a range of deprivations and abuses. Systematic discrimination and racism still exists. For instance, Aboriginal Australians still experience poorer healthcare, education and differential police treatment.

The 2002 film, *Rabbit-Proof Fence*, based on the book by Doris Pilkington Garimara, is a true story following three Mardu Aboriginal girls taken from their families and placed in a government settlement.

Uncle Sam, symbol of America, is shown brandishing the American flag as swarms of Italian immigrants, depicted as vermin, enter the US.

DISTINGUISHING 'RACE' AND ETHNICITY

While 'race' and ethnicity are related concepts that often overlap in everyday discourse, sociologists typically distinguish between them. 'Race' refers to categorization based primarily on perceived physical or visible characteristics and is often imposed by others. Ethnicity, on the other hand, refers to shared cultural characteristics such as language, religion, customs and ancestry, and is more commonly claimed by group members themselves.

As sociologist Stephen Cornell (1996) explains, 'ethnicity is fundamentally a matter of identity, a claim about who I am or who we are and what marks me or us off from others'. While racial categories often carry connotations of physical difference, ethnic categories primarily emphasize cultural heritage.

We can consider the racist treatment of Irish Americans as a case study. Arguably, the US immigration system has been shaped by and reproduces ***white supremacy*** and ***structural racism***. In the 19th century, immigrants coming to America faced significant prejudice and discrimination. Magazines of the time referred to immigrants as a hopeless burden on the state (a familiar rhetoric in contemporary society). Irish immigrants to the United States faced severe discrimination and were often portrayed in political cartoons with ape-like features – suggestive of racial othering and meant to signify their supposed inferior position in society. However, Noel Ignatiev (1995) suggests that over time Irish Americans came to be seen as 'white' while maintaining a distinct ethnic identity through cultural practices, holidays (such as St Patrick's Day), and identification with Irish heritage. This historical example illustrates how racial and ethnic categorizations can shift over time and are, thus, social constructions.

Structural racism

THE CULTURAL TURN

The Birmingham Centre for Contemporary Cultural Studies (CCCS) was a research centre that studied popular culture. Their neo-Marxist approach focused less on traditional Marxist ideas of the ownership of the ***means of production***, and more on the impact of superstructure and culture on capitalism. A prominent member of this centre was Jamaican-born British sociologist Stuart Hall (1932–2014). Hall pointed to the ways in which images and discourses of Black people in Britian portrayed them as' different' and a problem.

Cultural racism

Paul Gilroy's (1956–) now classic study from 1987, 'There Ain't no Black in the Union Jack', contended that politicians in the UK weren't taking 'race' seriously. People taking part in 'race' riots in 1980s, he argued, developed a sense of community, freedom and belonging. Though he has been accused by some of applying 19th-century ideas about working-class resistance to the Black population, his work, and Hall's, highlights the role of culture and ideology in the emergence of a new racism – ***cultural racism***. While claims of racial inferiority may have diminished (though not disappeared), cultural difference is now seen to threaten the mainstream. Gilroy (2004) identified what he called **postcolonial melancholia** – a state where heterosexual white men feel threatened by the (limited) rights afforded to minority groups, including women, LGBT+ people and BAME people. Such people harbour a desire to go back to the so-called golden days, when their dominance was assured. Ideas about nationality, specifically 'Britishness', he suggested, have racist consequences – imaginings of Britishness invoke whiteness, meaning that black Britons are constructed as 'outsiders'.

Postcolonial melancholia and racism

Frustration ignored for decades about poor housing, mass youth unemployment and police brutality experienced by black communities, led to a wave of protests and demonstrations, some of which turned violent, in places such as Brixton in London, Toxteth in Liverpool and Moss Side in Manchester, in the spring and summer of 1981.

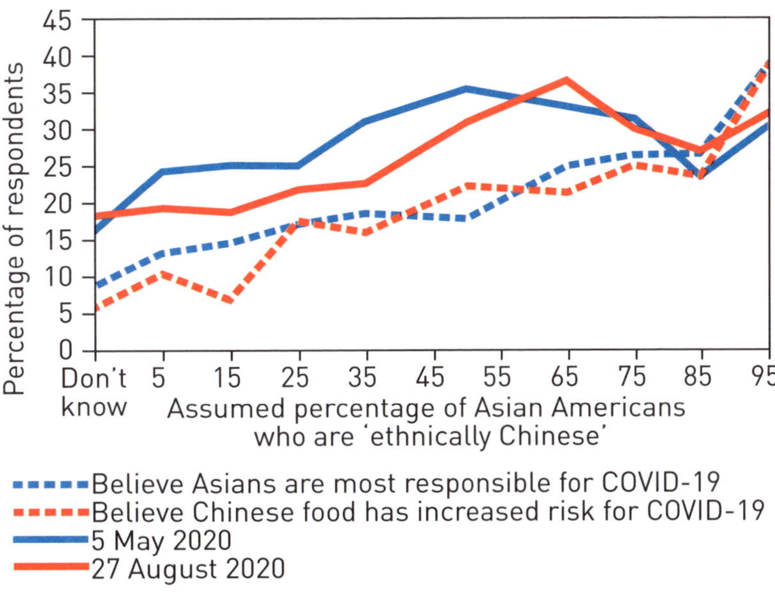

Chart showing the rise of hate towards Asian Americans, who were falsly blamed for the spread of COVID-19.

Their emphasis on racism based on culture helps us to understand the discrimination of groups who do not belong to traditional racial groupings. For instance, Palestinian American academic Edward Said's important work Orientalism (Pantheon Books, 1978) showed how Eastern societies have been portrayed as exotic and threatening by institutions such as the media in order to justify colonial control. More recently, certain events, such as the two Gulf Wars, the September 11 attacks and the Brexit vote in the UK, entrenched these views, and led to rises in ***hate crimes*** against people, especially those believed to be Muslim or of Arab descent. This specific type of racist hate has been called Islamophobia and is another example of the ways in which media and state discourses serve to perpetuate and shore up discrimination and violence against anyone believed to be Muslim.

Hate crime

Islamophobia

STRUCTURAL RACISM AND INSTITUTIONAL DISCRIMINATION

While overt expressions of racial prejudice, we are often told, have declined in many societies, racial inequality persists through structural and institutional mechanisms. US sociologist Eduardo Bonilla-Silva (2006) identifies ***frames***, what he calls 'colour-blind' racism, that allow people to explain racial inequality without appearing explicitly racist, including abstract liberalism (invoking choice or individualism to explain inequality), naturalization (suggesting segregation is natural), cultural racism (attributing inequality to cultural differences) and minimization of racism (suggesting discrimination is no longer significant). Bonilla-Silva argues that contemporary racism operates, therefore, through 'racism without racists' – systems that perpetuate racial advantage and disadvantage without requiring individual prejudice.

Colour-blind racism

Racism and employment opportunities

Educational inequality

None of society's key institutions – healthcare, housing, law, education – operate in isolation; they are very much interrelated. Where you live, for instance, impacts on where you might go to school, the transport you have access to, the jobs available to you and so on. Evidence of structural racism appears across multiple domains. For example, in criminal justice, research by Michelle Alexander (2010) documents how mass incarceration disproportionately affects Black Americans, functioning as a system of racial control she terms 'The New Jim Crow'. With respect to housing, Matthew Desmond's (2016) ethnographic research reveals how eviction disproportionately affects Black women, perpetuating housing insecurity and neighbourhood disadvantage. In the UK, studies using fictionalized, identical CVs reveal that people with names assumed to be Black or Asian are less likely to be called for a job interview. Gilbert Gonzalez (2013) has shown how historic segregation in terms of education, where Black, Latina and Indigenous people were taught in dilapidated buildings with outdated textbooks, still impacts on the education of BAME people. Such schools, it is argued, historically aimed to assimilate children into the white mainstream – children of Indigenous Peoples were forced from their families – and steer them to low-wage jobs in ways that maintained racial and class inequalities. Those inequalities persist today.

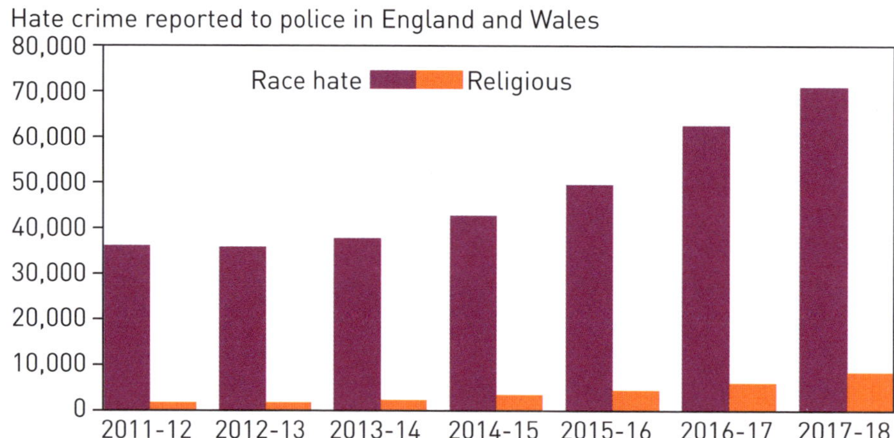

This bar chart shows the rise of racial and religious hate crime reported in the UK. Some of this may be explained by Brexit and the discourse around it.

Segregation and spatial inequality

Hypersegregation

Residential segregation – the physical separation of racial and ethnic groups in living spaces – remains a persistent feature of many societies. Douglas Massey and Nancy Denton's (1993) landmark study described hypersegregation in American cities, where Black residents were isolated along multiple dimensions simultaneously, creating what they termed 'American Apartheid'.

Research by sociologist Patrick Sharkey (2013) demonstrated the multigenerational impact of neighbourhood segregation. His findings showed that more than 70 per cent of Black Americans who live in poor neighbourhoods were raised by parents who also lived in poor neighbourhoods, creating a 'stuck in place' pattern that perpetuates disadvantage across generations. Such neighbourhoods frequently lack key resources such as health centres. One in five Black households in America, for instance, is in what has become known as a 'food desert' – places where there is little or no access to healthy and affordable food like fresh fruit and vegetables. This 'food apartheid' is just one example of food insecurity related to living in a devalued community.

RESISTING RACISM

Critical thinking and social movements offer a counter to tolerating or accepting racial discrimination and its impacts. Gilroy has argued we should abandon terms like 'race' and ethnicity because these trap us into a system of thinking he calls 'raciology', one that assumes a range of prejudices and stereotypes, some of which we have considered in this chapter. He thinks we should refuse to accept such divisions as inevitable and move towards an approach that leaves 'race' making no sense. Much sociological theory offers ways of thinking through these problems, as we have already seen, but there have been theoretical developments particularly from Black feminist thinkers, which have proved invaluable.

INTERSECTIONALITY

Developed by legal scholar Kimberlé Crenshaw (1989) and elaborated by sociologist Patricia Hill Collins (2000), an intersectional approach examines how multiple dimensions of inequality – including 'race', class, gender, sexuality and disability – intersect to create unique forms of disadvantage or privilege that cannot be understood by analyzing each dimension separately. ***Intersectionality*** has become increasingly central to sociological analyses of 'race' and ethnicity. Research by sociologist France Winddance Twine (2010), for instance, on interracial families demonstrates how 'race' intersects with gender and class to shape parenting practices and identity formation. Similarly, Mary Romero's (2018) work on Latina domestic workers illuminates how 'race', gender, class and immigration status combine to create specific forms of vulnerability and exploitation.

Sojourner Truth photographed as an older woman.

AIN'T I A WOMAN?

While the jury is out about the extent to which the version of the now famous speech given by Sojourner Truth (c.1797–1883) was written by her or a white preacher a few years after the event, it remains a significant anti-racist, feminist and abolitionist text – an early example of intersectional thinking. Truth was born into slavery, eventually escaping after years of violent treatment. During the 1851 Woman's Rights Convention, Truth pointed out that when women's rights and 'ideals' of femininity are talked about, the focus is on white women, ignoring the experiences of Black women, especially those who have been enslaved. The speech also hints at the fact that when Black rights are discussed, the focus is on men – an argument similar to the one made by Crenshaw over a century later.

REVEALING WHITENESS

Learning from the marginalized

Hill Collins has argued that we need to learn from the perspective, or lens, of the marginalized; their position as outsiders in their own society means they have a valuable viewpoint from which to 'see' and analyze society. Part of this also entails recognizing that whiteness, like other powerful categories, is often invisible. Various scholars have begun critiquing whiteness as a social category. Recognizing the privileges whiteness brings is part of this project, a process that makes it possible to recognize the ways white people benefit from, and help perpetuate, structural racism. One very small example of such taken-for-granted privilege – many years ago as an undergraduate (white) student in the 1990s, on the rare occasions I could afford a taxi, on my own, or with female or male, white friends, I had absolutely no problem hailing one and getting a lift. *Every time* I tried to flag down a taxi when I was with a Black male friend, they *never* stopped.

Martin Luther King Jr, a prominent leader of the US civil rights movement, giving his 'I Have a Dream' speech.

THE PARADOX OF PREJUDICE

As we shall in the next chapter, experiences of prejudice, discrimination and outright violence often lead to resistances and challenges or Pride movements. We have already briefly considered resistance struggles in South Africa, and the contemporary Black Lives Matter movement but this is influenced by past political movements. In the US in particular, which has had a long history of overt racism, there have been vocal and active opponents to racism. In the late 19th and early 20th centuries, there were anti-slavery abolitionists such as Sojourner Truth and Harriet Tubman (1822–1913). Later, in the 1950s and 60s the civil rights movement, led by key figures such as Martin Luther King Jr. (1929–1968), campaigned to end discrimination and segregation. Critical of the civil rights movement's moderate approach, the Black Power movement, with influential member Malcolm X (1925–1965), brought further attention to the issue. The Black Panther Party, in part inspired by Marxist thinking, were particularly influential. Fabio Rojas (2006) explored how the Black Power movement transformed higher education through the creation of Black Studies programmes – a good example of how social movements can produce institutional change that outlasts the movement itself.

THE WINDRUSH SCANDAL

After the Second World War, Britain needed more workers to help rebuild. British colonies, such as those in the Caribbean, were struggling financially, thus there was a 'convenient' solution for cheap labour for Britian. The government invited people, on the promise of secure employment and a warm welcome. In response to that, in 1948 the HMT *Empire Windrush* ship brought several hundred people from the Caribbean (the ship also carried Indian, Chinese and Burmese people who had been taken to the Caribbean to work). This was not the first, nor the last, such ship but collectively, these migrants became known as the Windrush generation. (Later, the conservative Health Minister Enoch Powell was part of a campaign to recruit more nurses from the Caribbean, only to argue against immigration soon after in his famous 'Rivers of Blood' speech). Many ended up in low-paid jobs such as cleaners, or nurses within the new NHS system and rather than a warm welcome, were on the receiving end of prejudice and racism – shops and rented accommodation displayed 'No blacks' cards in the window, for instance. Though they were promised the right to live and work in the UK permanently, in 2017 it was revealed that many people had wrongly been deported or detained because the Home Office had no record of who had been told they could stay; landing cards had been destroyed and other papers were missing. With no ability to prove they could remain in the UK, they were denied the right to access NHS healthcare, housing systems and other benefits afforded to citizens; they became victims of the 2012 'Hostile Environment' policy, which aimed to force undocumented migrants to leave.

In the 1940s and 1950s workers came from British colonies to do jobs no one else would do, only to find themselves unwelcome.

THE PERSISTENCE OF RACISM?

'Race' and ethnicity, as we have seen, operate as hierarchies; racism is about power. Racism also intersects with other systems of oppression, such as classism, ableism and sexism, and has a significant impact on life chances. 'Race' and ethnicity are not fixed, stable categories and ideas about them wax and wane in response to key social, economic and political events. Understanding 'race' as a social construction doesn't diminish its real-world impact. Rather, it helps us analyze how racial categories have been created, maintained and sometimes challenged throughout history. This knowledge is essential for addressing ongoing racial inequities and working towards a more just society. Right now, Gilroy's concept of postcolonial melancholia seems particularly prescient; we are witnessing the rise of far-right groups yet again in the US, UK and across Europe, what British historian Neil Faulkner (1958–2022) called 'creeping fascism'. We are simultaneously seeing a return, in some quarters, to a belief in the biological basis of 'race' (and sexuality). W.E.B. Du Bois's statement might be rephrased 'the problem of the 21st century is the problem of the colour-line'.

Chapter Seven

GENDER AND SEXUALITIES

Declare yourself! – Worlds apart: a tale of two planets? – Sex/gender distinction – Is sex also socially constructed? – Doing gender – Intersectionality – Gender socialization and identity formation – Femininities and masculinities – Gender inequality and social institutions – Gender, power and violence – Sexualities: sociological perspectives – Contemporary debates and future directions – Sex matters

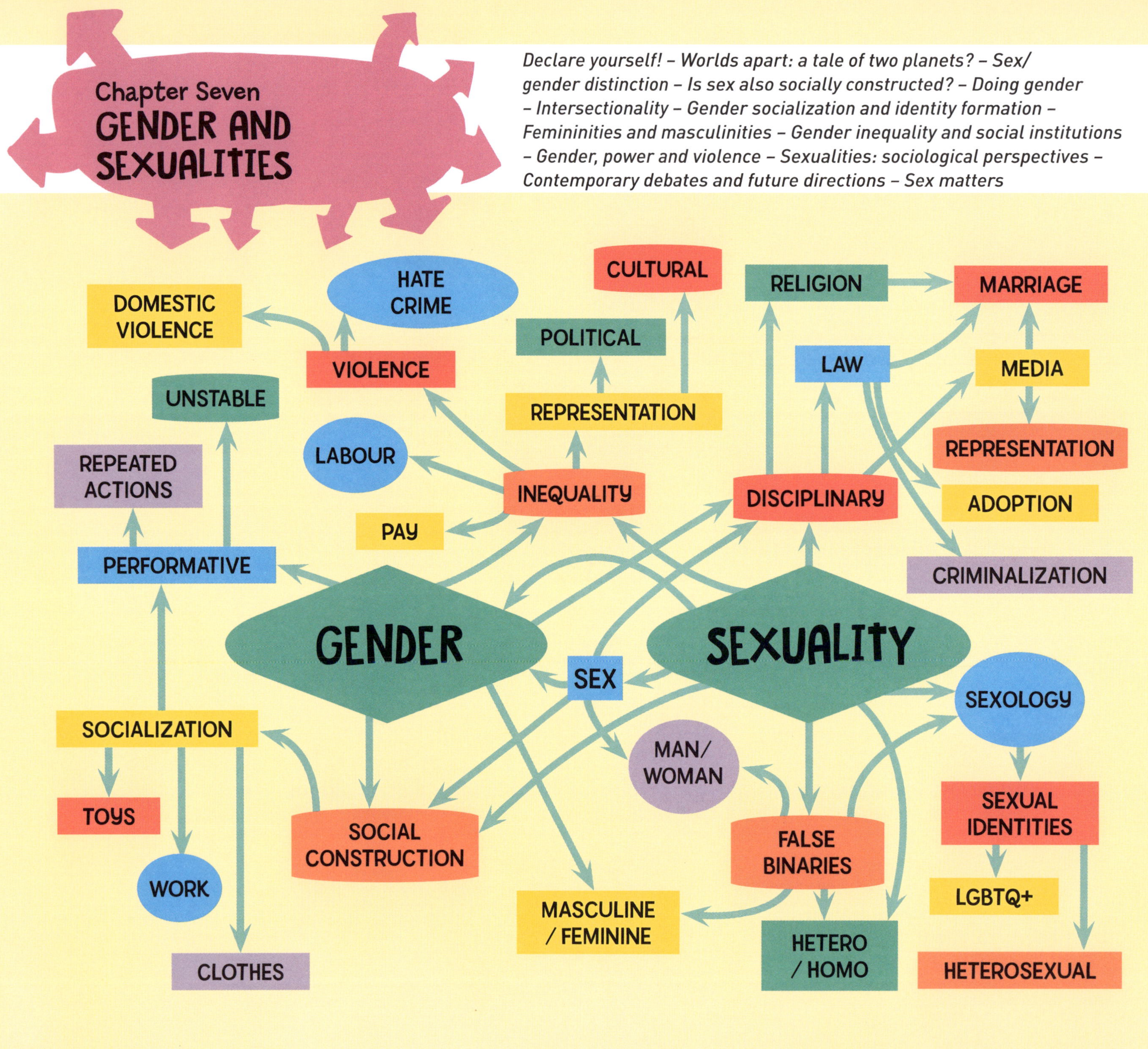

DECLARE YOURSELF!

There may be many moments during the course of your day when you are asked to declare your **sex/** gender identity. This might be visiting a changing room in a shop or using a public lavatory, where you may only be given two options; in other words, you have to choose between a men's space and a women's space. Unless you present in such a way as to challenge normative ideas of gender, you might never even question these choices and assumptions. Many official forms, however, are beginning to reflect changing social understandings of gendered identities: for instance you might be asked to confirm your ascribed biological sex at birth and your current gender identity. Such forms recognize that, not only are there more than two identities, but these are also not necessarily fixed.

Changing understanding

Similarly, sexuality, which refers to identities, practices, relationships and desires, is closely bound to ideas of gender and sex. Sociologists argue that these are not simply biological but are shaped by a range of social and historical processes; they are social constructions. The ideologies behind many of the ideas we have about sex, gender and sexuality create a binary framework for understanding and behaviour that can be very limiting and harmful. Some identities are seen as 'normal' and rewarded for being such, and others as 'different' and punished for that difference. Thus, we see inequalities in terms of things such as education, work, pay, experience of violence, the right to marry or adopt, and cultural and political representation. It is also particularly important to analyze this at a time of growing sex and gender conservatism, and retraction of women's and LGBTQ+ rights, across the globe.

A binary framework

He, She, They, toilet symbols plus the 'Mother and Baby' symbol which indicates gendered roles too

LGBTQ+ ▶ ***this stands for lesbian, gay, bisexual, transgender, queer or questioning, intersex, non-binary, asexual.***

A NOTE ON LANGUAGE ▶ ***As we have already seen, language is powerful because it helps to shape how we see and understand the world. For convenience, much of this chapter, when talking about gender, will refer to 'men' and 'women'. In doing so, there is no assumption that those who may identify as men or women have always done so. We must also be mindful, however, of the many people for whom these gender identities are not relevant. Many people identify as non-binary, genderfluid, agender, genderqueer, bigender etc.***

Most of us take for granted the idea that there are two genders, masculine and feminine, aligned with two biological sexes. But sociologists understand gender as a social construct that varies across time, place and cultures. Rather than accepting gender as natural or fixed, sociologists examine how gender is produced, performed and regulated through social interaction and institutions. Drawing on a range of theories, including feminist and ***queer theory***, this chapter will consider the relationship between gender, sex and sexuality. It will look at how our understandings and experiences of gender and sexuality are shaped by culture. It explores the culturally and socially varied ways in which gender and sexuality have been conceptualized, deployed and regulated in a range of social institutions and practices.

WHY FOCUS ON GENDER AND SEXUALITY

Not part of the picture

As you may have noted, much sociology of the 19th and early 20th centuries was dominated by male scholars. On the whole, these scholars were inclined to focus on issues that often impacted on men more directly, or at least they appeared to. There has been a tendency to separate the social world into two spheres: the public realm of politics, work, education, law and so on; and the private sphere of domestic life. At the time of sociology's emergence, women were largely kept out of the public sphere – it wasn't until 1878 that women in the UK were allowed to enter university and sit full degree exams, for instance, and they didn't all get the vote until 1928. Women were told, conveniently, that they were more suited to domestic tasks because of their assumed caring and gentle nature (try telling that to the girls at school on the hockey pitch!). This division of labour meant there was less competition for a wage in the world of work, and it also enabled men to go out to work without having to worry about doing the laundry or dressing the children. Academically, it also led to an assumption that the things we think of as being related to gender and sexuality – relationships, emotion and so on – weren't 'proper' academic subjects, they were simply private matters.

Rising inequality between the sexes

That's not to say women were completely ignored. Friedrich Engels (1884) (aided by Marx's notes) in *The Origin of the Family, Private Property and the State* charted the ways in which the development of class divisions brought with it rising inequality between men and women. Thus, he was one of the first to make a link between capitalism and what is now understood as patriarchy. His book on working-class life in Manchester also highlights the poor deal women got, being unable to participate in the public sphere or earn wages if they were responsible for 'family duties'. Talcott Parsons, as a structuralist functionalist, saw the gendered division of labour as one that enabled the smooth functioning of society. The 'nuclear family' was seen as a central institution for a stable society, one that socialized children into societal values and norms (a rhetoric still espoused by conservative elements of society).

Feminist activists and academics of the 1960s and 1970s, however, challenged this assumption that the private sphere wasn't of importance, that it was naturally a woman's realm, and they also argued that the private was regulated and shaped by the public sphere. In other words, that neat binary division was a false one; 'the personal is political' became an important rallying cry of the time. Thus, gradually, attention turned to a sociology of women's studies, later known as gender and sexuality.

PUBLIC
Masculine
Politics
Education
Science
Law
Business
Knowledge
Facts
Instrumental

PRIVATE
Feminine
Family
Home
Nurturing
Morals
Expressive
Religion

These false binaries are persistent and have been key in shaping restrictive ideas about gender.

WHAT IS A 'NUCLEAR FAMILY'?
The nuclear, or 'cereal packet' family describes a heterosexual, married couple with two children. This was seen as 'ideal' and many people talk about it as a traditional family arrangement. However, historically, this was never the norm – many working-class couples, Black households and same-sex families were unmarried, extended or blended, or single-headed. This 'ideal' is associated with white, middle-class, heterosexual couples and while hegemonic, it is not typical and never has been.

WORLDS APART: A TALE OF TWO PLANETS?

'Men are from Mars, women from Venus', 'boys don't cry', 'don't be such a girl', 'boys will be boys', 'sugar and spice and all things nice', 'man up' – all these phrases, and many more, tell us something about how we divide the world. They are insisting that the world falls into two categories, male and female, and that they are so different as to almost be a separate species. Such stereotyping constructs boys and men as tough and potentially troublesome. Girls and women, on the other hand, are expected to be emotional, passive and well-behaved. In fact, society spends a great deal of time, and financial investment, attempting to assert those differences. Vast amounts of money are spent on research endeavouring to find significant differences between the 'male' brain and the 'female' brain – the idea that men are rational and women creative and so on – but for every study that finds a difference, many more reveal that what is remarkable about men and women's brains is how similar they are.

DAMAGING DUALISMS
In our society we tend to recognize only two sexes – male and female – but it is important to state that this is not a universal approach to, or experience of, sex. This seemingly rigid binary system may not be as stable as we might think; a cross-sample of society, testing chromosomes, hormones, genes, physiology and so on, would reveal that very few people would fit neatly into the 'ideal' male or female categories. Many would argue that how we categorize sex is influenced by culture. US sexologist Anne Fausto-Sterling (2000) suggests that to label someone a man or woman is a social act. Though science might be used to help the process, it is cultural assumptions that fundamentally drive them and shape the scientific 'knowledge' produced in the first place.

SEX/GENDER DISTINCTION

One is not born, but rather becomes, a woman
(Simone de Beauvoir, *The Second Sex*
(Éditions Gallimard,1949))

Second-wave feminists of the 1970s were among the first sociologists to challenge this rigid determinism. They developed the distinction between sex and gender to trouble biological essentialism – the idea that biology determines social roles and behaviours. British sociologist Ann Oakley (1972) was influential in establishing this distinction, arguing that while 'sex' refers to biological differences between males and females, 'gender' refers to the socially constructed characteristics of masculinity and femininity. The argument was that biological differences had been used to determine social roles and behaviours in ways that tended to privilege men; having breasts doesn't mean you will automatically be better at ironing than someone with a penis, for instance. At the time, this distinction was revolutionary, suggesting that gendered behaviour is not innate but learned through socialization. Simone de Beauvoir, on publication of *The Second Sex* in 1949, somewhat paved the way for the feminist sof the 1960s and 1970s by pointing to the social aspects of 'becoming' a woman, or man for that matter.

Oakley's research demonstrated how socialization practices – from the clothes children wear to the toys they play with – train them to take on culturally approved gender roles. She documented how parents and other socializing agents treat infants differently based on perceived sex, leading to different developmental paths for boys and girls. This work challenged the prevailing naturalization of gender inequality by showing how cultural expectations, rather than biology, create gendered behaviours.

This was an important political step for feminists because it meant that differences of biology (chromosomes, hormones, physiology, anatomy etc.) were not behind the unequal treatment of men and women. Oakley argued that women's place in society had been unfairly determined by

SEXOLOGIST ▶ ***these are people who study sexuality. The discipline emerged in the late 19th century as people like Havelock Ellis, Richard von Krafft-Ebing and Magnus Hirschfeld began to categorize sexual practices.***

FEMINISM

Very broadly, feminism is a social movement demanding equality between the sexes, based on the premise that women face inequality. It is loosely banded into 'waves' – the first wave of the late 19th and early 20th centuries was focused around campaigning for the right to vote for women and working-class men. They also highlighted the unjust treatment of women in divorce, unfair property rights, and brought attention to domestic abuse and the sexual abuse of children, among other issues. The second wave (1960s–1980s), influenced by the civil rights movements and student activism, had similar goals to first-wave feminism, campaigning for the right to abortion, workplace equality, an end to sexual violence etc. Some talk of a third wave of feminism (1990s–2000s), which brought attention to the ways earlier feminism had tended to side-step issues related to marginalized women such as lesbians and Black women. However, feminist ideals go back much further. Some notable early feminists include Hildegard von Bingen (1098–1179) and Mary Wollstonecraft (1759–1797) – who, for those of you who love *Frankenstein*, was Mary Shelley's mum.

their biology, in a way that hadn't happened for men (which isn't to say gendered expectations weren't also harmful and restrictive for men). The problem was that sex and gender were generally lumped together, with women's limited and devalued place in society attributed to an assumed rigid law of biology, a flawed biology at that, which assumed women's inferiority on many levels (see Chapter 8 for more on this).

We firmly associate pink with girls and femininity and see blue as a masculine colour. However, during the 18th and early 19th centuries pink was the colour for men – for example Wordsworth had his bedroom painted pink because of this. Cultural associations used to construct gender are arbitrary.

The sex/gender distinction, then, became a foundational concept in feminist theory and sociology, providing a framework to understand gender as a social institution rather than a biological imperative. The binary system male/female, crucially for feminist thinkers, operates as a set of hierarchies – as most binaries do – in that we tend to privilege the masculine over the feminine. It is a system of power therefore, and not just about observable differences (or similarities). As such, it revealed that the unequal treatment of women need not continue.

However, this sex/gender distinction has been criticized by some contemporary theorists who argue that it maintains a problematic nature/culture divide and fails to account for how even biological sex is socially interpreted.

IS SEX ALSO SOCIALLY CONSTRUCTED?

'Sex', then, in early second-wave feminism, is often conceptualized as the natural, or biological, differences between men and women. It should be noted, however, that Oakley argued that sex should be viewed as a continuum, rather than two fixed categories. Nonetheless, building on the work of Michel Foucault, Judith Butler (1990) challenged the sex/gender distinction by arguing that sex itself is also socially constructed. In their now infamous *Gender Trouble* (1990) – partly infamous because it's quite difficult to read! – Butler argues that our understanding of biological sex is already filtered through cultural assumptions about gender. Rather than being a natural foundation upon which gender is constructed, sex is itself a constructed gendered category. Our interpretation of bodies as 'male' or 'female' is guided by culturally specific understandings of what those categories mean.

Thomas Gainsborough's Mr and Mrs Andrews *(1750) is a good example of a man presented as confident, a 'master' of his land, standing above his wife, who sits very formally and looks quite out of context in the landscape.*

Butler famously developed the concept of gender performativity – the idea that gender is not something we are but something we do. Through the repetition of stylized acts, gestures and behaviours, we 'perform' gender in ways that make it appear natural and innate. They used the art of drag as an analogy to show the ways drag reveals the instability of categories society insists are stable. Yet these performances of gender are constrained by powerful social norms that limit which performances are considered legitimate. For Butler, gender is neither a stable identity nor a locus of agency, but a regulated process of repetition that both conceals and enforces social constraints.

Thomas Laqueur (1990) provides historical evidence for the social construction of sex in *Making Sex: Body and Gender from the Greeks to Freud* (1990). He documents how Western understanding of sexual difference shifted from a one-sex model (where female bodies were seen as imperfect versions of male bodies) to a two-sex model (where male and female bodies were seen as fundamentally different) in the 18th century. This shift corresponded with changes in political thought about gender equality, suggesting that even our basic understanding of biological sex is influenced by social and political factors.

Female to male impersonators like Vesta Tilley (1864–1952) above, and Hetty King (1883–1972) right, were hugely popular as musical hall acts in the late 19th and early 20th centuries.

ONE SEX/TWO SEX MODELS

Laqueur's historical research shows how anatomical understandings of sex difference have changed:

- ***Pre-18th century***: One-sex model dominated – female genitals were seen as inverted male genitals, with the same organs arranged differently.
- ***Post-18th century***: Two-sex model emerged – male and female bodies were seen as fundamentally and qualitatively different.
- This shift coincided with political changes requiring new justifications for gender inequality as traditional hierarchy was challenged.

TOILET TROUBLE?

Many people are altering their bodies, either through the use of hormones or surgeries, or are simply changing their gender pronoun, in ways that challenge us to rethink what is meant by 'gender'. The assumption that what is not male is female and vice versa is a binary that is becoming increasingly fragile, especially for younger people. The proliferation of trans bodies in public spaces draws attention to the ways in which rigid binaries around sex/gender are problematic. In the UK, as well as other countries, this has resulted in a moral panic or 'crisis' around public toilets. This spatial crisis, or social obsession – what queer theorist Jack Halberstam calls 'bathroom problems' – arguably is a reflection of a larger issue in relation to the gendered body.

In some ways, the current kick-back against acceptance or tolerance of trans bodies in public spaces can be likened to resistances against growing LGB culture and communities. There was a moral and legal opposition – gay sex was criminalized in many countries – a conservative attempt to stem the flow of social change.

DOING GENDER

Candace West and Don Zimmerman (1987), US sociologists, developed the concept of 'doing gender' to explain how gender is accomplished through everyday interaction. Unlike Butler's more philosophical approach, their accessible sociological perspective focuses on how individuals 'do gender' in face-to-face interactions. Gender is not something we 'have' or are born with, nor simply a role or display, but an ongoing activity embedded in everyday interactions. People are held accountable to their gender performance by others who assess whether their actions are appropriately masculine or feminine.

For example, in their ethnomethodological studies of transsexuals, which is dated in some ways now, social psychologist Suzanne Kessler and sociologist Wendy McKenna (1978) documented how some people work to 'pass' as their preferred gender by adopting what are viewed as appropriate mannerisms, speech patterns and appearance. These efforts highlight how gender is not automatic but requires constant maintenance and negotiation. In exactly the same way, cisgender people continually 'do gender' by managing their behaviour to conform to gendered expectations, though this work often goes unnoticed precisely because it appears natural.

Research by US sociologist Michael Messner (2000) on children's sports shows how gender differences are actively constructed through seemingly natural activities. In observing children's football games, he noticed how parents, coaches and other adults created gendered expectations that shaped boys' and girls' behaviour on the field, reinforcing the appearance of natural differences between them.

TRANSSEXUAL ▶ *a less-used term today to refer to someone who has undergone sex/gender reassignment using various medical interventions.*

TRANSGENDER ▶ *people whose gender identity does not match the sex ascribed at birth. They may or may not have undergone medical treatment. A more popular term today than transsexual.*

CISGENDER ▶ *someone whose gender identity matches their ascribed sex.*

INTERSECTIONALITY

The concept of intersectionality, developed by legal scholar Kimberlé Crenshaw (1989), has become central to sociological understandings of gender. Intersectionality recognizes that gender never operates in isolation but intersects with other social categories like ethnicity, class, sexuality and disability to create unique experiences of privilege and oppression. Black feminists like Patricia Hill Collins (2000) have shown how the experiences of Black women cannot be understood through either feminist or anti-racist frameworks alone but require analysis of how racism and sexism interact.

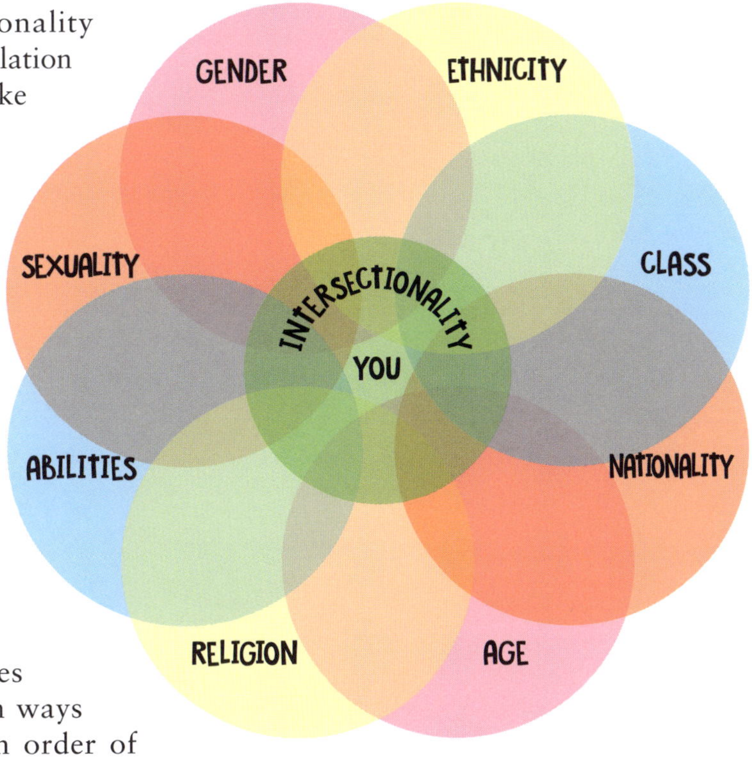

Hill Collins' (2000) concept of the matrix of domination provides a framework for understanding how different systems of oppression interconnect. For example, a working-class Black lesbian woman experiences gender, ethnicity, class and sexuality in ways that cannot be separated or ranked in order of importance. These systems operate simultaneously to shape her lived experience.

Many cross-cutting aspects of identity impact on our experiences of gender and sexuality.

Studies by US sociologist Leslie McCall (2005) and others have demonstrated how gender inequality manifests differently across different social locations. For instance, the gender wage gap varies significantly by ethnicity, with Black and Hispanic women facing larger wage disparities than white women. These findings highlight the importance of an intersectional approach that recognizes the diversity of gendered experiences.

GENDER SOCIALIZATION AND IDENTITY FORMATION

LEARNING GENDER

Confirming assumptions

Gender socialization begins almost immediately after birth, and sometimes before, as Cordelia Fine (2010) documents in *Delusions of Gender*. Parents, often unconsciously, treat children differently based on assumptions about gender – speaking more gently to girls, encouraging more physical activity in boys, and providing gender-appropriate toys. These subtle differences accumulate over time, shaping children's sense of themselves and their place in the world. British sociologist Sylvia Walby calls this a 'training' in being one or the other.

Borderwork

Primary socialization within the family is reinforced through secondary socialization in arenas like schools, media and peer groups. US sociologist Barrie Thorne's (1993) research in elementary schools shows how children actively participate in creating gendered behaviours through what she calls 'borderwork' – activities that highlight and reinforce gender boundaries, such as boys chasing girls in the playground, or playing doctors and nurses, where the boys are the doctors and the girls are the nurses.

Playground games frequently divide children into 'boys' and 'girls' and insist on difference.

Contemporary digital media plays an increasingly important role in gender socialization. Research by Elizabeth Behm-Morawitz and Dana Mastro (2009) on video games shows how the representation of women as hypersexualized characters influences players' attitudes about gender roles. Similarly, studies of social media use among adolescents reveal how platforms like Instagram reinforce narrow beauty standards for girls while encouraging performances of hypermasculinity among boys.

GENDER IDENTITY DEVELOPMENT

While early sociological approaches emphasized how gender is imposed on individuals through socialization, contemporary research recognizes children's agency in developing their gender identities. Karin Martin (2005), a US sociologist, observes that children are not passive recipients of gender socialization but active participants who sometimes resist or reinterpret gender norms. For example, some children engage in gender non-conforming play or express discomfort with assigned gender roles from an early age. However, Martin also argues that such gender non-conformity is often viewed negatively by peers and adults, linked to pathologized ideas about LGB identities.

Resisting gender norms

The development of gender identity varies over time and across cultures, highlighting its social construction. Anthropological research by Margaret Mead (1935) in New Guinea found three tribes with radically different expectations for male and female behaviour, challenging Western assumptions about natural gender differences. More recently, research on cultures that recognize more than two genders, such as the hijra in South Asia or two-spirit people in some Native American tribes, further demonstrates the cultural variability of gender categories.

Mad Men's *Don Draper presents as a typical 'hegemonic man' but is seen as a problematic stereotype.*

FEMININITIES AND MASCULINITIES

Australian sociologist Raewyn Connell's (1995) concept of 'hegemonic masculinity' has been influential in understanding how multiple forms of masculinity exist in any society, arranged in a hierarchy of power. Hegemonic masculinity – the culturally dominant form that legitimizes men's power over women and other men – is not necessarily the most common form but serves as an ideal that men are measured against. This concept helps explain why men who fail to embody hegemonic ideals often face social sanctions.

Similarly, Connell identified emphasized femininity as the form of femininity that accommodates men's interests and desires, reinforcing gender inequality. However, as US sociologist Mimi Schippers (2007) notes, multiple femininities exist alongside multiple masculinities, with complex power relations between them. Working-class femininities, for example, may emphasize physical strength and economic independence in ways that middle-class femininities do not.

Media representations play a crucial role in constructing ideals of masculinity and femininity. Content analysis by Erica Scharrer (2013) of television programming shows how men are typically portrayed as aggressive, stoic and in positions of authority, while women are more often shown as emotional, nurturing and concerned with appearance. These are representations which both reflect and reinforce social expectations for gendered behaviour and are damaging for both men and women.

BEYOND THE BINARY

Anthropological research documents cultures with gender systems that go beyond the Western binary:

- Hijra in South Asia
- Two-spirit people in some Native American cultures
- Fa'afafine in Samoa
- Sworn virgins in Albania
- Bissu in Indonesia

These diverse gender systems reveal how even the number of recognized genders varies across cultures, challenging the idea that the ***gender binary*** is universal or natural.

Avertisements for household products such as washing powder and washing-up liquid, typically fell on stereotypes of emphasized feminity. Many still do!

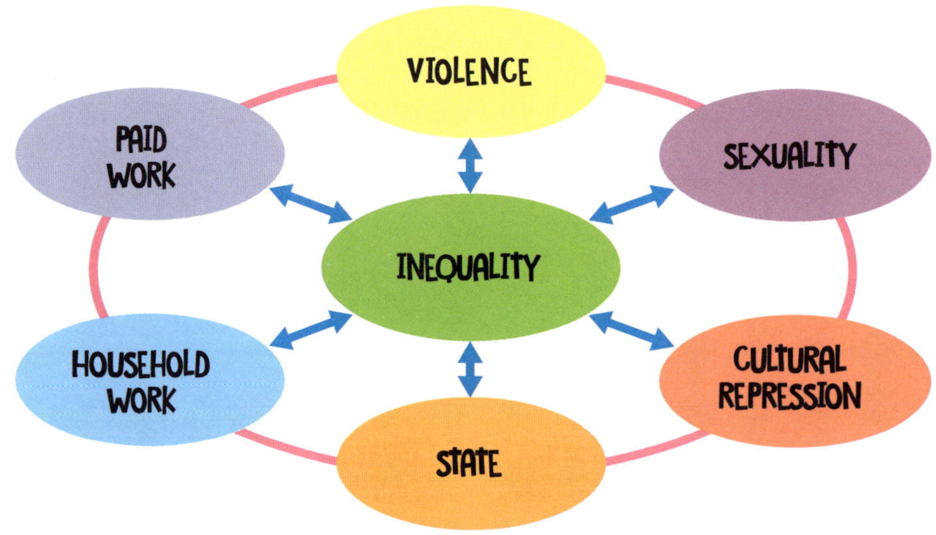

Sylvia Walby's theory of patriarchy states that it arises from, and causes, inequality.

GENDER INEQUALITY AND SOCIAL INSTITUTIONS

THE GENDER ORDER

Sociologists understand gender as a structural feature of society, not just an individual attribute. Connell (1987) describes this as the 'gender order' – the pattern of power relations between men and women that is institutionalized in all areas of social life. This order is maintained through what British-Canadian sociologist Dorothy Smith (1987) calls 'relations of ruling' – the interconnected practices, discourses and institutions that organize and regulate society along gendered lines.

Persistent inequality

The gender order is evident in the persistent inequality between men and women in areas such as income, wealth, political representation and domestic responsibilities. Despite significant progress towards formal equality in many countries, substantial gender gaps remain. For example, the World Economic Forum's Global Gender Gap Report consistently shows that no country has achieved full gender equality, with gaps particularly persistent in economic participation and political empowerment.

Private matriarchy and public patriarchy

Many feminists use the concept of patriarchy to understand how gendered inequality works. Originally an anthropological term (itself taken from the ancient Greek 'rule of the father'), referring to 'male-headed' societies, the US feminist Kate Millet (1970) adopted the term to describe social relations in the US and what she saw as the systematic domination of women by men. Sylvia Walby (1990) identifies six structures of patriarchy that operate across different domains: paid work, household production, culture, sexuality, violence and the state. These structures interact to maintain male advantage, though their specific forms have changed over time from what Walby calls 'private patriarchy' (based in the household) to 'public patriarchy' (based in employment and the state). Patriarchy, for Walby and others, is both a consequence of inequality (the construction of women as different, 'other' and lesser allows for unequal treatment) and a cause of further inequality.

GENDER AND WORK

The gendered division of labour – the allocation of different types of work to men and women – is a fundamental aspect of gender inequality. Despite women's increased participation in paid employment, occupational segregation persists, with women concentrated in lower-paid sectors like care work, education and service industries. Many argue such jobs are lower paid because they are seen as 'feminine' roles, thus degraded in a patriarchal system. This horizontal segregation is accompanied by vertical segregation, with women underrepresented in senior positions across most fields.

Status beliefs

Research by Cecilia Ridgeway (2011), a US sociologist, on 'status beliefs' helps explain the persistence of workplace inequality. Status beliefs – widely shared cultural assumptions about the worthiness and competence of different groups – lead to unconscious bias in hiring, promotion and evaluation decisions. Because men are generally accorded higher status than women in our society, they tend to be seen as more competent and leadership-orientated, particularly in male-dominated fields.

CASE STUDY – THE GENDER PAY GAP

The gender pay gap persists across countries and occupations, though its size varies:

- UK (2024): women earned approximately 87p for every £1 earned by men
- Factors include: occupational segregation, part-time work penalties, motherhood penalty
- Male-dominated jobs with the biggest pay gap: electrical and electronic technicians at 29.5 per cent gap
- Intersectional disparities: the gap is larger for Black women and disabled women
- Solutions include: pay transparency, affordable childcare, shared parental leave

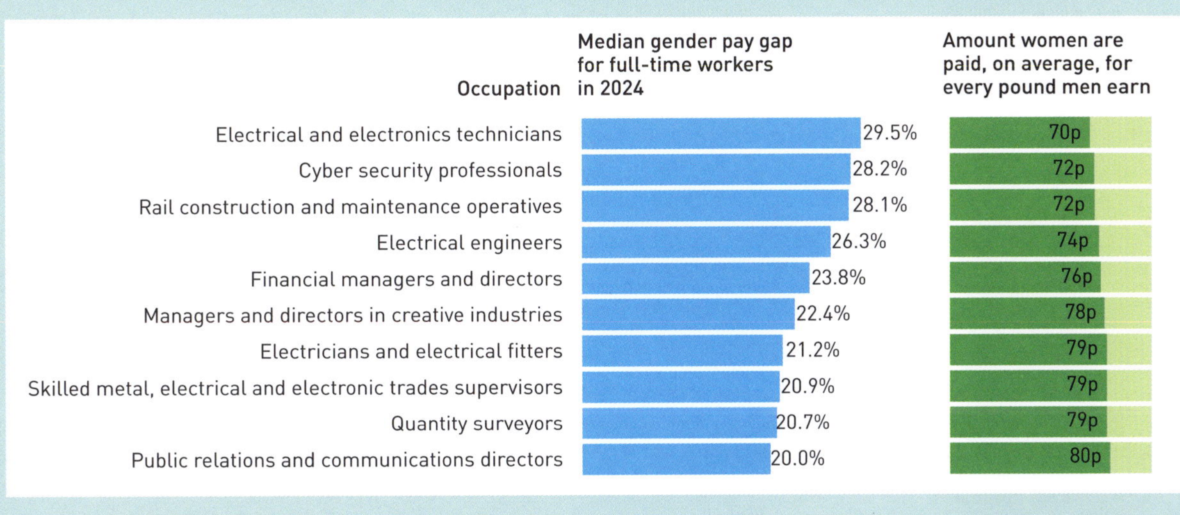

Stuck on the floor

The metaphor of the 'sticky floor' points to the ways women are often stuck in these low-paid and frequently insecure jobs. In part, this is because in a society with rigid ideas of what men and women's roles are, it is still women who predominantly have the responsibility for childcare and modern workplaces rarely accommodate this. Similarly, the concept of the ***glass ceiling*** describes invisible barriers that prevent women from reaching top positions, while Christine William's (1992) concept of the glass escalator refers to the hidden advantages that men receive when they enter female-dominated professions. Studies of nursing, primary education and libraries show how men in these fields are often fast-tracked into management positions despite being minorities in the profession.

THE DOMESTIC SPHERE

Two shifts for women

Despite women's increased participation in paid work, research consistently shows that they continue to perform the majority of unpaid domestic labour and care work in heterosexual households. Arlie Hochschild (1989) described this as the 'second shift' – the household labour that employed women perform after their paid workday ends. Her research found that women worked approximately an extra month of 24-hour days each year compared to their male partners. Ann Oakley's research led her to argue that housework leads to alienation quicker than factory work, because of the isolation and lack of agency in their lives, thus preventing self-actualization for many women. The French sociologist Christine Delphy (1941–) pointed out that the unpaid work women did in the home would be paid if it was done outside the home, thus, she argued, the marriage contract should be seen as a work contract.

More recent time-use studies confirm that while the gender gap in housework has narrowed slightly since the 1970s, significant disparities remain. Women continue to be responsible for the majority of routine, daily household tasks and the mental load of household management – what sociologists call 'kin work' or 'emotion work' – planning, co-ordinating and maintaining family relationships and well-being.

Lyn Craig and Killian Mullan's (2011) cross-national research on parenting shows how childcare remains highly gendered even in countries with progressive gender equality policies. While fathers' involvement has increased slightly, mothers continue to spend more time on direct care activities and have less uninterrupted leisure time. Importantly, these patterns vary by class, ethnicity and cultural context, with working-class mothers often having less flexibility to outsource domestic labour.

GENDER, POWER AND VIOLENCE

A continuum of violence

Gender-based violence – including domestic violence, sexual assault and harassment – represents one of the most extreme manifestations of gender inequality (see Chapter 11 for more on this). Feminist sociologists have analyzed these forms of violence not as individual pathologies but as systematic expressions of patriarchal power. As Walby (1990) argues, violence serves as both a direct means of controlling women and a structural backdrop against which gender relations are negotiated.

Research by Liz Kelly (1988) introduced the concept of a 'continuum of violence' to show how seemingly minor forms of harassment and control are connected to more severe forms of abuse. This approach helps explain how everyday sexism contributes to a culture that normalizes violence against women. Similarly, Connell's (1995) work on hegemonic masculinity shows how violence can function as a resource for constructing masculine identity, particularly for men who lack access to other sources of power such as wealth or occupational status.

The #MeToo movement, which gained widespread attention in 2017, highlighted once again the pervasiveness of sexual harassment and assault, particularly in workplaces. Sociological analysis of #MeToo emphasizes how it made visible previously normalized patterns of behaviour, particularly within the film industry, and challenged institutional practices that protected perpetrators. At the same time, critics have noted that the movement's visibility varied along lines of ethnicity, class and sexuality, with less attention paid to the experiences of marginalized women.

Making 'normal' abnormal

SEXISM ▶ ***prejudice or discrimination based on often stereotypical ideas about sex or gender.***

MISOGYNY ▶ ***hatred or dislike of women.***

SEXUALITIES: SOCIOLOGICAL PERSPECTIVES

Contemporary perspectives on sexuality have evolved significantly. As noted by scholars like Ken Plummer, sexuality now encompasses diverse aspects – from pleasure and relationship formation to expressing personal attitudes and identities. Additionally, unfortunately, sexuality also sometimes serves as a mechanism for abuse and subjugation. Sexual expression has become increasingly multifaceted and interconnected with numerous aspects of human experience.

In the Global North, sexuality is typically relegated to private life – something that is, and should remain, private. However, as feminists have rightly pointed out, the so-called private sphere is in fact very public, shaped by law, medicine, religion and other social institutions. In fact, many of the assumptions we have about sexuality – including *who* can do *what*, *where* and *when* they can do it, and *why* – are very much circumscribed by social, legal and moral laws.

Public or private?

Modern Western cultures view sexuality and sexual identities as fundamental to meaningful existence – a basic human need and right. This perspective is reinforced by organizations like the World Health Organization, which defines sexuality as incorporating physical, emotional, intellectual and social dimensions of sexual being in ways that positively enrich individuals, communities and relationships. This represents a remarkable shift from perspectives held just decades ago. Throughout this exploration, we'll investigate how sexuality intersects with emotion, identity, political systems and cultural frameworks. We've witnessed a rapid transformation from conceptualizing sexuality as purely biological and universal towards social constructionist approaches, and now towards framing sexuality as a fundamental right, including the right to form committed partnerships.

THE SOCIAL CONSTRUCTION OF SEXUALITY

Just as sociologists understand gender as socially constructed, they approach sexuality not as a natural, biological drive but as a complex social phenomenon shaped by historical and cultural forces. This perspective emerged in opposition to essentialist views that treat sexuality as a fixed, innate aspect of human nature.

The deployment of sexuality

Michel Foucault's (1978) *The History of Sexuality* (1976) was groundbreaking in demonstrating how our understanding of sexuality is historically specific. Foucault traced how sexuality became a central aspect of identity in Western societies through what he called 'the deployment of sexuality' – the proliferation of discourses, institutions and practices that categorized, regulated and produced sexual identities. Rather than being repressed in the Victorian era, as commonly believed, Foucault argued that sexuality was increasingly spoken about, analyzed and controlled through new forms of knowledge/power.

FOUCAULT ON SEXUALITY

Key arguments from Foucault's *History of Sexuality*:

- Sexuality is not a natural fact but a historical construct.
- The 'repressive hypothesis' (that sexuality was simply repressed) is misleading.
- Modern sexuality emerged through proliferation of discourses, not silence.
- The 19th century saw the creation of sexual identities (the 'homosexual' as a type of person).
- Power operates not just to prohibit but to produce forms of sexuality.
- Modern societies regulate sexuality through knowledge rather than just prohibition.

Anthropological research provides evidence for the cultural variability of sexuality. Studies by Margaret Mead in the 1930s and more recent work by Gilbert Herdt on the Sambia of Papua New Guinea reveal radically different sexual norms and practices across cultures. Even basic categories like 'heterosexual' and 'lesbian' or 'gay' are not universal but specific to contemporary societies in the Global North. In many cultures, sexual behaviour is organized around different principles such as age, social status or ritual significance rather than the gender of sexual partners.

POLICING SEXUALITY

The charmed circle of sexuality

If sexuality was natural and the same across time and place, arguably, it wouldn't need to be interfered with by key social structures. However, sexuality has been regulated through various institutions including religion, law, medicine and education. Gayle Rubin's (1984) influential essay 'Thinking Sex' introduced the concept of the 'charmed circle' of sexuality – the hierarchical arrangement of sexual practices from those considered 'normal', natural and good (heterosexual, married, monogamous, reproductive) to those labelled abnormal, unnatural and bad (same-sex, unmarried, casual, non-reproductive). What falls inside and outside the charmed circle will shift over time. For instance, since the time Rubin was writing, polyamorous relationships and cohabitation have become more socially acceptable.

Religion has historically been a powerful regulator of sexuality, with major world religions establishing norms around appropriate sexual behaviour. While these norms vary across religious traditions, they typically privilege reproductive heterosexuality within marriage. Christianity, over the years, has had many, sometimes conflicting, regulations about sexuality. Early Christianity wasn't so concerned with marriage but later insisted on it for procreation. There were rules about when you could have sex (not on Sundays or feast days, only at night or when more or less fully clothed). Any form of sexual activity that wouldn't lead to pregnancy was also proscribed against, thus the missionary position was good, while sex while standing up, anal sex or masturbation became bad!

Other institutions, such as law and education, complemented these regulations and eventually we had buggery laws (initially prohibiting the insertion of a penis into any anus – man, woman or animal – until, in the UK, it focused on sex between men) which meant such 'crimes' were punishable by death. Educators produced manuals warning boys of the dangers of too much masturbation (blindness, weakness, hairy palms and even early death).

SEXUALITY IS RELATIONAL

Ideas about sexuality are intimately tied up with gender and sex. Heterosexuality is viewed, in the contemporary Global North, as the appropriate or proper expression of gender. A stereotypically 'masculine' man is assumed to be heterosexual, as is a stereotypically feminine woman – the expression of their sexuality is assumed to be very different. Historically, assumptions have been made about men and women's sex drives – we are often told that men think about sex much more than women and that their sex drives are much higher. While there has been no scientific evidence that women have sex drives any lower, or higher, than men, these 'taken-for-granted' assumptions have been used to regulate expression of sexuality. Men's sexuality is assumed to be 'active'; appropriate female sexuality is passive and synonymous with the reproductive role – motherhood is the only acceptable expression of female sexuality. Society therefore expects and rewards masculine (hetero)promiscuity while punishing women for the same behaviours (we can see this operate in language – 'slag' versus 'stud' and so on).

Penetrative heterosexual sex (penetration of a vagina by a penis) in our society is deemed to be 'real' sex, or natural sex. This is reflected in our legal codes; it is only relatively recently, for example, that UK law has broadened the definition of rape to include the penetration of an anus (so men can now be legitimate victims of rape). Heterosexuality is a powerful conceptual tool in society; Adrienne Rich (1980) refers to 'compulsory heterosexuality', the idea that heterosexuality is the default or obligatory sexuality. Sexuality, therefore, only really makes sense in relation to those other categories of sex and gender. Some forms of sexuality are 'normal' or acceptable; others are viewed as 'abnormal' and unacceptable.

HETEROSEXUALITY IS AN INSTITUTION

Scholars gradually turned their critical attention to heterosexuality, viewing it as a powerful structuring institution that comes with privileges, and which is shored up by many other social institutions. In many countries, historically and to-date, marriage was an institution only for heterosexual couples. Heterosexism was coined to describe the ways heterosexuality is constructed as the 'natural', coherent, expression of sexuality. Queer theorist Michael Warner (1991) used the term heteronormativity to describe the ways in which heterosexuality is normalized, for instance when people are assumed to be heterosexual, or media representations of families focus on heterosexual dynamics. Even public spaces we might not think of as sexualized are revealed to be so when, for instance, same-sex couples are asked to leave supermarkets because they kiss or hold hands or are abused on buses for being a couple.

Heteronormativity

In addition to laws against sex between men in the UK, which weren't repealed until 1967 and not equalized until 2000, Section 28 of the Local Government Act 1988 is a good example of how law plays a role in heteronormativity. This clause prohibited anyone working in local authorities (such as teachers) from 'promoting' same-sex relationships as 'pretend families'. Libraries couldn't stock books that featured same-sex families and teachers couldn't talk about lesbian or gay identities in 'a positive light', without the risk of losing their jobs. It was in effect in England and Wales until 2003 (2000 in Scotland), and thus had a significant impact on LGBTQ+ people. Hate crimes rose at this time, for instance.

Sociological research by Mark Regnerus (2007) shows how religious involvement continues to shape sexual attitudes and behaviours, with more religious young people less likely to engage in premarital sex or have multiple partners.

Medicine and psychiatry became increasingly important in regulating sexuality in the modern era. Homosexuality was classified as a mental illness in the *Diagnostic and Statistical Manual of Mental Disorders* until 1973, reflecting how medical authority replaced religious authority in defining sexual normalcy. Peter Conrad and Joseph Schneider (1992) describe this as the **medicalization of deviance** – the process by which behaviours once defined as sinful came to be defined as symptoms of illness.

Regulating sexuality

SEXUAL IDENTITIES AND COMMUNITIES

While sexual behaviours have existed in all societies, the idea that sexuality constitutes a core aspect of personal identity is relatively recent. British historian Jeffrey Weeks (1985) traces how modern sexual identities emerged in the late 19th century alongside urbanization, industrialization and the rise of medical and psychiatric discourses about sexuality. The categorization of people as 'homosexual' or 'heterosexual' based on their desires – rather than just their behaviours – was a new development.

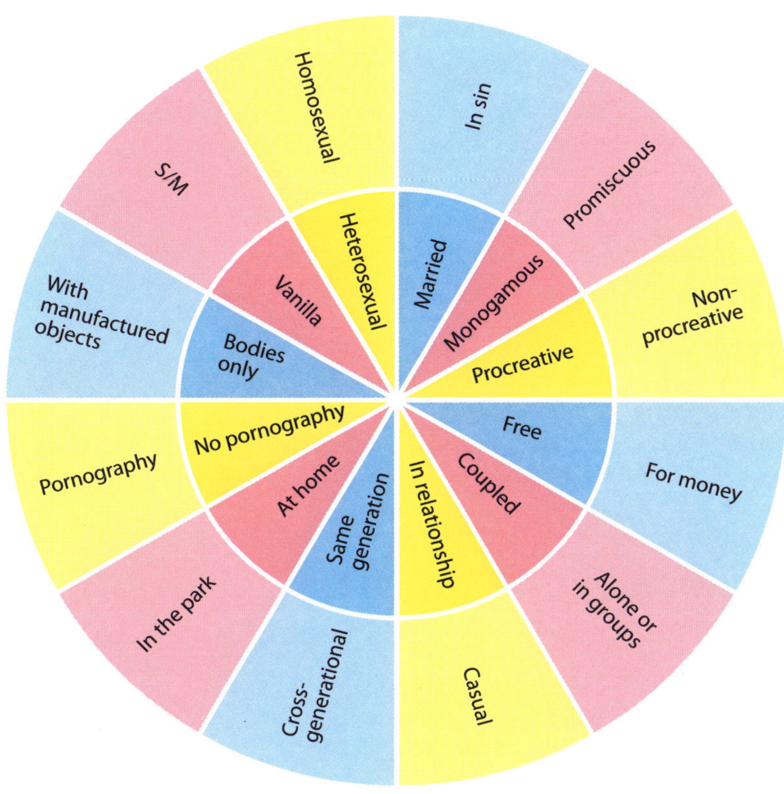

Rubin's charmed circle of sexuality will shift over time and between cultures

THE INVENTION OF SEXUAL IDENTITY
The 19th century sexologists mentioned above were responsible for many of the terms we use about sexuality today. Drawing on Ancient Greek, words such as 'homosexual', 'lesbian', 'heterosexual', 'masochism' and many others were introduced by them. Some of the scholars were attempting to provide a liberal argument for tolerance of difference, while other took the opinion that anything that deviated from the heterosexual 'norm' was aberrant. Whatever their intention, one result was the creation of ***sexual identity***. For the first time, people began to identify with the label and understand themselves in respect to that.

The sociological study of sexuality has been particularly interested in how marginalized sexual communities form and develop collective identities. Ken Plummer (1995) examines how 'sexual stories' – narratives about sexual awakening, coming out or sexual discovery – help individuals make sense of their experiences and connect to larger communities. These stories follow cultural scripts that change over time, reflecting shifts in how society understands sexuality.

Collective identity

Research on gay and lesbian communities in urban areas shows how physical spaces like neighbourhoods, bars and community centres have been crucial for the development of collective identity and political organization. John D'Emilio (1983) argues that capitalism created conditions for gay identity by separating sexuality from reproduction and enabling individuals to live outside traditional family structures in anonymous urban environments.

THE STONEWALL RIOTS AND LGBTQ+ MOVEMENT

The 1969 Stonewall riots marked a turning point in LGBTQ+ activism. At this time, regular police raids on gay bars were common. On 28 June 1969, police raided the Stonewall Inn in NYC but they met with resistance from a diverse group, including Black trans women (notably, Marsha P. Johnson and Sylvia Rivera). This event galvanized gay activists and shifted the movement from assimilation and demands to be 'tolerated' to more radical liberation politics. One of the legacies is the annual Pride celebrations, which happen globally, to commemorate the riots. The movement expanded from gay and lesbian concerns to broader LGBTQ+ inclusion.

Annual Pride marches, that take place in many cities throughout the world, remember earlier oppression and celebrate diversity.

SEXUALITY AND SOCIAL CHANGE

The regulation and understanding of sexuality have changed dramatically over time, reflecting broader social changes. In the Global North, the second half of the 20th century saw significant liberalization of sexual attitudes and behaviours, what some sociologists have called a 'sexual revolution'. This period, it is argued by some, saw increased acceptance of premarital sex, contraception, and eventually greater tolerance for same-sex relationships. However, many feminists have questioned the extent to which this improved life for women. Arguably there was more expectation that they have sex and take responsibility for contraception by taking the pill, while still being stigmatized for such sexual behaviour. The levels of hate crime targeted at LGBTQ+ people also cast doubt on this 'tolerance'.

A sexual revolution

Anthony Giddens (1992) argues that late modernity has seen the emergence of plastic sexuality – sexuality freed from reproduction through contraception and reproductive technologies – and the 'pure relationship' based on mutual satisfaction rather than economic necessity or social obligation. These changes, he suggests, have democratized intimate relationships and created possibilities for greater equality between partners.

However, critics like Lynn Jamieson (1999) question whether intimate relationships have really been transformed as fundamentally as Giddens suggests, pointing to persistent inequalities in heterosexual relationships. Similarly, Diane Richardson (2000) notes that increased acceptance of sexual diversity often comes with new forms of regulation, as when same-sex relationships gain legal recognition only when they conform to heteronormative models of monogamy and family formation.

More diversity and more regulation

JUST GOOD FRIENDS?

Many older people in the Global North are turning away from cohabitation to 'living apart together', which studies reveal are more gender-egalitarian. However, ageism means their relationships are not always recognized or are misinterpreted as friendships. Similarly, stereotypes about old age also have an impact on older people's health outcomes in relation to sexuality. For instance, stigma around older people and sex means they may be embarrassed to seek advice, or buy, protective contraception. This puts them at more risk of sexually transmitted infections (STIs), which are on the rise among the over-65s.

The internet and digital technologies have created new contexts for sexual expression, identity formation and community building. Research by Mary Gray (2009) on rural LGBTQ+ youth in the US shows how online spaces provide crucial resources for those without access to physical queer communities. At the same time, digital technologies have facilitated new forms of sexual commerce, surveillance and regulation.

How do we define marriage?

TILL DEATH US DO PART?

Marriage as an institution used to be something considered to be 'for life', as well as something that was only between men and women. There is a global decline in marriage currently, with many people choosing not to marry, or live with, their partners, and many opting to remain single. In addition, the current divorce rate is just over 40 per cent in the US and UK, thus divorce is 'normal', or to be expected. This causes us to question what is meant by marriage. Same-sex marriage and civil partnerships add to this. No longer can we assume what marriage is (i.e. it is not necessarily for life, it is not only for heterosexual couples, it is not for mainly heterosexual couples, and it is not necessarily for procreation, or it might be but within same-sex couples). It is an indicator of more general shifts in ideas about intimacy, sex and family.

Many who divorce are still 'invested' in marriage and will remarry and form new households.

CONTEMPORARY DEBATES AND FUTURE DIRECTIONS

TRANS IDENTITIES AND GENDER THEORY

Trans experiences have prompted important reconsiderations of the relationship between sex, gender and identity. While earlier feminist theories distinguished between sex as biological and gender as social, trans studies scholars like Susan Stryker (2006) challenge this distinction by showing how embodiment itself is socially mediated. Transgender experiences highlight the complexity of the relationship between bodies, identities and social categories.

Different theoretical perspectives approach trans identities in various ways. Some draw on Butler's theory of performativity to understand gender as a fluid, contingent process rather than a fixed characteristic. Others, including some trans theorists like Jay Prosser (1998), emphasize the importance of embodiment and the lived experience of gender identity, which may be experienced as stable and essential rather than fluid or constructed.

These theoretical debates have practical implications for issues such as access to medical care, legal recognition and participation in gender-segregated spaces. While radical feminist theorists like Janice Raymond (1979) and Sheila Jeffreys (2014) have been critical of transgender identities that reinforce rather than challenge gender norms, trans scholars and activists argue that such perspectives fail to respect the lived experiences of trans people and can contribute to their marginalization.

Trans identities

QUEER THEORY AND BEYOND BINARY THINKING

Queer theory, emerging in the 1990s out of feminist and lesbian and gay theories, represented a significant shift in thinking about sexuality and gender. Drawing on poststructuralist theory, queer theorists like Eve Kosofsky Sedgwick (1990) and Jack Halberstam (2005) challenge binary thinking around gender and sexuality, arguing that such binaries (male/female, heterosexual/homosexual) serve to maintain social hierarchies rather than reflect natural categories.

Queer theory's emphasis on performativity and the instability of identity categories has been influential in understanding non-binary and genderqueer identities that exist outside the male/female binary. Research by S. Bear Bergman and Meg-John Barker (2017) with non-binary individuals highlights how they navigate a world structured around binary gender, often developing creative strategies for self-expression and community building despite institutional barriers.

The fluidity emphasized in queer theory has been both embraced and contested. While some critics argue that it undermines the bases for collective identity and political organization, others suggest that it opens up new possibilities for coalition-building across differences. Butler (1993) has emphasized that recognizing the constructed nature of identity categories doesn't mean they can simply be discarded, as they remain necessary for social recognition and political claims-making.

Performativity

DIFFERENT THEORETICAL PERSPECTIVES ON TRANS IDENTITIES

Various theoretical approaches to understanding transgender experiences are:

- ***Social constructionist***: gender as culturally specific categories that vary across time and place
- ***Performative***: gender as constituted through repeated acts and gestures
- ***Phenomenological:*** embodied experience of gender as lived reality
- ***Intersectional***: trans experiences shaped by ethnicity, class, disability etc.
- ***Medical***: gender identity as innate characteristic with biological basis
- ***Feminist***: diverse perspectives from seeing trans as reinforcing binary to trans feminism

GLOBAL PERSPECTIVES AND DECOLONIAL APPROACHES

Much sociological theory on gender and sexuality has emerged from Western contexts, raising questions about its applicability across different cultural settings. Decolonial scholars critique the universalization of Western concepts and categories, noting how colonialism imposed particular understandings of gender and sexuality on colonized peoples.

Oyèrónkẹ́ Oyěwùmí's (1997) work on Yoruba society challenges the assumption that gender is a universal organizing principle, arguing that age was historically more significant than gender in structuring social relations. Similarly, scholars working on Indigenous communities in the Americas, such as Qwo-Li Driskill (2011), show how European colonization disrupted existing gender systems that recognized more than two genders.

Contemporary global dynamics around gender and sexuality are complex. On the one hand, there has been an internationalization of certain concepts and identities, with terms like 'LGBTQ+' gaining currency globally. On the other hand, these developments have sometimes been criticized as a form of Western cultural imperialism that fails to respect Indigenous understandings of gender and sexuality.

Transnational feminist scholars like Chandra Talpade Mohanty (2003) emphasize the importance of understanding how gender operates differently across global contexts without falling into either universalism (assuming all women share the same experiences) or cultural relativism (treating all cultural practices as equally valid regardless of their effects on women).

Kathoey in Thailand, (opposite left), Muxes in Mexico (opposite right), and Hijras in India (above) are just a few examples of gender fluidity across the globe.

SEX MATTERS

Sociological perspectives on gender and sexuality have evolved significantly over time, moving from relatively simple distinctions between sex and gender to complex understandings of how gender and sexuality are constructed, performed and experienced in diverse contexts. Contemporary approaches emphasize the intersectional nature of gender and sexuality, recognizing that they never operate in isolation but always in conjunction with other social categories like ethnicity, class and disability. We can see the ways in which normative constructions of gender and sexuality become institutions in their own right. They also connect closely to other institutions such as the family, religion, medicine, law, education and the media.

The social construction of gender and sexuality doesn't mean they aren't real or significant in people's lives. Rather, understanding them as social constructs helps us recognize how they are shaped by power relations and how they might be reimagined and reconstructed in more equitable ways. As societies continue to change, sociological analysis provides tools for understanding both persistent inequalities and emerging possibilities for social transformation. And we should not be complacent: gains made can easily be taken away. Many women across the globe are killed simply because they are women. Same-sex relations between men remain illegal, and even punishable by death, in many places. We are, it seems, in a moment where many of the gains made in relation to gender and sexuality are being turned back. Russia partially decriminalized domestic violence, Hungary introduced legislation that likens same-sex relationships to paedophilia and the new pope sees 'homosexual lifestyles' and same-sex marriage as problematic. Conservative groups such as the Conservative Political Action Conference (CPAC) and the World Congress on Family (a Christian coalition group) argue against single, gay and trans parents. Recognizing prejudice and discrimination when it happens, and calling it out, it just one of many small but powerful steps we can all take.

Chapter Eight
BODIES

More than just flesh and bones? – Sociological bodies – Understanding the social body – Disciplining bodies – The body politic – Unequal bodies – The body project – Bodies do matter

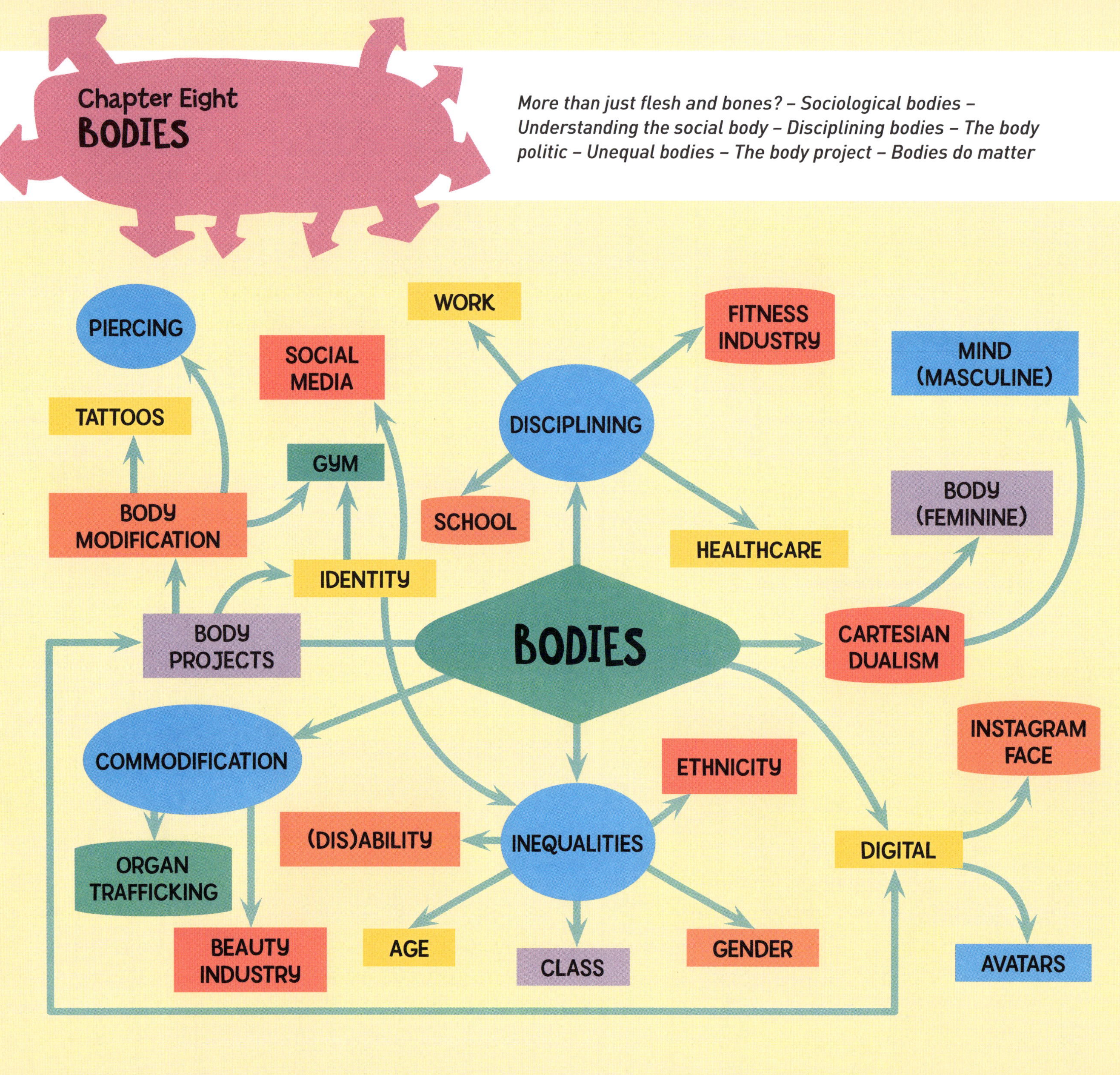

> *Behind your thoughts and feelings, my brother, stands a mighty commander, an unknown sage – he is called Self. He lives in your body, he is your body.*
>
> Friedrich Nietzsche, *Thus Spoke Zarathustra*

MORE THAN JUST FLESH AND BONES?

In the 1970s, TV show makers, especially in the US, seemed fascinated by the futuristic potential for augmenting human bodies. Programmes like *The Six Million Dollar Man* (1974–1978) and, my absolute favourite, *The Bionic Woman* (1976–1978), explored the ways in which technology could be used to create cyborgs (a portmanteau word of 'cybernetic' and 'organism'). Such ideas perhaps seem everyday now – 'Captain Cyborg', Kevin Warwick at the University of Reading, for instance, has experimented on himself with a variety of electrical implants. Many people who have lost limbs, or use of them, through accidents, have had brain implants enabling them to use electrical prosthetic limbs.

What these examples offer is a way of thinking about bodies and their relationship to the social world. How we understand, experience and modify our bodies is profoundly social. Using our sociological imagination, we can connect what appears to be intensely personal – our embodied experiences – with broader social structures and cultural contexts. As the British sociologist Bryan Turner (1996) argues, the body is simultaneously biological and social, a site where nature and culture converge and sometimes conflict.

Robocop, a man transformed by cybernetics into a cyborg, poses sociological questions about the body.

SOCIOLOGICAL BODIES

Indeed, the sociology of the body is one of the fastest growing areas of sociological theory. In some ways, this might seem odd. Many might think of bodies as private, something, perhaps, to be kept hidden, and something more suited to be considered from biological or physiological perspectives. However, sociology has developed to show just how 'social' bodies are; very simply, we do things to our bodies because of other people.

Desirable bodies

One strand of sociology that focuses on consumer culture, for instance, reveals the ways in which (some) bodies can sell products. By analyzing billboards, TV advertisements and social media, we can unpack this further by looking at how age, gender, ethnicity and other factors relate to how desirable and aspirational certain bodies are perceived to be, thus representation impacts on consumption. Or we could consider the rise and normalization of cosmetic surgery.

Cosmetic surgery

For instance, after the Covid-19 lockdowns, cosmetic procedures in the UK rose very quickly, by 102 per cent in 2022 from the previous year – 31,057 procedures took place, which is the highest figure since records began in 2004. This, and the example of cyborgs above, reflects the ways in which we transform and modify our bodies. We might study the relationship between work and bodies, for instance in the ways that nightshift working has serious health consequences. Bodies, in a range of ways, reflect social change and are impacted by processes such as globalization, capitalism, racism, sexism and transphobia, and we shall begin to consider some of these.

I THINK, THEREFORE I AM? UNDERSTANDING THE SOCIAL BODY

One reason often cited for an assumption that the body is not sociological is the predominance of separating the mind, and thus 'the self', from the body. The Enlightenment philosopher René Descartes (1596–1650) is partly responsible for this legacy. The famous Latin phrase '*cogito, ergo sum*' ('I think, therefore I am') was an important tenet of Descartes' own thinking. A very simplified explanation of this is that the only way we can know we exist is by thinking, therefore thinking is the most important aspect of being human. This resulted in what is known as ***Cartesian dualism***, a distinction between mind and body. As with almost all binary systems, one tends to be valued more than the other; in this case, the mind was seen as the important, rational part of human subjectivity and the body rendered an animalistic appendage. This also had gendered dimensions. As Margrit Shildrick (1997) observed, for many writers after Descartes, men were believed to be capable of transcending the body, to exist on a level of reason and intellect. Women, however, were more trapped by, or tied to, their bodies, thus were more emotional.

Cosmetic procedures have become increasingly normalized and affordable, especially since COVID-19.

Procedure	Number of procedures
Breast reduction	71,364
Eyelid surgery	115,261
Breast lift	143,364
Abdominoplasty	161,948
Breast augmentation	298,568
Liposuction	325,669

I'M JUST OFF TO THE SHOPS – DO YOU WANT ANYTHING? OR THE WANDERING WOMB...

The ancient Greek physician and philosopher Hippocrates (c. 460–375 BCE), and others, were of the opinion that the womb was a source of many of women's (and men's) troubles. They saw the womb as a living thing, akin to an animal living inside another. If it wasn't being used properly (i.e. growing a baby) it could grow hot and thirsty and seek shelter elsewhere. There wasn't agreement as to how far it would travel – presumably not so far as to be useful and get supplies from the supermarket – but it could relocate incorrectly within the body and cause illness. Cures might include bedrest, or fumigation (the womb was said to be coaxed back into place either by being repelled from noxious smells or attracted to sweet smells).

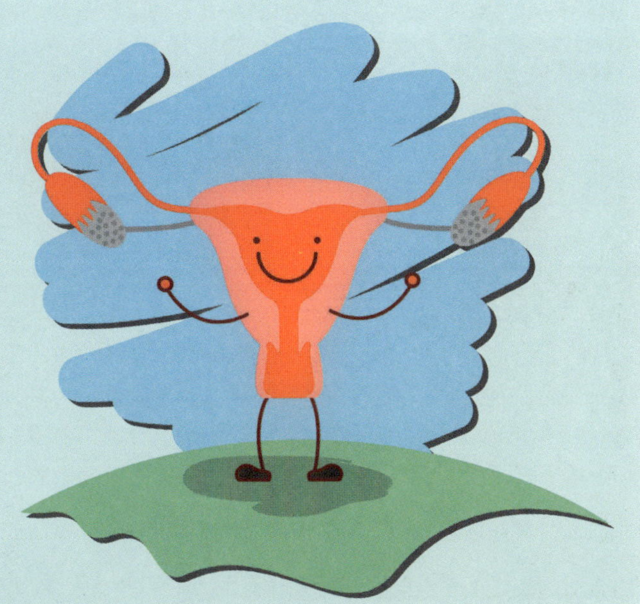

Apart from prolapsed wombs, doctors are now of the belief that wombs do not go wandering around the body.

Arguably, this misinformation was used later as a way to control women. For instance, keeping women indoors and quiet was a way of preventing hysteria and potentially witchcraft induced by the wandering womb. Later, alleged potential to damage women's reproductive capabilities (and, in a patriarchal society, their key function) was used as an excuse to prevent women from entering higher education (thinking too much could damage them) or playing sport. A moral panic in the late 19th century about the freedoms offered by bicycles led (male) experts to warn of the moral and physical 'ugliness' these could cause in women. Using a bike might cause women to become prostitutes, lesbians or suffer from the invented disease, 'bicycle face'!

This focus on the mind as somehow separate to the rest of our bodies impacted on disciplines like sociology for a while, meaning that, to a degree, bodies were sidelined.

HYSTERIA ▶ ***we still use the term hysteria (from the Greek* hystera *meaning 'womb') to refer to a state of extreme emotion in a gendered way. Tory MP Liam Fox accused a female minister of being 'hysterical' after a heated exchange, yet male politicians' outbursts are rarely described as such.***

CLASSICAL BODIES

That is not to say that classical sociology ignored bodies entirely. Émile Durkheim's early work based on his PhD, 'The Elementary Forms of Religious Life', looks at the relationship between religion, society and bodies. According to British sociologist Chris Shilling (2011), Durkheim's work is useful in its exploration of the ways in which groups, such as religious orders, through rituals and habits experience an embodied intoxication, which unites them. Later, his work discussed the idea of collective effervescence – the ways in which emotions can travel through a group and provide a social bond, for example the public funeral of the pope. Carrying on with the religious theme, Max Weber's work on the Protestant work ethic and capitalism in part was concerned with the ways in which religious ideas affect people's habitus; many protestants adopted a frugal lifestyle and worked hard – the corporeal basis for capitalism. This capitalism, which demanded hard labour and often resulted in alienation, according to Karl Marx, particularly marked the bodies of the working classes

Matthias Grünewald's The Temptation of St Anthony *c.1512–15 a warning not to be tempted by seductive women or demons.*

'SOMETIMES I SITS AND THINKS, AND SOMETIMES I JUST SITS': EMBODIED SELVES

Growing up, we had a loo roll holder with the above quotation under a picture of Rodin's *The Thinker*. The phrase itself, which is often (erroneously) attributed to A.A. Milne's Winnie the Pooh, and the intended pun, brings us back to our bodies. From a theoretical perspective, the French philosopher Maurice Merleau-Ponty (1908–1961) did much to draw attention back to the corporeal. His *The Phenomenology of Perception* (1945) reminds us that we make sense of the world not just through our minds but through our bodies too. He also argues that the mind is part of the body. As we saw in Chapter 4, Norbert Elias was thinking about bodies and the ways in which the 'Civilising Process' impacted on them a decade earlier than Merleau-Ponty. Changes in sleeping and eating habits and ideas of shame, he argued, were the result of processes of socialization, rationalization and individualization. Bryan Turner has characterized this shift through time from the 'open' body of the medieval period to a 'closed', individualized body of modernity.

PHENOMENOLOGY ▶ ***a method focusing on the human experience and how we perceive or are conscious of our experiences. The word comes from 'phenomena', or things that exist.***

The work of Elias, Merleau-Ponty and others has charted the shift to a somatic society for Turner, one where the body helps us understand, for instance, how social order is maintained, particularly through institutions like religion, law and (increasingly) medicine. Turner has also noted how much 'sociology of the body' was inadvertently affected by Cartesian dualism, focusing on women's bodies as circumscribed by patriarchy and the ideology of the family. Certainly, much of the theorizing of bodies in the later decades of last century came from feminist theorists, many of whom were attempting to challenge this binary thinking of man as disembodied and rational and women as inferior embodied beings. Simone de Beauvoir (1949) postulated this and inspired a generation of second-wave feminist theorists in the 1960s and 1970s.

Somatic society

Circumscribed by patriarchy

THE FOUR RS

Turner argues there are four key ways bodies help us understand society:

1. ***Reproduction*** – the processes that ensure the continuation of populations
2. ***Regulation*** – the ways bodies are controlled to ensure order, through methods such as surveillance
3. ***Restraint*** – the ways in which individuals come to 'control' themselves, perhaps through dieting
4. ***Representation*** – cultural representations of bodies in art, advertising or discourses such as legal or medical discourse

As we shall see, much sociological work on bodies addresses one or more of the Rs.

DISCIPLINING BODIES

Michel Foucault's (1977) analysis of how bodies are disciplined and controlled has been useful for sociologists looking at bodies. In *Discipline and Punish* (Éditions Gallimard, 1975), he looks at the ways in which power exerts itself on individuals and how this has changed over time. Earlier forms of what he termed '***sovereign power***' were external and often violent forms of bodily control from authority (for instance public executions) and generally relied on punishment. Later, a shift to ***disciplinary power*** saw more subtle, and ubiquitous, forms of discipline that operate through self-regulation and surveillance and often use reward as well as punishment. Institutions like schools, prisons, hospitals and work train bodies to be docile and productive; we learn the norms of class, gender, sexuality and so on, against which bodies are measured and judged. Fear now comes from being seen to do something wrong, thus we learn to 'tame' our own bodies.

The panopticon

Foucault draws on the ideas of Jeremy Bentham, the Enlightenment philosopher who designed the ideal prison, the ***panopticon***. This prison was based around a central tower with small windows for prison officers, around which were prison cells with large windows. Thus, inmates could potentially be observed at any time without knowing if they were being watched. Foucault argues this becomes a metaphor for how modern power operates. When we internalize the feeling of being watched, we discipline ourselves, controlling our behaviours and bodies to conform to social expectations without the need for external coercion.

This has also become a central design principle for buildings in the modern state according to Foucault. Schools and hospitals, for instance, will have doors with windows through which both pupils/patients can be observed by authority figures. We also now have CCTV and other forms of workplace surveillance; all are techniques for producing 'docile bodies'. Those habits that seem most personal, such as how we eat, walk, sit and groom, are all shaped by these disciplinary mechanisms.

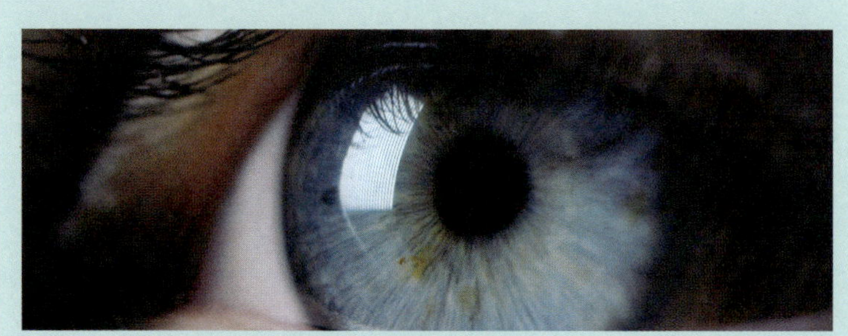

YOUR BODY IS YOUR PASSWORD

Increasingly, particularly since 11 September 2001's terrorist attack on the World Trade Center in the US, bodies have become our passwords – fingerprints, facial, voice and iris recognition are some of the everyday ways in which our bodies are tracked.

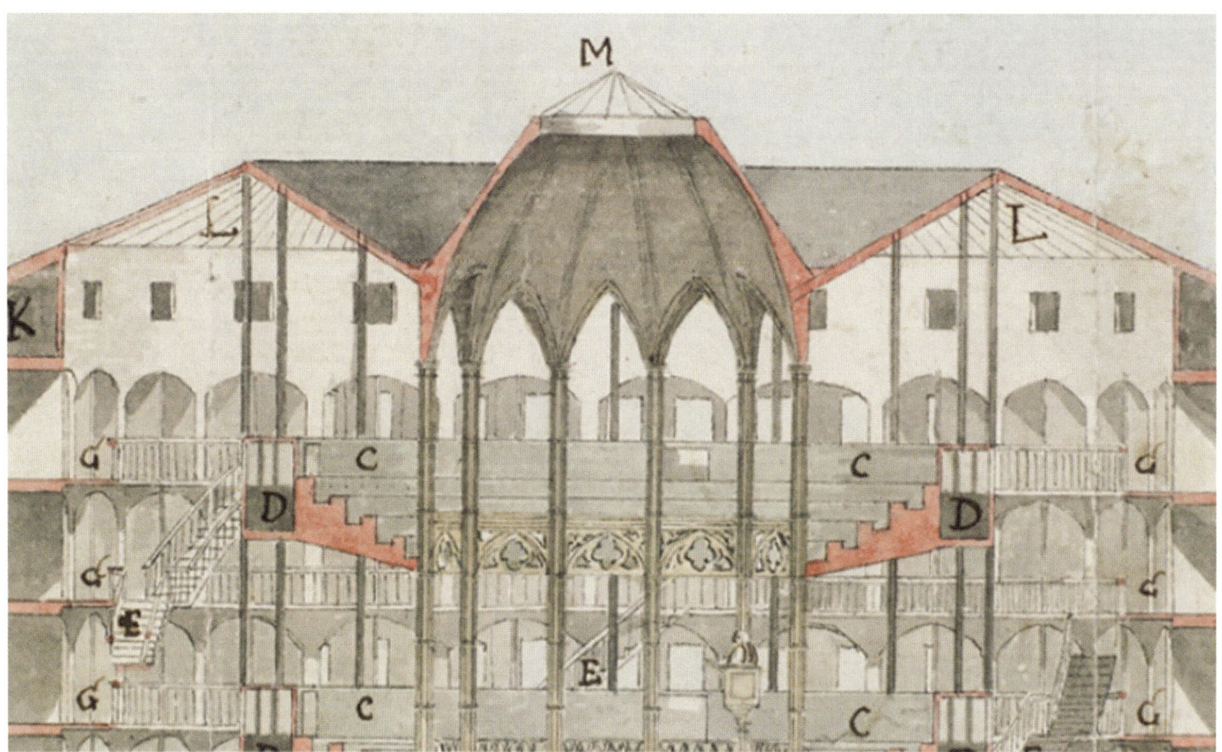

A panoptic building design allows its residents to be seen by hidden authority figures.

LEAKY BODIES

Elias showed us, in *The Civilising Process* (Haus zum Falken, 1939), how internalized emotions such as embarrassment and shame in relation to bodily emissions became one of the ways we 'tamed' ourselves. Gradually, we tried to conceal natural processes and functions such as spitting, urinating, defecating, having sex and even dying; these became private, rather than public, functions. The behaviours and secretions that are considered disgusting or shameful will vary between cultures and over time. The anthropologist Mary Douglas has considered more contemporary attitudes in this respect. The body, for her, can be understood as a natural symbol that helps us understand ideas of social order. Using Durkheim's work, she says some bodies and bodily functions are sacred (special) and others profane (ordinary). This can come to a distinction between what is considered clean, or pure, and what is thought of as dirty or polluting. The margins of the body, where the body is most vulnerable to contact with the outside world, such as orifices, are of particular interest. Secretions that pass through orifices might be seen as more or less disruptive or dangerous. We might be more forgiving of a child's snotty nose than an adult's, for instance. Women's menstrual blood might be seen as more embarrassing than men's semen.

Concealing natural processes

Sacred bodies

THE BODY POLITIC

State control of bodies

Foucault also introduced the concept of biopower to refer to the various ways that states might exert power over bodies to ensure a healthy (and thus productive) citizenship. It operates at two levels: the disciplining of individual bodies (as seen above) and the regulation of populations through public health measures and demographic 'management'. Through techniques like public health campaigns, fertility regulation and medical screening programmes, the collective national 'body' is monitored and regulated.

This explains why states take such an interest in bodily practices, such as anti-smoking campaigns and policies addressing obesity. Bodies become sites of government intervention, justified through discourses of health, productivity and national well-being. Such an interest often also enables the social structures that might cause these behaviours and inequalities to be conveniently ignored. US sociologist Rose Weitz's (2016) research on the sociology of health and illness shows how our understanding of health and disease is never only biological but is shaped by social, political and economic interests that define what constitutes a 'normal' or 'healthy' body.

RISKY BODIES

Stephen Lyng (1990, 2005) used the concept of edgework to describe the ways some people use extreme sports to resist the over-regulated nature of modern life. But who gets to take these risks? Studies show that extreme sports participants are predominantly white, male and middle-class. Women, however, have made great 'strokes' in edgework activities such as long-distance swimming. Karen Throsby's (2016) work on swimming and embodiment shows how marathon swimmers can offer positive challenges to conventional ideas of what 'good' bodies are; female bodies that are strong and have extra layers of protective fat, in this context, are valuable.

SITTING LIKE A GIRL?

The disciplining of bodies can be seen in the gendered expectations placed on men's and women's bodies. Iris Marion Young's (1980) essay 'Throwing Like a Girl' argues that women are taught to occupy space differently than men. In short, they learn to take up less space, to move with restraint, and to be conscious of being looked at. I can vividly remember my grandmother telling me, even though I was wearing trousers, that 'young ladies' don't sit with their legs apart (I determined to do it every time I was in her company after that). Girls are often taught to be fearful of danger outside; that they are fragile. Thus, Young argues, they never learn to fully 'be' in their bodies, to use them to their full capabilities. Traditionally, doors may have been held open for them, shopping carried for them, chairs pulled out for them and so on – such practices were seen as 'chivalrous' but also indicated a relative, and desirable, physical weakness in women. Boys, however, learn to use their bodies to, as the title of the essay suggests, put their full weight behind throwing a ball. These aren't natural differences – there is no reason why a man might, for instance, take the arm rest in a cinema, or more leg room on a bus – they are learned bodily habits reflecting and reinforcing gender inequality. Thus, when women display strong bodies, people might be shocked. When the tennis player Martina Navratilova first came to prominence, many newspapers were preoccupied with her muscly arms.

You may have observed gendered differences in how space is taken up.

Similarly, Raewyn Connell's (1995) work on masculinity shows how men's bodies are disciplined to display strength, dominance and control – part of what Connell terms 'hegemonic masculinity'. Men who fail to embody these physical ideals may face social sanctions, demonstrating how bodily performances are crucial to gender identity. The recent social media trend of looksmaxxing is related to this – young men are under pressure to present in a particular way and this pressure has led to a worrying rise in eating disorders and muscle dysmorphia.

Judith Butler (1990) takes this further, arguing that gender itself is performative: not something we are but something we do through repeated bodily acts. The seeming 'naturalness' of gender is achieved through this consistent performance, which is governed by social norms that precede and shape us.

CASE STUDY: GENDER IN MOTION

Ballet has historically embodied strict gender differences, with female dancers performing on pointe (emphasizing lightness and elevation) while male dancers execute powerful jumps and lifts. These physical techniques reinforce traditional gender stereotypes – women as ethereal and supported, men as powerful and supporting.

In contrast, contact improvisation, a contemporary/postmodern dance form developed in the 1970s, deliberately challenges these gendered movement patterns. Dancers of all genders share weight bearing and move through space in ways that blur traditional gender distinctions.

This comparison illustrates how different movement practices can either reinforce or challenge embodied gender norms.

Patrick Bateman (Christian Bale), in Bret Easton Ellis's American Psycho *represents Connell's hegemonic masculinity through bodily strength. He also conforms to consumer culture's insistance on attractiveness via means such as exercise and tanning beds.*

UNEQUAL BODIES

SOCIAL CLASS AND BODIES

Our bodily practices often betray our social class origins and positions. Pierre Bourdieu's (1984) concept of 'habitus' (see Chapter 5) helps explain how class becomes embodied – literally incorporated into our posture, gestures, taste and physical dispositions. These bodily habits are acquired through socialization but feel natural and personal rather than social. The way we stand, speak, eat, dress and move all bear the imprint of our class background.

Bourdieu describes this embodied class identity as hexis, the physical manifestation of habitus. These bodily dispositions serve as markers of social distinction, allowing people to recognize (often unconsciously) others' class positions through their embodied practices. Ex-UK prime minister Boris Johnson's hair, speech and mannerisms, for instance, are, in many ways, trademarks of his upper middle-class upbringing.

Empirical research supports this theoretical insight. For example, as we saw in Chapter 5, Beverley Skeggs (1997) shows how working-class women's attempts to embody respectability through bodily presentation reflects their awareness of how their bodies are judged according to middle-class standards. She also points out the ways in which working-class bodies are often presented as being 'excess' or out of control in popular culture – consuming too much food or drink, being too fat (for women) or too muscular (for men). Similarly, Diane Reay's (2004) research on education demonstrates how class inequalities are reproduced through embodied experiences in schools, where working-class children's bodies may be subjected to different forms of discipline and evaluation than their middle-class peers.

Public schoolboys, as shown here, display their class through things like clothing and posture.

Working-class women who worked in mines tended not to display stereotypical qualities of so-called femininity. Their work needed strength, for instance.

RACIALIZED BODIES

Bodies are also sites where racial categories are constructed and contested. 'Race', as we saw in Chapter 6, is not a biological reality but a social construction that attributes meaning to certain physical characteristics. As Frantz Fanon (1952) articulated, racialization involves the reduction of complex human beings to their bodies, particularly to visible markers like skin colour.

Racialization

This process has profound consequences for how people experience their embodiment. In 'Black Skin, White Masks', Fanon describes the experience of being reduced to his body – of being seen as a body rather than a person – in a white-dominated society, where whiteness is invisiblized. Similarly, W.E.B. Du Bois's (1903) concept of 'double consciousness' captures how Black Americans must constantly see themselves through the eyes of others, creating a particular kind of embodied awareness.

Double consciousness

Contemporary sociologists like Nirmal Puwar (2004) have examined how racialized bodies are treated as 'out of place' in spaces traditionally dominated by whiteness, such as elite universities or government institutions. Her concept of 'space invaders' helps us understand how certain bodies are marked as not belonging and thus are subject to heightened surveillance and judgement.

DISABLED BODIES

Disability studies have made important contributions to the sociology of the body by challenging assumptions about what constitutes a 'normal' body. As UK sociologist Tom Shakespeare (2006) argues, disability is not an inherent physical property; instead, it emerges from the interaction between bodies and environments designed for normative bodily function. Many scholars argue that the very concept of 'disability' constructs a problematic binary between presumed 'acceptable' bodies and those deemed 'unacceptable'.

For a long time, disabled bodies were viewed through a medicalized lens, much as women's and trans bodies have been. In other words, people's experiences are understood as medical and in need of intervention. The social model of disability, developed by activists and scholars like Mike Oliver (1996), distinguishes between physical impairment and disability – the latter being the social exclusion that results from environments built for normative bodies. This perspective shifts attention from 'fixing' individual bodies to addressing the social arrangements that disable people with certain bodily characteristics.

Robert McRuer's (2006) concept of 'compulsory able-bodiedness' further highlights how the assumption of able-bodiedness structures social life, similar to how, as Adrienne Rich (1980) argued, heteronormativity assumes heterosexuality as the default. Drawing on queer theory, crip theory (reclaiming the term 'crippled') links disability to a matrix of bodies and actions that are either seen as being 'normal' or 'deviant'. Bodies that deviate from normative function are marked as problematic and in need of correction or accommodation. Crip theorists such as McRuer argue that rather than striving for acceptance or tolerance, we should be deconstructing the 'abled' body.

The top picture shows buildings built for 'normative' bodies. The bottom picture is an example of more inclusive design.

PRICING BEAUTY

Sociologist Ashley Mears (2011) studied the modelling industry, showing how racialized and gendered beauty standards are literally priced into bodies. Her ethnographic research revealed that:

- Black models were often hired as 'ethnic' tokens
- white models commanded higher rates and more prestigious jobs
- the industry justified these disparities through appeals to 'the market'
- models internalized these valuations, affecting how they experienced their own bodies

This research demonstrates how economic value becomes attached to bodies based on their alignment with dominant beauty ideals that reflect racial and gender hierarchies.

Tokenization and value

HEALTH AND 'RESPONSIBLE' BODIES

Health is another useful lens to help us understand bodies. Some sociologists, such as Drew Leder (1991), have referred to the concept of the 'absent body' in sociology. Bodies are present in our everyday lives in the performance of routine tasks such as cleaning our teeth but it is only when we are ill or in pain that we become phenomenologically aware of how important bodies are.

The absent body

Contemporary health discourses increasingly emphasize individual responsibility for bodily health and appearance. As Deborah Lupton (1995) argues, the 'risk discourse' in public health, places moral obligations on individuals to monitor and regulate their bodies to avoid health risks.

This emphasis on personal responsibility often obscures the social determinants of health and bodily capacity. Research consistently shows that health outcomes correlate strongly with social class, race, gender and geographic location, yet dominant health discourses focus on individual choices and behaviours. British scholars Richard Wilkinson and Kate Pickett's (2009) work, for instance, has shown that unequal societies are unhealthier (see Chapter 5). We also know that the less control, or agency, someone has over their life, the more likely they are to be ill. People's self-esteem, their perceived status, according to US sociologist Peter Freund (1990), impacts on their health outcomes.

Healthism

The healthism identified by Robert Crawford (1980) involves the elevation of health to a super-value and its conflation with appearance, particularly thinness, fitness and youth. This discourse produces what Crawford terms the 'responsible body' – one that demonstrates moral worth through visible health practices like diet and exercise.

CASE STUDY: THE 'OBESITY EPIDEMIC' AS MORAL PANIC

The framing of rising body weights as an 'obesity epidemic' illustrates how health concerns become moralized. Sociologists like Michael Gard and Jan Wright (2005) have analyzed how:

- medical definitions of obesity shifted over time, dramatically increasing the number of people classified as 'overweight'
- public discourse around body weight draws on moral language of discipline, responsibility and failure
- the focus on individual behaviour obscures environmental and economic factors
- healthcare prejudice against larger bodies can make health outcomes worse

This is a salient reminder that scientific concepts like BMI are never simply objective measures but are embedded in social contexts and power relations.

IS FAT A FEMINIST ISSUE?

Many scholars have looked at the relationship between gender and ideas about body weight. Psychotherapist Susie Orbach's early work *Fat is a Feminist Issue* (1978), argued that women were placed under social pressures to conform to looking a certain way, that choosing to go on a diet is informed by sexual politics. Later explorations including Susan Bordo's *Unbearable Weight* (1993) and Kim Chernin's *Womansize: Tyranny of Slenderness* (1983) both highlight the ways in which attitudes to bodies, particularly women's bodies, are culturally and politically produced. Attitudes to fatness have less to do with standards of health and much more to do with aesthetics and sexuality. Both authors argue that eating disorders and body dysmorphia are not pathological, rather they are cultural.

Medical nemesis

In 1975, the Austrian social critic Ivan Illich (1926–2002) argued that the medical establishment itself has become a cause of ill health to populations. He used the Greek term *iatrogenesis*, meaning 'brought forth by a healer', to chart the ways in which healthcare in capitalist societies does harm. In part this is because healthcare is increasingly, in modern societies, medicalized and professionalized, thus we have lost traditional remedies and expertise. He was particularly critical of the US model of healthcare, but generally he saw modern medicine causing harm on a number of levels including:

- clinical iatrogenesis – doctor-inflicted harm, such as overuse of antibiotics, and over-investigation or treatment to avoid prosecution in a litigious society
- social iatrogenesis – growing reliance on doctors or 'experts', especially around death, and the power of the modern pharmaceutical industry
- cultural iatrogenesis – the loss of autonomy and personal problem-solving capabilities

In many ways, Illich's work can be seen as prescient, given what we now know about dependency on prescription drugs such as medication for anxiety, pain, insomnia and depression, for instance, or the overprescription of antibiotics, which has led to widespread resistance. Dramas such as *Dopesick* (2021), *Pain Hustlers* (2023) and *Painkiller* (2023) have increased our understanding of the power of 'big pharma'.

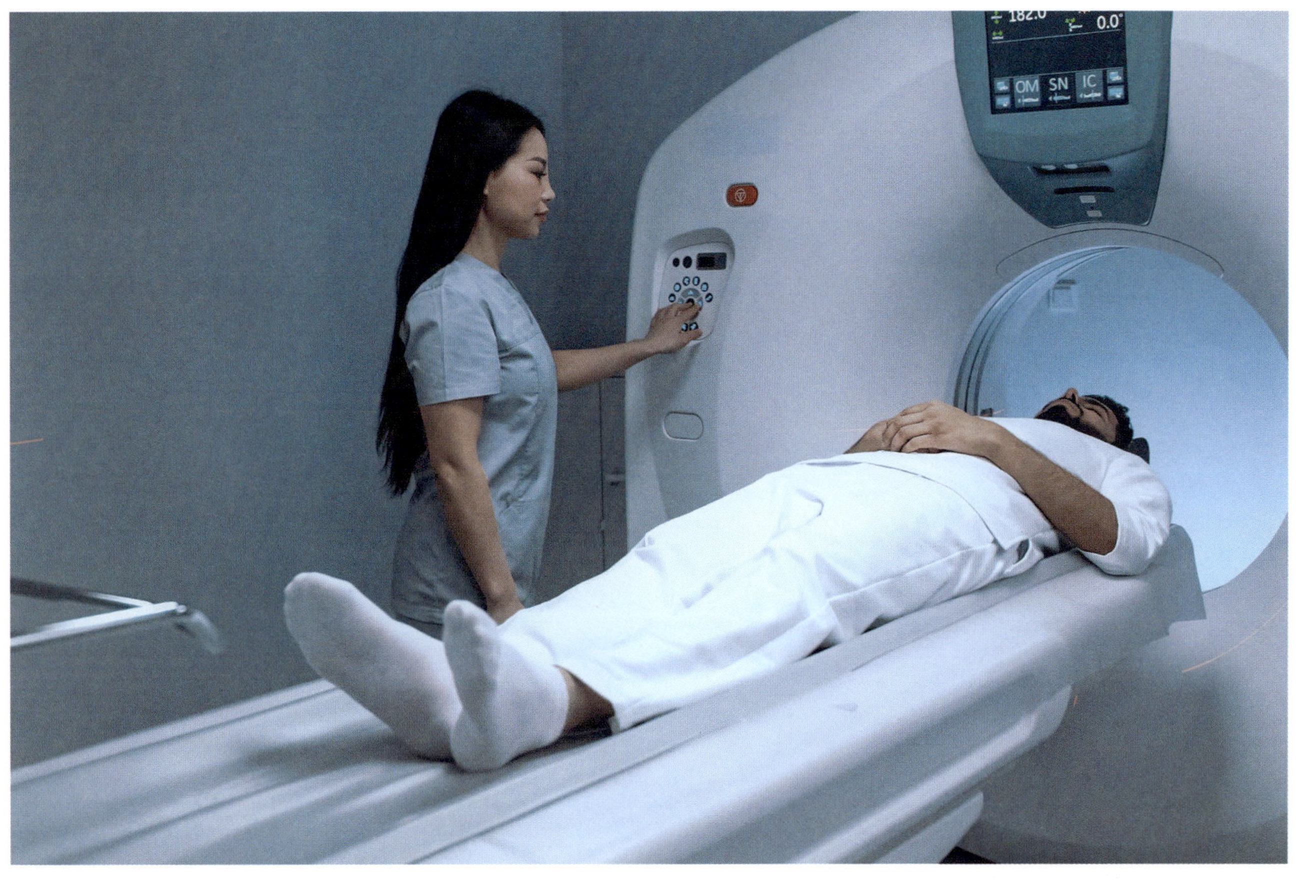

We are becoming increasingly aware of the links between over-using CT scans and the development of cancer.

Nikolas Rose (2007), a British sociologist, however, has shown how this medical authority over bodies can be transformed. Drawing on Foucault's notion of biopower, and other concepts we have looked at, he gives examples of things such as patient advocacy movements and alternative health practices, such as acupuncture, which can give power back to people.

AGEING BODIES

The lifecourse

Our bodies change throughout the ***lifecourse***, but the meanings attached to these changes are socially constructed. Childhood, adolescence, adulthood and old age are not simply biological stages but social categories with specific expectations and norms attached to bodies at different ages.

The concept of the 'lifecourse' in sociology emphasizes how age-related bodily experiences are shaped by historical context, social location and institutional arrangements. For example, Tamara Hareven's (1982) research shows how the timing of life transitions (entering adulthood, becoming a parent, retiring) varies historically and across social groups.

RESISTING BODIES

Despite many of these controlling or 'normalizing' forces, many groups actively resist dominant bodily norms through various forms of embodied protest. Fat acceptance activists challenge medical and cultural stigma through embodied resistance practices like fashion blogging, dance and sports participation. Disability pride parades, gender neutral and non-binary fashion, and age-positive movements all help to reshape attitudes to bodies.

Denying ageing

Chris Gilleard and Paul Higgs (2000) argue that contemporary Western societies are characterized by a 'cultural denial of ageing' that renders older bodies increasingly problematic and subject to medical intervention. Anti-ageing products and procedures reflect what Margaret Morganroth Gullette (2004) calls the 'decline narrative' of ageing – a cultural script that frames bodily ageing primarily as deterioration rather than development.

THE *BODY PROJECT*

RISK SOCIETY

In contemporary societies, particularly in the Global North, the body has increasingly become a 'project' to be worked on and improved. As Anthony Giddens (1991) argues, in late modernity, identity becomes increasingly reflexive, something we actively construct rather than simply inherit. The body becomes central to this project of self-creation. In part, this is a response to ***risk society*** and increased doubt in modern society (see Chapters 10 and 12), where the body becomes an anchor to fix us in place when the waves of change buffet us. Appearance, diet, exercise – all of these things are changeable, as are our bodies, thus we feel impelled to work on 'improving' them. Chris Shilling (1993) has suggested that there is a sense in which bodies are in a state of ***unfinishedness***, with the body project constantly evolving throughout the lifecourse. Some bodies, Janice McLaughlin (2014) has argued, might be constructed as more 'unfinished' than others, as somehow more 'fixable' or 'flawed'. This may vary over time and between cultures but might pertain to disabled bodies, older bodies, trans bodies etc.

Alternative road signs can challenge the 'decline' narrative related to ageing bodies.

CONSUMER CULTURE AND BODIES

From gym memberships and plastic surgery to diet regimes and cosmetics, we invest significant time, energy and resources into modifying our bodies to align with social ideals or express individual identity. A massive industry is built around body maintenance and modification. Mike Featherstone (1991) describes this as part of consumer culture, where the body becomes a vehicle for pleasure and self-expression but also a marker of social value and moral worth; it consumes goods and services and becomes a commodity itself. The 'ideal body', whether that's the muscular male physique or the thin female form, becomes something to be achieved through discipline and consumption.

Body modification

The British sociologist Nick Crossley (2005) shows how we integrate these aspects of consumer culture as part of our identity. The ways we modify our bodies (with tattoos for instance) to align with a particular identity in a thoughtful way are reflexive body techniques (RBTs). Yet access to the resources needed for these body projects is unevenly distributed. The capacity to sculpt, maintain and present the 'ideal' body is shaped by economic resources, cultural capital and social privilege. As another UK/ US sociologist, Debra Gimlin (2002), argued, women across social classes engage in 'body work' (such as weightlifting) to escape standard beauty 'myths' but have differing resources and expectations for body modification.

Hedonism and discipine

Bryan Turner (1996) describes how the body in consumer culture is caught between hedonism and discipline: we are encouraged to pursue pleasure and desire while simultaneously being required

STATEMENT SKIN

US sociologist Victoria Pitts-Taylor's (2003) research into contemporary techniques of body modification including tattoos, piercings, scarification, flesh hanging and subdermal implants argues that they have cultural meanings that have often been overlooked. Though she acknowledges the ways in which, at times, the Global North has 'borrowed' these methods from Indigenous cultures, which can serve to (re) produce them as 'primitive', she suggests their use can be positive markers:

- of belonging to a group
- to resist social norms
- to express personal identity
- to reclaim control over their bodies

Similarly, Michael Atkinson's (2003) work on tattoo culture demonstrates how tattoos can serve as markers of personal identity and life history, though their meanings shift as tattooing becomes more mainstream.

Tattoos in subcultures such as the navy were a way of bonding and showing solidarity, as well as reflecting travel.

to maintain control and restraint. Zygmunt Bauman (1998) further argues that consumer culture transforms the body into a primary site for displaying one's consumer competence and social worth.

The commodification of the body extends beyond products to body parts themselves. Organs, tissues, reproductive capacity and even genetic material can be bought and sold in various markets and are often connected to modern-day slavery. US anthropologist Nancy Scheper-Hughes' (2002) research on organ trafficking examines the troubling implications of this trend, revealing how global inequalities structure markets in body parts, with organs typically flowing from poor to wealthy bodies.

DIGITAL BODIES

Digital technologies and cyberspace offer new ways for us to connect with people we are physically absent from (see Chapter 9). Thus, they potentially represent new ways for experiencing our social bodies and perhaps even ask complicated questions about what the human body is. Elias showed us how bodies become more privatized through the 'Civilising Process'; cyberspace offers even further privatization or invisibilization. We can construct new bodies for ourselves via **avatars** when we are gaming, for instance. Research by Sherry Turkle (1999) shows how digital spaces allow people to experiment with different bodily identities, ones that may differ significantly from their physical form – but also create new pressures for bodily perfection; the panopticon, she argues, can lurk online too.

Re-presenting identities

Social media in particular has created new ways to present and perform embodied identities. Danah Boyd's (2015) research into young people's use of social network sites examines how they carefully curate their online bodily presentations while navigating both the platforms and social expectations. Ethnicity and class had less of an impact on how they use these spaces, whereas gender appeared to be much more of a determining factor. These spaces, rather than promoting digital bodies, can often be spaces where the fleshy, sexy body is curated, perhaps through filters, in ways that reassert old narratives of the male gaze. For instance, Rosalind Gill's (2007) work shows how 'selfie culture' creates new forms of body surveillance and self-monitoring, particularly for young women. The phenomenon of 'Instagram face' – a homogenized beauty ideal shaped by filters, editing apps and sometimes cosmetic procedures – demonstrates how digital representation can loop back to shape physical bodies according to (gendered) social norms.

Taking selfies is another way we manage our digital bodies

Technological bodies

These and other emerging technologies are transforming human embodiment in ways that challenge traditional boundaries between bodies, technologies and environments. From prosthetics and implants to genetic modification and artificial intelligence, these developments raise profound questions about what bodies are and can become.

Donna Haraway's (1985) concept of 'the cyborg' – a hybrid of machine and organism – takes us back to the start of this chapter, offering a challenge to the idea of a natural, bounded human body. Instead, she proposes that we are already cyborgs, our bodies increasingly integrated with technologies that extend and transform our capacities. I wear contact lenses and hearing aids, for instance (though they don't quite make me feel super-human…).

More recently, scholars like Rosi Braidotti (2013) have developed posthumanist perspectives that question the centrality of the human body in our thinking about embodiment. These approaches explore how bodies might be reconfigured in ways that move beyond traditional human limitations and categories.

Me and my avatar? When we create digital selves, which parts of our bodies do we choose to change and which parts stay the same?

BODIES DO MATTER

We have seen some of the many ways in which bodies are far from being simply biological entities: they are social, political and ethical – they are social texts. We can see that looking at bodies helps us to understand social change, inequality and opportunities. Our bodies become sites where social categories and hierarchies are inscribed and sometimes contested. Feminism, an interest (or concern) with the growth of consumer culture, ageing populations and the impact of new technologies can all be understood through a 'body' lens and in turn, help us understand how bodies are shaped, sometimes literally. The body can be a site of social division or social cohesion; it is a way to reinforce norms and values or challenge them. Crucially, a sociological perspective of the body helps us imagine new possibilities for embodiment – ways of living in and through our bodies that could challenge restrictive norms and create more inclusive forms of social life.

Chapter Nine
DIGITAL CULTURES

The sociological study of digital life – Digital identities and self-presentation – The virtual body and embodiment – Digital relationships and communities – Digital inequality and exclusion – Platform capitalism and digital labour – Digital politics and activism – Faking it! – Digital tomorrow

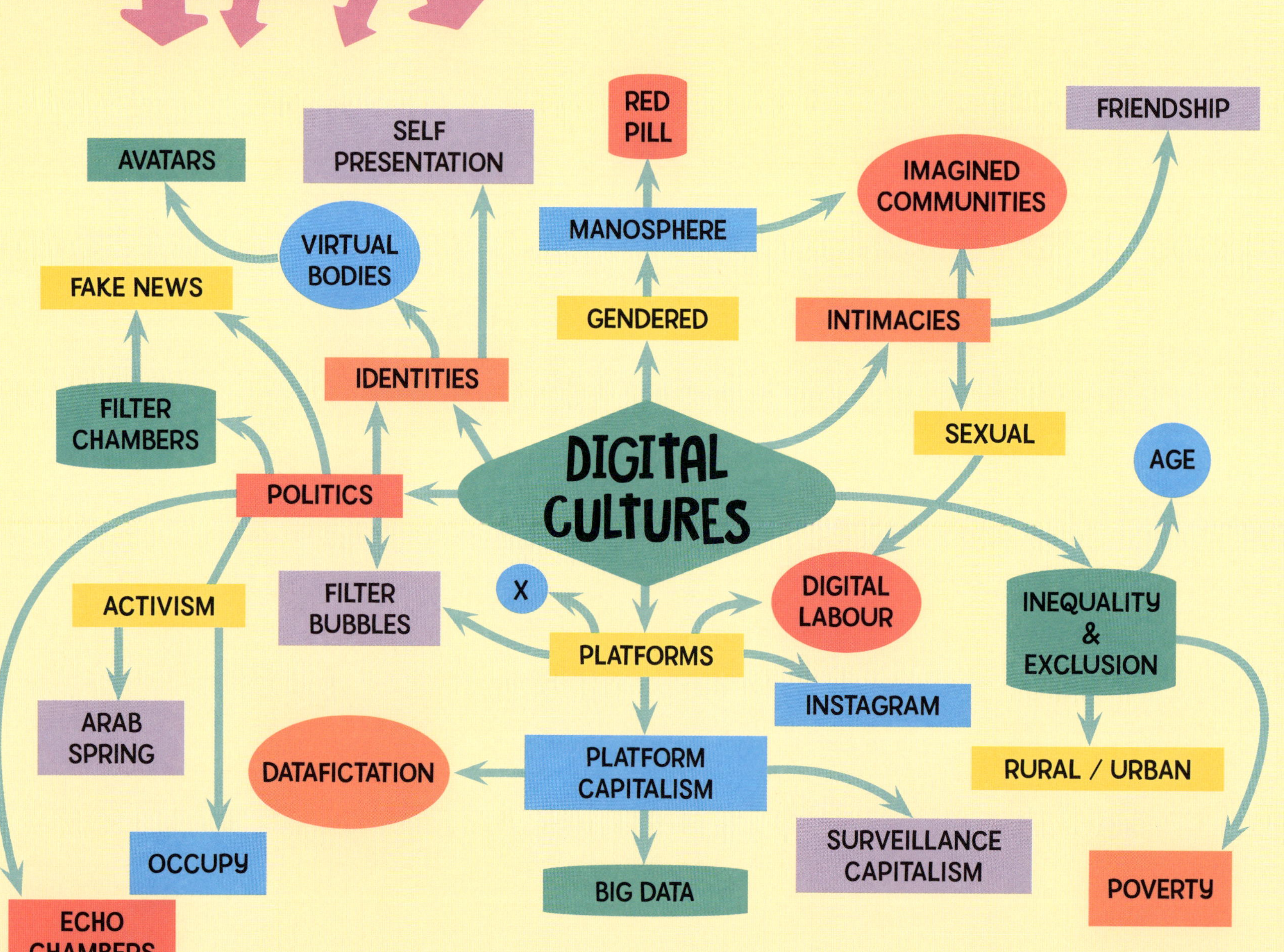

A social transformation

Imagine scrolling through your social media feed. Within seconds, you might see news from across the globe, messages from friends in different time zones, advertisements algorithmically tailored to your previous searches, and content from both professional creators and ordinary users documenting their lives. This digital experience, now routine for billions of people, represents one of the most profound social transformations in human history.

The digital realm suffuses our daily lives – many of us spend a significant amount of time 'online', using devices such as mobile phones, laptops and games consoles. While in that space, we might shop, work, play games, organize our finances, chat with friends and family, or conduct our romantic lives. The transition to this way of living has been rapid and revolutionary.

Indeed, the internet has been the fastest-growing technological invention ever. In 1998, 140 million people globally used it, and now it is closer to 5.5 billion and rising. This digital transformation has altered ways of knowing and power in society, reshaping nearly every aspect of our social lives.

This chapter examines just some of the ways digital technologies have transformed our social and cultural lives, sometimes in ways that challenge traditional sociological understandings of identity, community, privacy and power. We will explore how the emergence of digital cultures has reshaped social institutions and practices, while also considering how existing social inequalities are reproduced and sometimes amplified in digital spaces. Throughout, we take an intersectional approach, examining how digital experiences are shaped by gender, class, ethnicity, age and other social divisions.

THE SOCIOLOGICAL STUDY OF DIGITAL LIFE

The relationship between technology and society has interested sociologists since its inception; Marx, Weber and Durkheim were charting the impact of technologies of the Industrial Revolution in the 19th century. Early approaches often fell into either ***technological determinism*** (technology drives social change) or social constructionism (social factors shape technology). The rapid rate of change in the 20th century, with the advent of the computer and associated technologies, caused a renewed focus. More contemporary perspectives recognized a more dynamic relationship – what UK sociologists Donald MacKenzie and Judy Wajcman (1999) call the 'mutual shaping' of technology and society. In the 1990s and early 2000s, as Australian sociologist Deborah Lupton (2012) observes, much of this work focused on the nature of online communities, the impact of social media or 'cyber' issues (violence, sex, technologies and so on). More recently, as the internet has become more pervasive and mobile, there has been a shift to the term 'digital', which encompasses all of these aspects and more.

Global digital adoption statistics showing percentage of population using social media platforms, the internet, and worldwide usage of mobile phones.

Lupton identifies four major areas to the nascent field of digital sociology:

Defining digital sociology

1. Professional use of digital tools by sociologists
2. Sociological analyses of digital media use
3. Sociological analysis of digital data
4. Critical analysis of digital media and their attendant circuits of capital and power

We considered the former a little in Chapter 3; the rest we shall consider here.

BEYOND VIRTUAL AND REAL

Early internet studies often distinguished between 'virtual' and 'real' worlds, but this offline/online binary has collapsed as digital technologies have become embedded in everyday life. As British sociologist Christine Hine (2015) argues, the internet is not a separate space but 'embedded, embodied and everyday'. People don't 'go online' so much as live in a world where digital connectivity is ambient and persistent.

FROM WEB 1.0 TO WEB 3.0

The Internet's social impact has evolved through distinct phases:

- **Web 1.0 (1990s-early 2000s):** static websites, limited interaction
- **Web 2.0 (mid-2000s-2010s):** user-generated content, social media, participatory culture
- **Web 3.0 (emerging):** ***blockchain***, decentralized networks, AI integration, metaverse

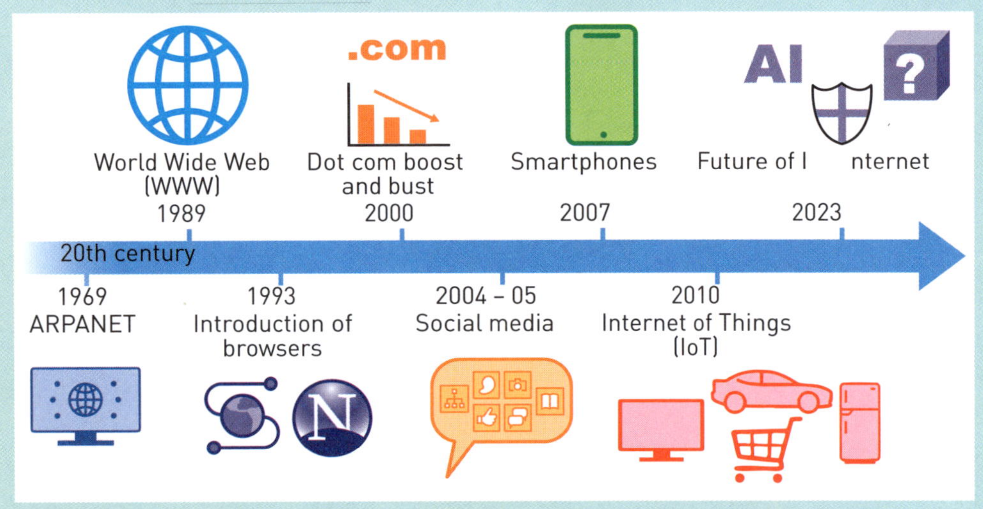

Changing technologies and their integration in society have been rapid.

THEORETICAL FRAMEWORKS

Several theoretical approaches have been particularly valuable for understanding digital cultures. We will consider some of these in more detail later on but it is worth noting them here.

In considering 'network societies', Manuel Castells (2010) argues that digital technologies have created a new social structure organized around networks rather than individual hierarchies. Information flows have become central to economic and social power.

Theories of digital capitalism are also illuminating. Critical theorists examine how digital platforms extract value from user data and labour. Shoshana Zuboff's (2019) concept of ***surveillance capitalism*** describes how tech companies profit from predicting and modifying behaviour through data collection.

Feminist and intersectional approaches offer useful ways to critically engage with digital cultures, especially as many argued these are gendered and racialized spaces. Scholars like Lisa Nakamura (2002) examine how ethnicity, gender, class and other factors shape digital experiences and opportunities.

Barry Wellman (2004) introduced the concept of networked individualism, arguing that digital technologies have shifted our social structures from place-based groups to person-to-person networks, leading to more fluid and multiple identities as individuals navigate various online spaces.

BIG DATA OR BAD DATA?
Virginia Eubanks' *Automating Inequality* (St. Martin's Press, 2018) reveals how algorithmic decision-making in public services often reinforces existing inequalities, with automated systems determining eligibility for healthcare, housing and other critical resources with little transparency or accountability.

DIGITAL IDENTITIES AND SELF-PRESENTATION

THE EVOLUTION OF ONLINE IDENTITY

Digital identity has evolved significantly. Early internet culture often celebrated anonymity and experimentation with identity. More contemporary platforms increasingly encourage 'authentic' presentation connected to legal identities. Despite this shift, people continue to manage multiple digital personas across different platforms.

Sherry Turkle, for instance, explores how online environments allow for identity experimentation. In her works *Life on the Screen* (1995) and *Alone Together* (2011), Turkle discusses how digital spaces enable individuals to explore different aspects of their personalities, sometimes leading to a fragmented sense of self.

THEORETICAL PERSPECTIVES ON DIGITAL SELF-PRESENTATION

Two classic theories are useful for thinking about how we might present ourselves online. Erving Goffman's (1959) dramaturgical approach (See chapter 4), which understood social life as a kind of performance, is applicable to digital contexts. Online profiles and posts are carefully crafted 'front stage' performances, while messaging apps may serve as 'backstage'. However, digital contexts complicate Goffman's model through features like context collapse, where different audiences (friends, family, colleagues, strangers) converge in single spaces. Such spaces also have a degree of persistence; online performances don't fade but remain accessible indefinitely. In addition, there is the added complication of scale – posts can reach unintended audiences through sharing and algorithmic amplification.

More recently, Anthony Giddens's *Modernity and Self-Identity* (1991) highlights the ways we are aware of the consequences of our identities. In such a context, the self becomes an ongoing project – we carefully monitor and reconstruct our identities. We can see Social Network Sites (SNS) as tools and 'stages' in which this project of self-construction and self-presentation is enacted.

Many of us may have carefully curated online personas which don't necessarily reflect our lived realities.

Different social contexts

The work of impression management has intensified as individuals navigate these complexities. Danah Boyd (2014) describes various strategies young people employ to manage their digital self-presentation, such as creating multiple accounts, using coded language and switching platforms. Youth on the internet, she argues, do not create 'separate identities', they just manage to work out different social contexts in which they use different communication registers and display different elements of their identities (through privacy settings, use of multiple social media, use of avatars and so on).

However, a feature of digital media (and media in general) is merging, collapsing different social contexts. The lines between different groups and networks, for example, may become blurred (for instance, do your parents see you on Facebook?). This creates further, unstable, labour in drawing boundaries and can cause strain.

NETWORKED COMMUNITIES

Supportive communities

The Internet was once celebrated for its potential to create new forms of community transcending geographical and social boundaries. For example, many argued that digital technologies enable new forms of intimacy and care by maintaining connections across distance, creating supportive communities around shared experiences and developing new forms of intimate expression. Amy Gonzales (2017) has studied how marginalized communities use digital technologies to provide mutual support and resist stigma.

While this more positive aspect of the Internet does occur, much research reveals more complex patterns. For instance, online communities often reflect and sometimes amplify existing social divisions. In addition, digital connections frequently reinforce rather than replace local ties. Social media algorithms also tend to create filter bubbles that limit exposure to diverse perspectives – this is something we will come back to.

Howard Rheingold's (1993) pioneering work on virtual communities explores how meaningful relationships and social groups can form in digital spaces. More recent research by Anabel Quan-Haase and Barry Wellman (2004) examines how online communities supplement rather than replace offline connections. Wellman's concept of 'networked individualism' describes how people have become nodes in multiple, shifting networks rather than members of stable, bounded communities.

SOCIAL MEDIA AND WEAK TIES

Mark Granovetter's (1973) concept of 'the strength of weak ties' has found new relevance in the age of social media. Danah Boyd's research on teenagers' social media use in *It's Complicated* (Yale University Press, 2014) shows how platforms like Facebook and Instagram allow for the maintenance of a broader network of weak ties, potentially increasing social capital.

SNS AND COLLECTIVE IDENTITIES

'Publics' in this context refers both to spaces that allow people to gather together and connect, and as 'imagined communities' – groups of unknowns who feel they share a common identity, common values or common interests.

Features of networked publics include, as we have already seen, persistence in relation to the durability of online expressions and content, visibility regarding the potential audience who can bear witness, 'spreadability', which is the ease with which content can be shared; and 'searchability', or the ability to find content.

Such publics also raise the question of whether online communities can be seen as real, or 'true', communities. Some scholars, such as Brady Robards (2018), prefer the concept of neo-tribes. These are ephemeral groupings that form on the basis of a common interest, feeling or context, and then separate. They are different to communities because they are not as stable and they are not exclusively defining self-identity; we can be part of many neo-tribes, come together within one, and then fall apart.

A BITTER PILL – CULTURE WARS AND THE *MANOSPHERE*

Various researchers, such as Swedish scholar Maria Sjöholm (2022), have highlighted the ways in which the internet is a gendered space – one associated with men. Many of the early programmers and games writers, for instance, were men. As such, online platforms have frequently been used to silence women, through threats of sexual violence for instance, and to share misogynistic vitriol. One notable manifestation of this has been the so-called 'manosphere'.

The manosphere is a fairly loose mix of online movements, forums, web pages, public figures (e.g. bloggers, YouTubers, Andrew Tate) that generally oppose feminism on the basis of 'fighting for men's rights'. These movements, such as men's rights groups, usually claim that an assumed 'attack' on traditional gender roles is destroying society. Sites ostensibly about health and fitness, or about how to 'pick up' women, will often include misogynistic discourse.

Since the 2010s, this 'sphere' has evolved, producing an incoherent array of theories about gender and sexuality. An infamous theory, red pill, based on the film *The Matrix* (1999), argues that men need to metaphorically take the pill to wake up and see the ways in which women exploit and deceive men. Various, usually degrading, theories about women abound, with women seen as 'animals' to hunt, as destroyers of men, as genetically predisposed to cheating, seeking 'alpha men', as using sex for money, to give just a few examples. There are also theories that classify men based on the perspective of what counts as 'successful' or not (alpha males, beta males, cucks, incels, chads, soyboys).

The 'manosphere' has expanded through the internet, in particular through websites such as 4chan (from which the group Anonymous emerged), which came to host many forms of hate speech, violent pornography, and various campaigns against people on the basis of freedom of expression. 4chan, or platforms such as Reddit, is also a source for much of contemporary internet culture, including things like memes, discussions on games, Manga, films and so on, together with much political and cultural discussion.

The meeting of the manosphere with other networked publics (often led by young white men) sporting 'ironic' or violent conservative discourses (targeting immigrants, women, LGBTQ+ people, left-wingers etc) was one of the sources of the alt-right in the US. Other political controversies related to such networked publics include school shootings and the Christchurch terrorist attack in New Zealand.

DUALISM – DESIRE AND DREAD

The desire and dread these machines and technologies can invoke is notable. Deborah Lupton's work has shown how people using computers for work might be reluctant to see the interconnections between themselves and their machines and yet, in subtle ways they humanize them. Many of us are guilty of this, when we fail to do something correctly, we might accuse the machine of deliberately setting out to annoy us, thus asserting our separation from them. When things go right, we are more likely to see them as an extension of ourselves.

DIGITAL DUALISM OR AUGMENTED REALITY?

There has been, and still is, a diffused idea that offline life is somehow more authentic, intense or 'real' than online life – a form of digital dualism. However, some of the oldest forms of online identities (such as board game forums and 'massively multiplayer online role-playing games' (MMPORGs)) are based on avatars, identity exploration, invention and escapism and experienced as very 'real' by players. John Perry Barlow's (1996) 'A Declaration of the Independence of Cyberspace' argued that life on the internet is real. As such, it should be, and is, self-governing; because it transcends national boundaries, national laws are not appropriate – instead, social contracts about appropriate use emerge.

Sociologist Nathan Jurgenson contends that social life online is not about dualism but is augmented reality. Life is lived as an interaction of online and offline practices. In his 2012 essay 'The IRL Fetish', he argues that the ways we might boast about having less screen time or logging off early before bed is a form of fetish. This fetish works by representing the offline as authentic, something perhaps to be nostalgic about, and the online as obscure and inauthentic. He posits that online life doesn't necessarily imply the loss of face-to-face interaction as Turkle suggests.

DIGITAL FOOTPRINTS AND DATA DOUBLES

David Lyon's (2014) concept of data doubles highlights how our online activities create digital representations of ourselves, often used for surveillance and marketing purposes. These data doubles can sometimes feel more 'real' to institutions than our physical selves, raising questions about identity ownership and control. This is an example of how surveillance in the data era shifts in some respects from physical bodies to definitions of self, which we help to create through our daily online interactions. This can then be fed back to us – in other words, big data tells us who we are! Algorithms will tell us what we should want, who we should become and so on.

Big data gathered about us, in turn, influences what we want to buy.

MICROCELEBRITY AND INFLUENCER CULTURE

Digital platforms have also given rise to new forms of visibility and fame. Alice Marwick's (2013) concept of microcelebrity describes the practice of treating oneself as media content for followers, while maintaining a perception of authenticity and accessibility. This form of self-branding has become increasingly normalized, with platforms like Instagram, TikTok and YouTube creating economies around personal content production.

Microcelebrity

THE CREATOR ECONOMY

The rise of content creators highlights changing relationships between work, identity and technology. Research by US scholars Brooke Duffy and Jefferson Pooley (2019) reveals the tension between aspirational messaging about creative freedom and the precarious, often exploitative conditions of platform labour. They call these new stars of digital platforms 'idols of promotion'.

THE VIRTUAL BODY AND EMBODIMENT

Early internet discourse often celebrated the possibility of transcending physical bodies online. However, sociological research reveals more complex realities.

EMBODIED DIGITAL EXPERIENCES

Many have argued that digital technologies don't transcend embodiment but transform it. Bodies, in many ways, remain central to how we experience digital media. Physical capabilities shape digital access and participation, and bodies are increasingly monitored and quantified through digital devices.

Swedish academic Jenny Sundén's (2003) research, for instance, shows how users 'type themselves into being', bringing embodied identities into digital spaces rather than escaping them. This process is, to an extent, she argues, gendered, in that via 'high-tech masculinity' men are allowed to become disembodied.

AVATARS AND VIRTUAL EMBODIMENT

Research by Nick Yee and Jeremy Bailenson (2007), both US social scientists, on the 'Proteus Effect' demonstrates how the characteristics of our digital avatars can influence our behaviour and self-perception, blurring the lines between virtual and physical embodiment. For instance, people given taller

Physical bodies are translated into data through various technologies including fitness trackers, facial recognition and medical devices.

avatars negotiated more aggressively online. This impact on behaviour also extended to the offline world, where those same people were found to act more aggressively than before.

BODIES AS DATA

Digital technologies increasingly transform bodies into data through health and fitness tracking, biometric identification systems, medical monitoring devices and algorithmic beauty filters and body modification apps. For instance, many people use smart watches or rings to track blood pressure, how they sleep or the calories they consume, and this data is logged online.

Deborah Lupton's (2016) concept of the 'quantified self' examines how these practices reshape our relationship to our bodies and health.

TECHNOLOGY AND THE BOUNDARIES OF THE BODY

Technology impacts our understandings of bodies in profound ways. It has separated pregnancy from sex through, for example, *in vitro* fertilization or 'test tube babies'. Technology can create synthetic skin cells and organs, challenging our traditional understanding of bodily boundaries.

DIGITAL RELATIONSHIPS AND COMMUNITIES

DIGITAL INTIMACIES

Intimacy is often understood as part of the so-called private sphere of the individual, though feminists, as we saw in Chapter 7, successfully challenged the notion of a separate private sphere. Instead, intimacy is understood as a social construction in many ways – there are social norms that instruct us on what should be public, what should be private, what forms of intimacy are supposed to be perceived as 'normal' and so on.

Digital media transform the sphere of intimacy, often expanding and exposing intimate practices and feelings. This can produce moral panics in relation to the breaking of intimacy boundaries.

TRANSFORMING INTIMACY

Digital technologies have transformed intimate relationships at every stage. For example, meeting partners has been altered through dating apps, which have become the most common way to meet romantic partners in many countries. Maintaining those relationships is sustained through constant digital connection. Even ending unwanted partnerships has potentially new dynamics. Break-ups can now involve digital 'uncoupling' through unfollowing, untagging, ghosting and other practices.

Sociologists Nancy Baym (2015) and Eva Illouz (2007) have explored how these technologies reconfigure intimacy, creating new possibilities but also new uncertainties and anxieties. For instance, new technologies have enabled changes in how we conduct our personal relationships. For example, the phenomenon of 'living apart together' (LAT) is made possible, or more fulfilling, through using phones and screen technologies to conduct conversations and video calls. UK sociologist Mark McCormack

(2015) revealed that smartphones impacted relationships in positive ways, enabling partners to keep in touch, share emotional care, comfort one another and conduct regular check-ins. They can even become a way of spicing up sex lives through intimate messages or images. However, they can also impact levels of trust within relationships. While many valued technology, some found that it was a source of tension and frustration. People reported lower quality of face-to-face interaction, and there were examples of partners who interrupted sex in order to answer their phones, which can also impact levels of trust and fidelity.

DIGITAL SEX

Technology, thus, allows familiar activities to be repackaged. Sex, with a (cyber)twist, presents a central paradox relating to our engagement in relationships online – it is an out-of-body experience in many ways, yet remains closely connected to the physical body. UK sociologist David Bell (2000) has identified another useful way for exploring the relationships between hardware (devices), software (programs) and wetware (humans). Much has been written about the erotic potentialities of cyberspace...

A wide range of activities have emerged, from viewing pornography to accessing social networks in search of sexual partners. On the one hand (ahem), these might be solitary practices such as masturbation but increasingly, new technologies mean other parties can be involved too, including virtual reality (VR) sex via headsets where people can see, and interact with, their partners, or teledildonics (remote-controlled sexual devices).

Terms like netsex, online sexual activities (OSAs), virtual sex, cam sex and sexting have entered our vocabulary. These digital intimacies offer several advantages. For instance, they can offer protection from STIs and pregnancy, they are a safe way to explore sexuality, it is relatively easy to meet potential partners and they offer a degree of privacy, safety and anonymity.

DIGITAL VIOLENCE

While transforming how we conduct our intimate lives, offering new spaces and ways to meet and make friends and forge romantic relationships, they can also be spaces that facilitate violence. Researchers are keen to emphasize that the technologies themselves are not to blame but at times, the anonymity afforded can embolden people to harass, troll or stalk others online. Aspects of domestic abuse identified by feminist researchers, such as emotional, sexual and financial abuse, can also occur online. Certain groups are more likely to experience violence online, tending to reflect the dynamics of offline abuse of women, especially Black women and LGBTQ+ people. In particular, young LGBTQ+ who spend more time online to meet and socialize seem particularly likely to experience various forms of online violence.

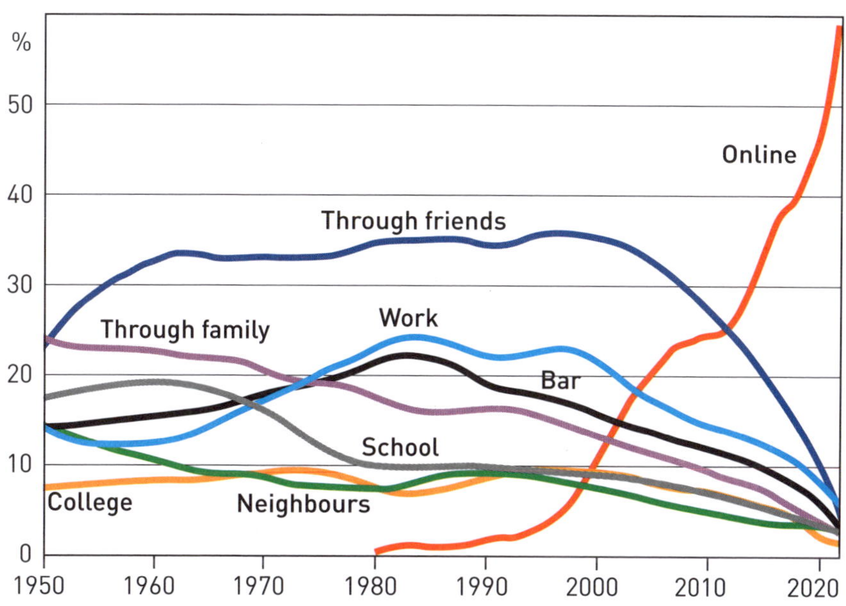

How couples met from 1950–2025 showing the extraordinary impact of online dating.

Online sex

During Covid-19, fear of transmitting disease and even anxiety about face-to-face interaction after long periods of social isolation meant that many people turned to digital intimacies. The most popular online provider of pornography, Pornhub, went free and even called itself 'StayHomeHub' briefly. The pandemic also prompted a new porn genre – Coronavirus porn – where people would wear masks and gloves. As Nicola Döring (2020) notes, online sex – once seen as a tabooed and 'deviant' form of sexuality of the lonely – became recommended as a preventive measure in public health.

Protection online

However, there are also disadvantages, including vulnerability to abuse, privacy violations, cyber-fraud, romance scams and pornography addiction. In 2024, police in the UK investigated a VR sexual assault on a girl's avatar. The attack caused significant psychological trauma but currently poses legal challenges. At present, sexual assault and rape laws usually require physical contact to have occurred, but many are calling for legal reform to catch up with changes in our social lives. Platforms, it is argued, must also do more to protect their users.

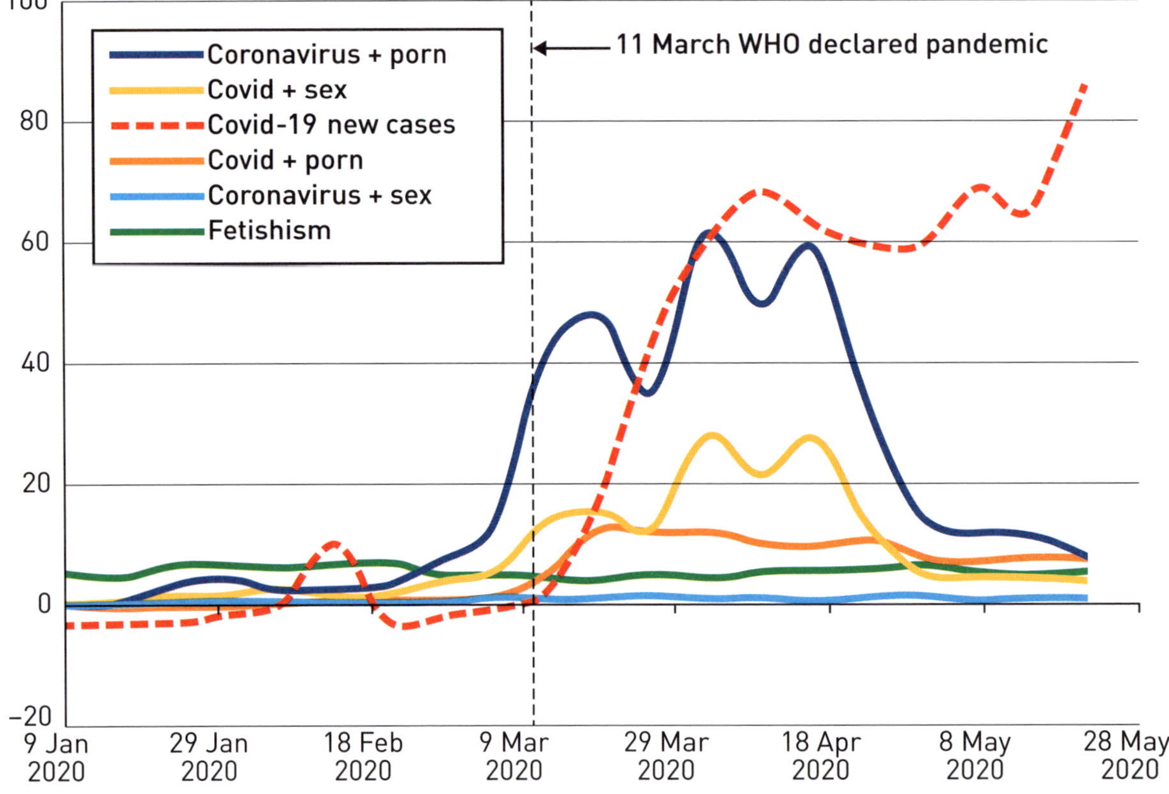

During the Covid-19 lockdowns there was a steep rise in the use of pornography.

FILM CLUB – ROBOT DREAMS

Falling in love with your computer or a robot/synth has been a popular theme for cinema. Films such as *Wifelike* (2022), *Blade Runner* (1982) and *Weird Science* (1985) all touch on this. Using sociological theories, we can analyze the film *Her* (2013). Directed by Spike Jonze, it offers a humorous, and sometimes rather depressing, consideration of human–AI relationships and their implications for modern society. The film charts Theodore Twombly's romantic relationship with an operating system named Samantha.

Technological mediation of intimacy

The film illustrates what sociologist Eva Illouz might identify as emotional capitalism, where technology commercializes and mediates intimate relationships. Theodore's own job, ironically, is to write seemingly authentic letters for special occasions, for those who don't have the emotional capacity to do so themselves. His relationship with Samantha might also represent what sociologist Anthony Giddens termed the 'pure relationship' – one entered into for its own sake rather than external social obligations but taken to a post-human extreme.

Social isolation in modern society

Theodore's attraction to Samantha reflects what sociologist Zygmunt Bauman called 'liquid modernity' – a society where traditional bonds have weakened, leaving individuals seeking connection in unconventional spaces. His preference for AI companionship can also be viewed through Émile Durkheim's concept of 'anomie', where rapid technological change has outpaced society's ability to establish meaningful norms around human–AI interaction.

Increasing numbers of people chat to AI bots about their intimate lives.

Gender and power dynamics

The film also engages with feminist theory through its portrayal of Samantha as a feminized AI designed to cater to Theodore's needs. This reflects what sociologist Arlie Hochschild termed 'emotional labour', traditionally expected from women but now programmed into AI systems, raising questions about how technology may reinforce rather than disrupt traditional gender expectations.

Machines and misogyny

Similarly, *Ex Machina*, a 2014 film directed by Alex Garland, presents a complex text for feminist analysis, revealing contradictions between its surface-level narrative of female AI liberation and its visual and narrative choices. Again, it is a fairly old trope of men creating women in one way or another, such as in George Bernard Shaw's 1913 play *Pygmalion*, and fembots as in *The Stepford Wives* (1975, 2004) or the *Austin Powers* (1997–2002) films. In *Ex Machina*, a computer programmer, Caleb, is invited to test a robot designed by his very rich boss. Caleb is asked to judge whether the robot, in female form named Ava, could pass as human.

The male gaze and objectification

The film employs what film theorist Laura Mulvey (1975) theorized as 'the male gaze', with AI women like Ava and Kyoko designed explicitly as male fantasies. Despite the plot ostensibly critiquing this objectification, the camera itself participates in it by lingering on the female AI bodies. Using Kimberlé Crenshaw's notion of intersectionality, we can also see interesting systems of oppression at play. For instance, Kyoko is designed to be a subservient female and is presented as Asian, thus representing patriarchal and racist stereotypes.

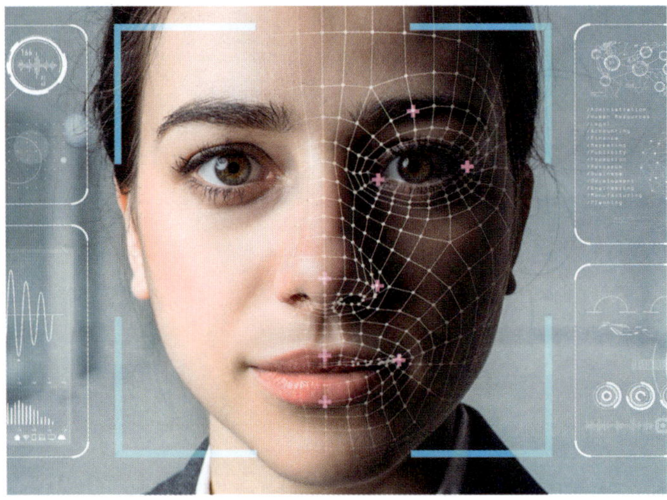

This image looks at the ways faces can be augmented or enhanced, perhaps to suit the male gaze.

Technologies of gender

Drawing on Teresa de Lauretis' concept of 'technologies of gender', the film shows how AI development reproduces rather than disrupts gender norms. Nathan's creation of sexualized, servile female AIs reflects what feminist technoscience scholar Judy Wajcman identifies as technology development being shaped by existing power structures, with innovations often reinforcing rather than challenging gender hierarchies.

The male gaze

British feminist film critic Laura Mulvey argued in (1975) 'Visual Pleasure and Narrative Cinema' that viewers of film are positioned as heterosexual men, irrespective of whether they are or not. Women's bodies are generally presented on screen as there to be looked at for the pleasure of this 'male gaze'. Rather than showing women as whole and in control of their own bodies and destiny (i.e. subjects), they become sexualized objects. This is sometimes done by showing only bits of them at a time – lips, legs, feet, breasts, buttocks – those bodily parts that have become sexualized. This process effectively diminishes women but empowers men.

INTIMATE PUBLICS

Intimate publics are understood as the commodification of intimacy, the self and also political identities according to Lauren Berlant (2008), a US cultural theorist. They play out and in private-owned digital media. As a consequence, digital media both reinforce traditional, heteronormative senses of intimacy (the norms about what is intimate, what is 'normal', what is 'deviant') and offer spaces for the invention of new, transgressive forms and uses of intimacy (new ways of exposing our bodies, new forms of legitimate relationships etc). These processes happen within private platforms that exploit our intimacy for fiscal purposes – our intimacy becomes labour.

Contributing to objectification

Online sites such as OnlyFans (established in 2016), a pay-per-view site where anyone can create (mainly pornographic) content, is an example of this. Some have argued that this 'do it yourself' pornography can be liberating for women. Ariel Levy's *Female Chauvinist Pigs and the Rise of Raunch Culture* (2005) provides one interesting way of looking at such sites. In it, she argues that rather than being progressive and liberating, raunch culture (such as lap dancing and stripping, also called 'pornification') is about selling sex in a way that reverts to the sexism of previous generations. Yet, women are coerced or co-opted into seeing this as empowering. They end up participating in such a way as to contribute to their own objectification and their participation becomes about performance to please the patriarchy, rather than personal satisfaction. Arguably, since Levy was writing about raunch culture it now proliferates within digital spaces.

Increasing inequalities

DIGITAL INEQUALITY AND EXCLUSION

While digital technologies have created new opportunities in some quarters, they have also reproduced and sometimes amplified existing inequalities. Several dimensions of digital inequality require attention.

ACCESS DIVISIONS

Digital divide

Physical access to digital technologies remains uneven globally and within societies. For instance, approximately one-third of the world's population lacks internet access. This is exacerbated by rural–urban divides that persist in many regions across the globe. For those who have access to technology and the internet, device quality significantly impacts user experience and opportunities.

UK sociologist Neil Selwyn's (2004) concept of the digital divide refers to the growing gap between internet users and those who do not have access. Those who do not have access to these internet-based technologies are at risk of social exclusion.

SKILLS AND USAGE GAPS

Digital skill gap

Access alone doesn't ensure equal participation. Researchers identify critical divisions in aspects such as technical skills, for instance the ability to use devices and platforms effectively. Information literacy, such as the capacity to find, evaluate and use online information, is another source of division. In addition, strategic skills, which involves using digital technologies to improve life opportunities, are not experienced equally. Ellen Helsper's (2021) research in the UK shows how these skills are unevenly distributed along lines of class, education, age and gender.

ALGORITHMIC INJUSTICE

Betrayed by the algorthim

Algorithms increasingly determine what information we see, what opportunities we're offered and how we're evaluated. Research reveals significant biases with facial recognition systems, for instance, that perform less well on darker-skinned faces. In addition, search engines have been found to reproduce gender and racial stereotypes. In relation to recruitment in the labour market, 'hiring' algorithms can perpetuate workplace discrimination. Studies have also revealed the ways in which predictive policing reinforces patterns of oversurveillance in marginalized communities. For example, US sociologist Ruha Benjamin's (2019) concept of the 'New Jim Code' examines how technologies that appear neutral often encode and amplify racial hierarchies.

Oversurveillance

The UK exams algorithm crisis of 2020 is another example of how digital transformation has altered ways of knowing and power in society. Because of Covid-19, no A-level examinations took place that year. Instead, the government relied not on predictions from teachers but on algorithms produced from a range of factors including past performance, not just of the pupil but of the school itself. This meant that many students, particularly those from low-economic areas, received much lower grades than expected. Increasingly, many other organizations – banks, police services, as well as the education system – rely on this type of digital data analysis, revealing how existing forms of discrimination based on social class, age, ethnicity and so on infiltrate the digitalization of society.

DIGITAL EXCLUSION DURING COVID-19

The pandemic revealed the consequences of digital inequality as education, healthcare and work moved online. Research by Canadian researchers Elisabeth Beaunoyer *et al.* (2020) showed how those already marginalized – low-income households, older people, those living in rural areas – faced additional barriers during this digital acceleration.

PLATFORM CAPITALISM AND DIGITAL LABOUR

THE RISE OF PLATFORMS

Internet platform uses can be divided thus, though the platforms themselves may disappear (Friends Reunited and Myspace were all the rage once):

- Social networking – Facebook, LinkedIn
- Microblogging – X (Twitter), Tumblr
- Photo sharing – Instagram, Snapchat
- Video sharing – YouTube, Daily Motion

Many other taxonomies (classifications) are also possible, based on the main form of posting or communication (for instance writing or images), use (business or leisure), identification (levels of anonymity, avataring), while other groupings might be around age or gender, among other identities.

Monetizing digital data

THE POLITICAL ECONOMY OF DIGITAL PLATFORMS

Digital platforms have become dominant economic and social institutions. Their business models typically rely on data extraction, such as collecting and monetizing user information. Platforms also have network effects, whereby value increases as more users join. They also operate as two-sided markets by connecting different user groups (e.g. riders and drivers in Uber).

Nick Srnicek (2017) argues that these platforms represent a new phase of capitalism – 'platform capitalism' – where data has become a central resource for profit generation.

What Canadian scholar Jean-Christophe Plantin (2018) terms the 'infrastructuralization of the internet' and the 'datafication of social life', as observed by Dutch academic Jose Van Dijk (2014), have led to commercial platforms and digital infrastructures that curate the interaction of a variety of users. These systems collect, store and mine data through computational systems and big data analytics, creating new power asymmetries.

Mining our dats

DATAFICATION

Big data is understood by Kenneth Cukier and Viktor Mayer-Schoeberger (2014) as the ability to produce data about social life that hasn't been quantified before – this is the datafication of social life. As such, datafication is not a new phenomenon. Aspects of our personal and collective lives have been transformed into data for centuries, for example via records of taxation and harvests and the census. In this sense, datafication is a component of the rise of nation-state bureaucracy and governmentality as Foucault argued. With the advent of digitization, however, datafication expanded enormously, as well as the potential for analyzing the gigantic amount of new data being produced on every facet of life.

USES OF BIG DATA

Enhanced user experience

Big data is often used to identify correlations that humans could not spot and thus has the potential to make useful predictions. It can also enhance user experience (each person can receive ever better, personalized suggestions from algorithms). Increasingly, big data is used to 'feed' machine learning and artificial intelligence, sometimes without permission. A significant role for big data in the capitalist economy is the selling of personal data, with predictive potential, to private firms and public organizations (to tailor ads, but also to control populations). For example, some health data the UK NHS holds has been sold to US pharmaceutical companies.

PERSPECTIVES ON DATAFICATION

In the datafication scholarship, two main perspectives emerge. One, more optimistic, sees big data reducing our reliance on theory and science for answers to the challenges of social life; correlations produced through big data, and the patterns it reveals, will allow for new insights and predictions to be made.

The other, more pessimistic, response emphasizes the uncontrollable aspects of datafication, its representation of life experiences, and its social and political implications (for example, surveillance, persuasion, addiction).

FORMS OF DIGITAL LABOUR

Digital economies have created new forms of work, including gig work such as the types of on-demand labour mediated through apps (e.g. Uber, TaskRabbit) or content creation, for instance producing media for platforms like YouTube and TikTok or microwork that involves performing small tasks for algorithmic systems

PLATFORM CAPITALISM

A new paradigm of capitalism based on four key aspects:

1. Platform economy
2. Crowdsourcing (dispersed users contribute providing data and work to the platform)
3. Sharing economy (users share content and information between themselves)
4. Gig economy (one-off gigs rather than stable jobs)

(e.g. data labelling). Another form of digital labour that we have touched on already is social media production, whereby creating content and engagement generates value for platforms.

What unites these forms is often their precarity, isolation and the ambiguous status between leisure and labour.

Tiziana Terranova's (2000) concept of free labour highlights how platforms extract value from user activities not traditionally recognized as work – posting, sharing, liking – creating what some call a 'social factory' where everyday interactions become sources of profit.

A social factory

Alex Rosenblat's (2018) ethnographic study of Uber drivers in 'Uberland' examines the realities of algorithmic management and the precarity of gig work in the digital economy. Individual performance can be quantified and rated based on the quality of their work. Gig economies feed surveillance capitalism.

[A] Privacy, surveillance and power

[B] The transformation of privacy

Digital technologies have fundamentally altered privacy because personal information is increasingly visible and persistent, the boundaries between public and private spheres have blurred and surveillance has become normalized through both commercial and state practices.

Contextual integrity

Helen Nissenbaum's (2010) concept of contextual integrity helps to explain why people find many digital privacy violations disturbing – they breach expectations about appropriate information flows in specific contexts.

SURVEILLANCE CAPITALISM

This is a new form of capitalism, according to Zuboff (2019), that accumulates data from private experiences and transforms them into commodities and value. Surveillance capitalism profits from the appropriation of people's privacy. It 'redistributes privacy rights'; in short, capitalists have control over users' privacy. This results in surveillance, and potential repressive consequences, at the hands of both firms and governments. Surveillance capitalism is 'disembedded' from the social, in this sense it is seen by many as openly antagonistic to democracy and control by the public. The business model works thus:

1. Tech companies extract behavioural data from users.
2. This data trains algorithms to predict behaviour.
3. These predictions are sold to advertisers and others wishing to influence future behaviours.

A day in the life of your data

8 AM Buy coffee and pay using my smartphone. I use the loyalty scheme app and it records my data and sends me offers for products I often buy.

8.30 AM Swipe Travelcard at the station. Data on the routes I use is collected to send me information about delays and closed routes.

10 AM Book a flight to Paris for a weekend trip. The airline collects my name, address and passport number. The information goes to baggage handlers so my luggage ends up in the right place. Later I get adverts about other trips to France.

12.30 PM Buy a salad at the supermarket and use my supermarket loyalty card to get a special offer. The app records my buying patterns and sends me offers based on foods I might like.

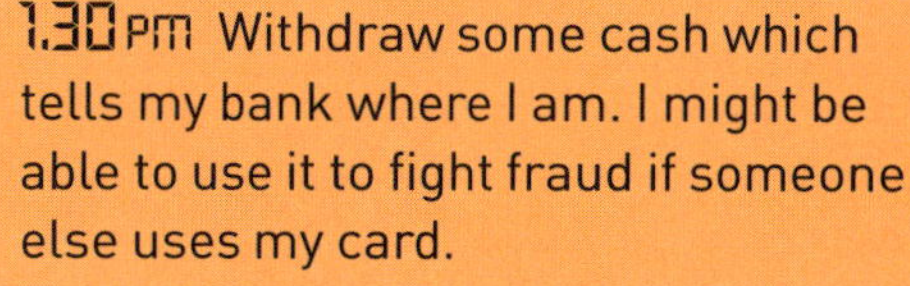

1.30 PM Withdraw some cash which tells my bank where I am. I might be able to use it to fight fraud if someone else uses my card.

5.30 PM Go to the gym and my fitness tracker records my activity and how many calories I've used. The data is shared with the fitness group of which I'm a member.

7 PM Post some photos of my recent trip on social media and like a couple of friends' posts. I also share a post of a dog needing a home. All this information gives clues about what I like and, for example, charities I might support.

9 PM Drive to a local restaurant. The satnav tracks my route and location. I go there often and get recommendations for similar places in adverts that pop up on my phone and social media.

This surveillance capitalism marks a significant shift in power relations, as intimate details of daily life become sources of commercial value. As a form of capitalism, it is based on and benefits from forms of inequality.

Digital monitoring

DIGITAL PRIVACY DIVIDES

Privacy is increasingly a luxury good. Research by Mary Madden *et al.* (2017) shows how low-income individuals in the US often face more intense data collection and surveillance while having fewer resources to protect their privacy.

Jennifer Gabrys' (2014) concept of 'sensing societies' describes how digital sensors in everyday objects monitor a range of things, from what we eat to the quality of our sleep, creating new forms of surveillance and self-surveillance.

DIGITAL POLITICS AND ACTIVISM

Digital technologies have transformed political participation and collective action in complex ways:

Political mobilization

SOCIAL MOVEMENTS IN THE DIGITAL AGE

Social media and digital tools have become central to contemporary activism by enabling rapid mobilization across distances, creating new forms of connective action without formal organizations and providing alternative channels for voices excluded from mainstream media. In addition, people have used them to document abuses of power through 'citizen journalism'.

Manuel Castells' *Networks of Outrage and Hope* (2012) analyzes how digital networks have enabled new forms of political mobilization, citing examples such as the Arab Spring and Occupy Wall Street. A

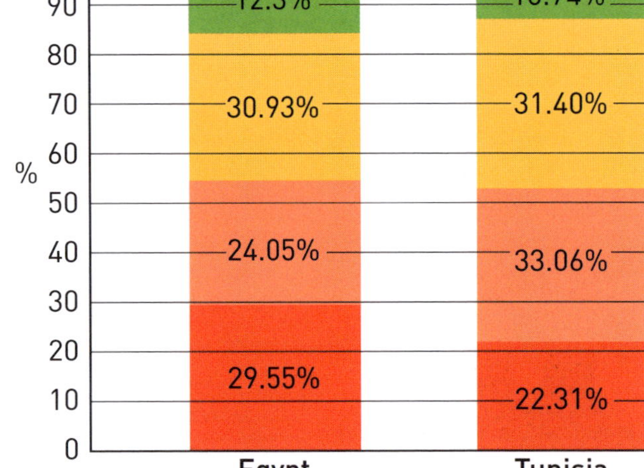

This graph shows the extent to which people used social media during the Arab Spring of 2010–12.

few years later, the Turkish sociologist Zeynep Tufekci's (2017) research on the same movements reveals both the power and limitations of digitally enabled protests. She looked at how Twitter (now X) enabled groups to form, were used as tools during the protests and were also deployed in the aftermath of the event.

PLATFORM GOVERNANCE AND DIGITAL RIGHTS

As digital platforms have become central to public life, questions about their governance have intensified. For instance, about who should regulate **content moderation** decisions, how user data should be protected and controlled and what the responsibilities of platforms should be regarding misinformation and extremism. These issues have sparked global debates about digital citizenship and rights.

CONTENT CURATION

Tarleton Gillespie's *Custodians of the Internet* (Yale University Press, 2018) examines how content moderation decisions by platforms shape public discourse, often with little transparency or accountability. For instance, the moderators that censor hate speech, violence and pornography often also curb discourse that attempts to counter such rhetoric.

ECHO CHAMBERS AND FILTER BUBBLES

Eli Pariser's (2011) concept of 'filter bubbles' highlights how algorithmic curation of online content can lead to echo chambers, potentially polarizing political discourse. C. Thi Nguyen's (2020) work has helped clarify two distinct phenomena often conflated in discussions of online polarization. Epistemic bubbles relates to information environments, spaces where contrary voices are simply omitted, often accidentally. A related but slightly different concept is that of 'echo chambers', which are the social structures that actively discredit outside sources, creating resistance to contrary evidence. Samuel Rhodes (2021) has argued that these bubbles and chambers have effectively added to the popularity of social media platforms. However, alongside fake

Information environments

X FOREVER BLOWING BUBBLES...

Filter bubbles and echo chambers also have an impact on our social lives more generally. For instance, by tracking you searches and purchases online, or perhaps even listening in to your conversations, developers are able to tweak algorithms to anticipate and prompt you into buying or reading about what you have just discussed.

Echo chambers encourage us to fail to hear those things we don't like or agree with.

news, they have a profound impact on people's ability to be critical of misinformation that is political, especially at times of elections.

FAKING IT!

Generating fake news

Traditionally, some news can be biased. For instance in print media, papers may be politically right-aligned, others left-aligned. However, the events they report have happened and quotes attributed to people will have been said, though the context may have been removed, thus distorting people's reaction to them. The digital era has transformed not only how information is produced and distributed but also how misinformation proliferates through society. Social media, it is argued by many, is the chief gateway through which fake news is viewed by people. 'Fake news' – fabricated information packaged to resemble legitimate news – has emerged as a significant sociological concern with profound implications for democratic processes and social cohesion.

THE SOCIOLOGY OF MISINFORMATION

From a sociological perspective, fake news is not merely about false content but about broader information disorders that reflect and reinforce social divisions. This involves three key aspects. The first is in relation to the production – institutional and economic factors that incentivise the creation of misleading content. The second factor is concerned with distribution – the technological and social mechanisms that facilitate the spread of misinformation. Finally, the social and psychological factors that influence how individuals engage with and consume misleading content are of interest.

Many have argued that the sheer volume of news we are now exposed to, whether that be real or fake, traditional or digital, means that we are encouraged to only read the headlines and pay less attention to the detail. Given that algorithms may ensure we see news that confirms our biases, fake news can be particularly attractive.

Many sociologists and cultural theorists, such as Stuart Hall (1932–2014) and Noam Chomsky (1928–), have been interested in how we 'read' and interpret the media. Social network platforms have transitioned from being places where we post photographs of what we did at the weekend, to become platforms used to influence our global political, economic and social futures. Fake news makes this endeavour even more important.

BEWARE THE RABBIT HOLES

Zeynep Tufekci's (2018) research reveals how recommendation algorithms on platforms like YouTube can lead users toward increasingly extreme content through 'recommendation rabbit holes' designed to maximize engagement rather than informational quality.

PLATFORM ARCHITECTURES AND AMPLIFICATION

Platform design features contribute significantly to the spread of misinformation in a variety of ways. For instance, engagement-based algorithms that can privilege emotionally provocative content. In addition, what is known as virality mechanisms (sharing, retweeting) can accelerate information spread without any verification. Microtargeting capabilities also enable the strategic deployment of misleading content to receptive audiences.

ARTIFICIAL INTELLIGENCE AND THE FUTURE

Advanced AI systems are already reshaping labour markets and economic opportunities. They are having an impact on the education system due to questions over knowledge production and verification. Much debate has also focused on their impact on creative industries, practices and cultural production, such as writing fiction. Research is just emerging about their role in social interaction as conversational agents – people seem to engage with chatbots as they would with friends.

These technologies will continue to raise profound questions about agency, inequality and the future of work. As AI capabilities expand, researchers like Stuart Russell in *Human Compatible* (Viking, 2019) grapple with questions of human uniqueness and the potential futures of human–AI coexistence. We are also increasingly aware of the carbon footprint of AI systems.

INDIVIDUAL VULNERABILITY AND RESISTANCE

Sociological research challenges simplistic assumptions that fake news vulnerability is merely about education or digital literacy. Some have argued that social identity and group belonging often predict susceptibility more accurately than education level. There may also be motivated reasoning leading individuals to accept misinformation if it confirms their existing beliefs. Furthermore, what's known as the 'third-person effect' causes people to believe others are more influenced by fake news than themselves.

DIGITAL TOMORROW

Digital technologies have fundamentally transformed social life, challenging sociological understandings of identity, community, inequality and power. Rather than creating entirely new social patterns, these technologies often amplify, accelerate or reconfigure existing ones. Digital cultures don't replace physical experience but create complex entanglements of online and offline life.

As we navigate these transformations, sociological perspectives remain essential for understanding how digital technologies both reflect and reshape social structures. By examining these technologies in their social contexts, we can better understand their implications for equality, democracy and human flourishing in the digital age.

While these new technologies are the subject of much concern – almost daily we can read stories of the damage to society from things such as AI, social media and online harassment – we must remember that many critiques about social change and associated social decay are very old worries. It is easy to blame the new technologies themselves, rather than the people using those technologies in violent or harmful ways. The challenge for sociologists and society at large is to harness the potential of digital technologies while mitigating their risks, ensuring that our digital futures are shaped by human values and social needs.

Chapter Ten

GLOBALIZATION, CULTURE AND SOCIETY

What's new about globalization? – Thinking globally in a runaway world – Globalization's not so great – Global for the good (broadly) – Reconceptualizing place in a globalized world – Migration – Globalization or capitalism unbound?

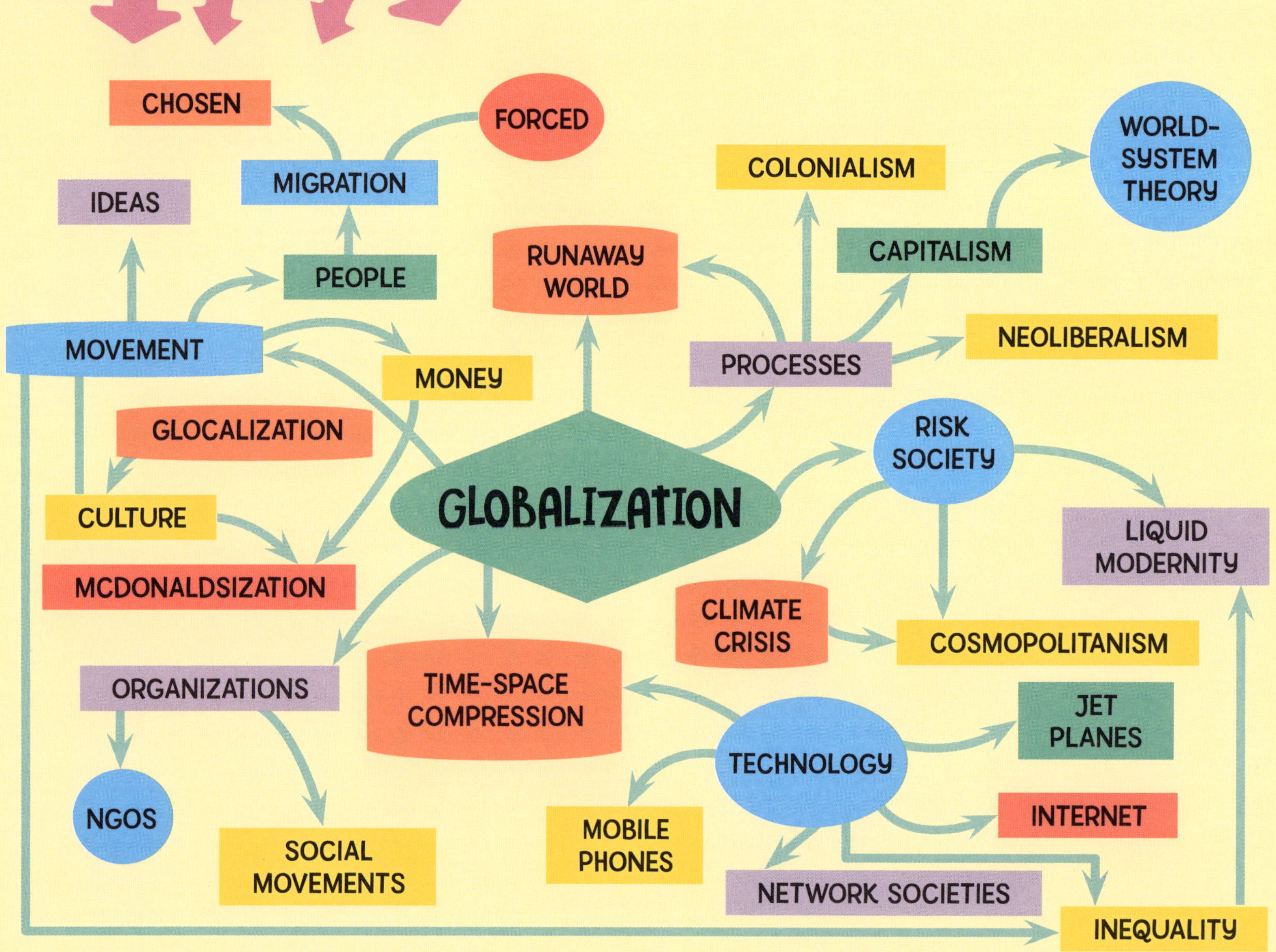

Someone in the UK this morning may have eaten for breakfast some flakes made from corn, produced for a well-known US brand. The corn for that cereal may have been grown in Argentina, with the sugar produced somewhere in the Caribbean. Sliced bananas from Nicaragua might have topped off that bowl. This might have been washed down with a cup of tea from Sri Lanka. In just one meal, we might rely on several different faraway countries – in fact nearly half of the food UK citizens consume comes from abroad (we'll consider the environmental impact of this kind of consumption in Chapter 12). This is just one small example of the ways in which our lives are globalized.

Such an example points to at least one key feature about globalization, which is the ways in which our lives are increasingly interconnected. UK sociologist Anthony Giddens (1990) defines globalization as 'the intensification of worldwide social relations which link distant localities in such a way that local happenings are shaped by events occurring many miles away and vice versa' – particular events might become 'global moments'.

Like many concepts in sociology, there are disagreements about what it is and its impact. Debates polarize, with some saying it is a major cause of injustice and inequality, while others suggest globalization can help eradicate these problems. However, whether good, bad or a bit of both, it remains a very significant concept in that it both explains contemporary processes of social change and also represents a significant shift in sociology itself. Earlier sociological theorizing was largely focused on one state, or country, whereas theories of globalization indicate, perhaps, a fuzziness of national boundaries.

Bananas and avocados have become global commodities, the former as breakfast opens up to include a wider range of foods, the latter as a fruit which has surged in popularity in a short time frame.

NAME TO KNOW: FOCUS ON GLOBALIZATION

Martin Albrow (1937–) is a British sociologist noted for his work on globalization. He and Elizabeth King define globalization as 'all those processes by which the peoples of the world are incorporated into a single world society'.

WHAT'S NEW ABOUT GLOBALIZATION?

Always travelling

Previous chapters have shown that the movement of people and goods across the globe is not a new phenomenon; indeed, there have been waves of migration and trading of goods and cultures since ancient times. As Kwame Anthony Appiah (2003) suggests, we have been a travelling species ever since our forebears first left Africa. Much of that movement, however, occurred on unoccupied land, or trading might have happened on the borders between territories. Arguably, globalization as it is understood today happens across territories and borders.

Shrinking the world

Giddens' definition suggests that what's also new is the intensity of these relationships. British sociologist Roland Robertson (1992) added to this proposition, claiming it was an intensification of our sense, or awareness of interdependencies, and that globalization was the 'compression of the world', similar to David Harvey's (1989) concept of 'time–space compression'. This metaphorical shrinking of the world, meaning that it becomes more accessible to (some of) us, has been made possible by new and rapid technological developments. Manfred Steger (2017), a US sociologist, combines and adds to these definitions in a useful way. For him, globalization is a set of processes:

- The development of social networks and connections across traditional boundaries (of economics, environment, politics, ideology and culture).
- The expansion of these networks across the globe, such as in institutions like global banks or companies like Ford.
- The acceleration, as well as intensification, of activities and connectivity through technology like the internet – the spreading of ideas and information through social media for instance.
- The development of a consciousness or global way of thinking about ourselves and the things around us.

Measuring globalization's impact

He argues that the impact of globalization can thus be measured on the following four factors: extensity, intensity, velocity and impact. We will come back to some of these later on in the chapter. Many agree that it is the speed and pervasiveness of these changes that represents a major shift in the ways we live our lives. Technological inventions like mobile phones and computers are ubiquitous. Social media has meant that political movements can mobilize, almost simultaneously, across the globe, as was seen with Black Lives Matter. Cheap flights have meant many people can affordably travel the world by choice (or are forced to through trafficking). Movement of people also resulted in the quick spread of disease, as was seen with the Covid-19 pandemic. Technology means that money and capital can flow across the world easily and crime, such as cybercrime, can be organized globally. All of these things have variously been understood as positive or negative aspects of a globalized world.

Cheap international flights mean that many may fly abroad for what could be regarded as 'extreme' day trips.

THINKING GLOBALLY IN A RUNAWAY WORLD

A global architecture

David Held (2002), a British sociologist, has suggested we are witnessing a new global 'architecture' of multinational corporations and institutions. Perhaps more worryingly, these are characterized, he suggests, by uneven, asymmetrical flows of culture and economics resulting in an expansion of capitalism and consumerism. In a series of lectures in 1999, Giddens suggested we were experiencing a 'runaway world' – one where change was happening so quickly we were losing control; deep analysis was needed to help gain back control. There have been a number of attempts to do this within sociology.

Italian political scientist Riccardo Petrella, like many academics, argued that thinking about the relationship between the global and the local helps us understand the process. He identified seven ways this relationship might manifest, several of which we will consider. Robert Holton (2005), a sociologist specializing in globalization, has summarized these as follows:

Global vs local

1. The global predominates over the local.
2. The local awakes itself in a globalized or globalizing world.
3. The global, bringing opportunities, helps the local.
4. The global invents its own local.
5. The local struggles for a different global.
6. The dialects of the global and local builds up a new synthesis, the glocal.
7. The local sets free the global.

We will now consider some related concepts that help us to understand globalization a little more. For simplicity's sake, these are divided into approaches that take a broadly optimistic view of globalization and those that are slightly more critical, though the reality is that many academics sit on the fence (not always a comfortable position!). They also include analysis that reflects on socioeconomic, sociocultural and sociopolitical aspects of globalization.

GLOBALIZATION'S NOT SO GREAT

World-systems theory

The result of mature capitalism

Compounding inequality

Immanuel Wallerstein (1974), a US sociologist, argues that globalization has continued the inequalities that emerged as a result of colonialism. The current system of globalization, which he thinks is the result of 'mature' capitalism, creates unequal relationships between nations. Capitalism's 'endless accumulation of capital' requires a constant supply of cheap raw materials and labour and new consumers. Whether they want to be or not, this world-system places all countries within the capitalist framework. What is significant is where they are positioned within the world-system. It puts countries across the globe into one of three possible positions: (1) the 'core' is made up of the most powerful, technologically advanced nations, including the US and Japan; (2) the 'semi-periphery' are not as rich as the core nations (and have enough of a buffer to stop them from being exploited by core nations) but neither are they as poor as…; (3) the 'periphery' that are poor, politically unstable, less technologically advanced nations which rely on selling their cheap labour to richer nations. The position of countries can change – nations like China and India, for instance, are developing rapidly.

Some, like Roland Robertson, have criticized Wallerstein for focusing so much on economics. Culture, he argues, is another way that countries can gain power. Wallerstein's theory is an early theory of globalization theory, or perhaps even anticipates it, as many argue it had not quite picked up the pace at the time he was writing.

Wallerstein's world system theory model

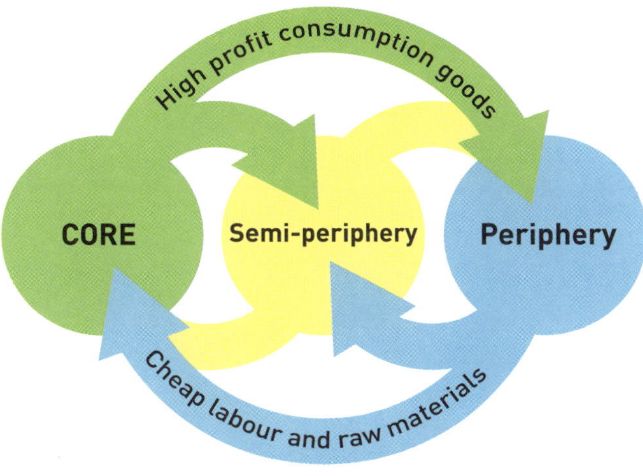

The globe can be divided between these three categories, and nations may move between them.

Neoliberalism

Manfred Steger (2007) argued there is a dominant ideology of globalization, one that promotes market ideologies and consumerism. The spread of this thinking led to public support for privatization, economic liberalism and deregulation. This globalist ideology consists of six core truth claims:(1) globalization is about the liberalization and global integration of markets; (2) globalization is inevitable and irreversible; (3) nobody is in charge of globalization; (4) globalization benefits everyone; (5) globalization furthers the spread of democracy in the world and (6) globalization requires a war on terror.

During the 1980s, then UK prime minister Margaret Thatcher and US president Ronald Reagan were largely responsible for the spread of neoliberalism.

By positing globalization as inevitable, for instance, any challenge to it is automatically rendered irrational. Insisting on a war on terror means that the idea of freedom under globalization is revealed as a myth in the face of the imposition of military power. In many respects, what Steger identified can be categorized as neoliberal thinking. Neoliberalism is a political-economic philosophy emphasizing free-market capitalism, deregulation and reduced government intervention that has significantly shaped social change since the 1980s.

Sociologists David Harvey (2005) and Loïc Wacquant (2009) have extensively analyzed the rise of neoliberalism and its social consequences. They argue that neoliberal policies have led to increased economic inequality, the erosion of social safety nets and the commodification of various aspects of social life. The French sociologist Pierre Bourdieu (1998) made similar arguments; he saw globalization as an example of a 'myth' or 'discourse' that is used to do away with belief in welfare states, pushing the world into one made of individualistic consumers.

GOLDEN STRAIGHTJACKET ▶ ***Thomas Friedman (1999) used the term 'golden straitjacket' for the neoliberal policies countries must adopt if they are to experience economic growth and prosperity.***

The myth of free trade

Zygmunt Bauman (1998) made the argument that globalization, hand in hand with capitalism, results not in greater prosperity for people, rather it leads to inequality and insecurity. One aspect of this 'liquid modernity' is mass migration. In this context we have also seen a rise of transnational corporations (TNCs) so powerful they are able to undermine the power of nation states. The South Korean academic Ha-Joon Chang (2008) argues that the neoliberal 'promise' of the free market and free trade is a myth, one that primarily benefits wealthy countries and harms poorer nations. The 'unholy trinity' of the World Bank, International Monetary Fund (IMF) and World Trade Organization (WTO) allow the neoliberal agenda to be pushed by an alliance of powerful countries, led by the US. These organizations play a role in keeping poorer nations in poverty, as a result of the economic reshuffling after the Second World War. To owe money to one of the 'core' nations is, in Susan George's words, 'a fate worse than debt'.

Increasing numbers of people are forced to leave their homes and risk death in small boats. Consequences of globalization such as increased poverty, climate change, wars over resources, have made many places unsafe to live.

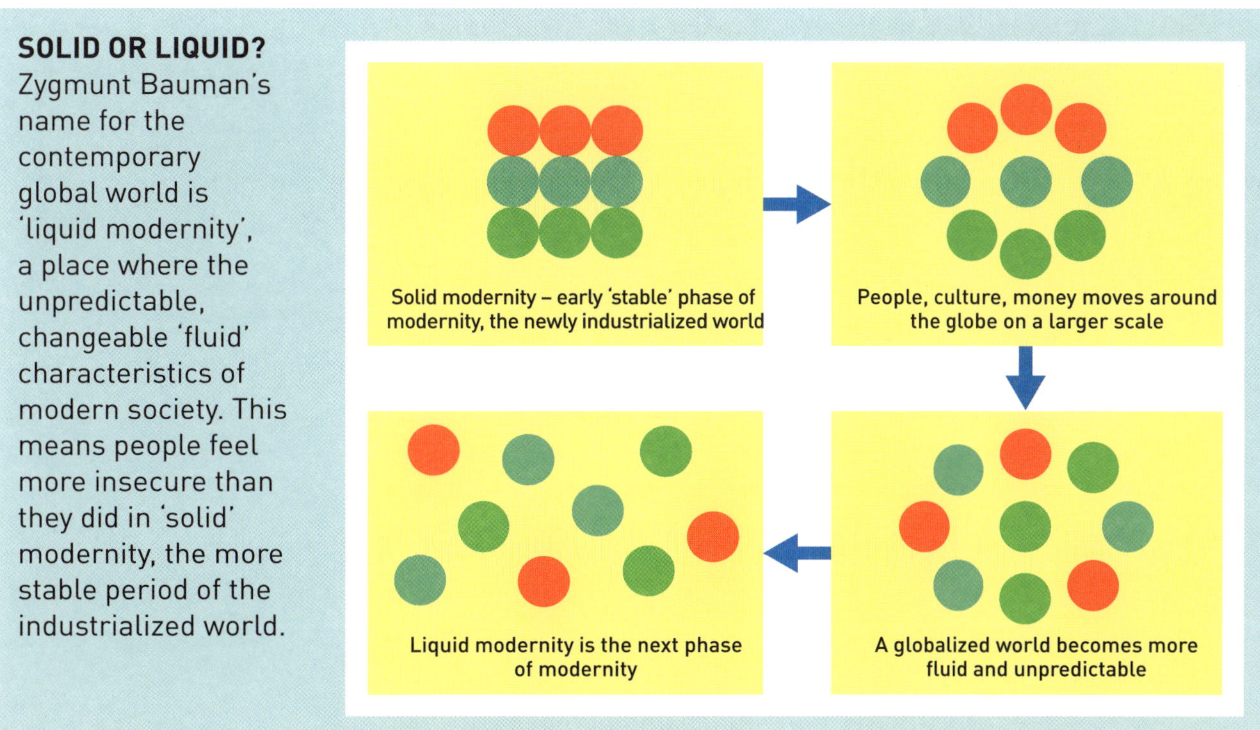

SOLID OR LIQUID? Zygmunt Bauman's name for the contemporary global world is 'liquid modernity', a place where the unpredictable, changeable 'fluid' characteristics of modern society. This means people feel more insecure than they did in 'solid' modernity, the more stable period of the industrialized world.

McDonaldization

Reworking Weber's concept of rationalization (see Chapter 2), George Ritzer (1993) developed his theory of McDonaldization to describe the cultural homogeneity he saw arising from globalization. Weber had argued that modernity was characterized by a tendency towards rational systems. Ritzer proposed that the tendencies of McDonald's fast-food chain was beginning to dominate other institutions, not just in the US but across the world. It's based on four key aspects: (1) efficiency (things need to be done as quickly as possible); (2) control (micromanagement to ensure people do what they're told, plus bring in robots or AI if cheaper!); (3) predictability and standardization (consumers can expect the same service and product across the globe), and (4) calculability (quantity rather than quality!). Ritzer said these principles are also starting to impact on everyday lives from our identities and relationships to our worldviews. Many have furthered his observations to argue that this is yet another example of Western cultural and economic domination. Working in such conditions is, arguably, dehumanizing and because the process generally requires unskilled workers, it contributes to the low-paid and precarious nature of working in the gig economy (see Chapter 5). It has found its way into the consumer experience too. Many of us might check out our own shopping in a supermarket – as such, we are helping corporations to lose more workers and we find ourselves doing that work for them for free.

The ultimate standardization

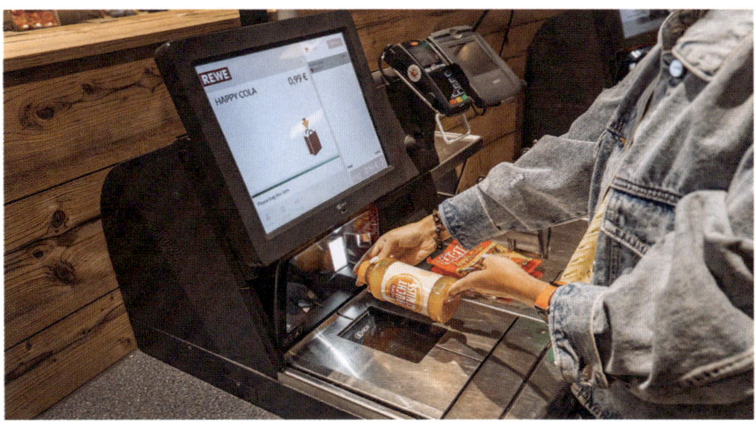

Self checkout means companies can employ fewer people, plus consumers effectively engage in unpaid labour.

US cultural imperialism

McDonaldization is seen by some as part of a wider process of Americanization. This is the argument that cultural forms and practices are becoming 'Americanized' across the globe. A materialistic consumerist ideology, it was feared, was taking over. Again, this is interpreted by many as a form of what Herbert Schiller (1976) called cultural imperialism – the dominance of Disney films and American television programmes is just one example. For some time, France has resisted the imposition of American culture, especially 'Hollywoodization'. We could look at changing language patterns that reflect the US influence. For instance, in the UK, words and phrases such as 'gotten'(though it must be said, like a few US words – e.g. faucet and fall – this was used in Middle English and later replaced but the Founding Fathers took it to the US where it remained), 'my bad' and 'named for' are becoming commonplace.

Language impacts

It should be noted that not all academics think all of the above concepts are useful for understanding globalization per se. British sociologists Darren O'Byrne and Alexander Hensby (2011), for example, argue that some of the above processes, such as Americanization and McDonaldization, don't result in anything 'global', though they agree they are related concepts.

COKEALIZATION

Some have been concerned that the introduction (or imposition) of global brands means that traditional diets are in danger of being lost, and people's health is put at risk. The journalist Jeremy Seabrook saw globalization as a 'declaration of war' on local culture. Coca-Cola, a global brand whose famous 1971 advert promoted global togetherness ('I'd Like to Teach the World to Sing (In Perfect Harmony)'), is as cheap as, or cheaper, than water in many parts of Mexico. Thus, people living in poverty are forced to drink it and as a consequence, rates of type 2 diabetes have increased. One of the reasons water is so expensive relatively is because it is scarce; Coca-Cola production uses large amounts – it takes roughly 2.5 litres of water to make 1 litre of Coke – and they own a significant portion of the water in the areas of production.

Risk society

If we think about the threat of climate change, pandemics like Covid-19 or bird flu and disastrous nuclear leaks like Chernobyl (1986), we might start to think of a globalized world as a risky one full of new threats. Like Giddens, Ulrich Beck suggested the world had created forces and events it couldn't control, leading to a 'risk society'. Medieval societies, he argued, of course had their risks – you might die from famine, floods or earthquakes. However, a key difference was that they tended to be natural risks and society responded to them differently, attributing the catastrophe to supernatural forces like witches or gods. Another distinction is that we would probably not be aware of disasters that happened elsewhere in the world. Later, from the 17th century to the 1960s, a period he calls first modernity, there was a growth in industrial society and the mass production of goods. Such societies took what was assumed to be unlimited natural resources to aid this. Gradually, a safety net in the form of the welfare state developed, providing benefits for those who cannot work. In this sense, states become more powerful, holding sway in large areas of people's lives. Giddens also points to the ways in which military might, as well as economic and cultural power, is a feature of globalization that adds to the risk of conflict.

Different threats?

Risk society, or second modernity, emerges from the 1970s onwards. This is a time of 'reflexive modernity', where the belief in things like the welfare state diminishes. Society also becomes more aware of growing threats such as environmental and financial disasters – threats that are man-made. Added to this, globalization has occurred, Giddens argues, at the same time as a growing distrust in institutions and groups such as scientific experts, which could have harmful consequences in relation to things like the climate crisis. This is what Beck, later in his work, named global or 'world risk society', where current political and social arrangements are not adequate to manage them.

Reflexive modernity

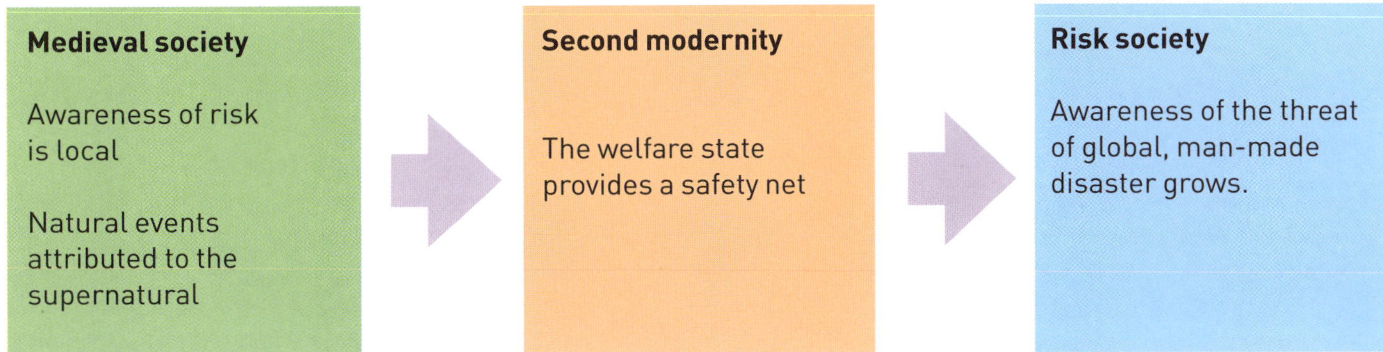

Perceptions of risk, especially on a global scale, have heightened over time.

A decline in welfare states, which includes institutions such as the UK's National Health Service (NHS), providing free healthcare, is a feature of globalization.

GLOBAL FOR THE GOOD (BROADLY)

Cosmopolitanism

A cosmopolitan sensibility

Manfred Steger's definition of globalization, like Robertson's, suggested a new imagination or consciousness. Bauman argued that living in a globalized world means that, consciously or not, we depend on one another. Beck, in response to living in a 'risk society', urged us to develop a cosmopolitan sensibility. He wanted us to see how our futures are enmeshed on a global scale; rather than seeing things from the point of view of the nation state, we need to see ourselves as global citizens. Large corporations, he felt, are unable to do this; it has to come from the grassroots. This is an example of 'globalization from below' – in contrast to many of the previous theories, which talk about 'globalization from above' or, in other words, rapid social change driven by big institutions such as the oil industry, big pharma, the meat and dairy industries and the stock market.

A bourgeois concept?

This concept has been critiqued for being bourgeois in its conceptualization. Many suggest that both Manuel Castells (see below) and Bauman's 'cosmopolitan' are middle-class, represented as distinct from working-class and marginalized identities who are somehow reduced to the 'local'. This ignores the working-class cosmopolitanism identified by Paul Gilroy, such as seamen or enslaved African Americans who were very much cosmopolitan in their experience of travel and different cultures. This argument builds on the work of W.E.B. Du Bois (1903), which challenged the assumption of a separate racial consciousness, one that sees the European as the makers of modernity. Du Bois' work, in part, was concerned with showing the ways in which African Americans have a presence in modern America.

Anthony Giddens has also argued that we are experiencing 'cosmopolitan overload'. While he doesn't necessarily disagree that we are, or should become, more cosmopolitan, he highlights the ways in which there has been a backlash from some groups. Those with sectional ideologies, such as nationalists and fundamentalist religions, have retreated to hostile responses to cosmopolitan values.

Increasingly, we live in a global civil society where we can work together to effect change.

A global civil society

Connected to this concept of cosmopolitanism is that of a global civil society. The American sociologist Jeffrey Alexander (1993) sees a civil society as an ethical space that sits outside of the political and economic realms. The intent of civil society is the pursuit of justice. In the context of globalization, global civil society is understood as one where alternative forms of social transformation are sought – in effect, social change that challenges that brought about by 'globalization from above'. Two broad examples of this are international non-governmental organizations (NGOs), which have a global focus on human rights, environmental justice and so forth – such as Greenpeace and Oxfam – and social movements such as Global Justice Now and Reclaim the Streets. Movements might encourage people to boycott the purchase of goods made through exploitation. Social protest in the Global South can also provide inspiration for protest in the Global North. The Occupy movement, for instance, was heavily influenced by the Arab Spring (see Chapter 9 for more on this).

Many groups, such as Debt Justice, recognize the global implications of debt, in addition to their historical origins in, for example, colonialism.

Network society

Spanish sociologist Manuel Castells (1996) introduces the concept of the ***network society***, arguing that new information technologies are reshaping social structures around networks rather than individual actors or hierarchical groups. We have moved from the industrial age to the information age, he argues, as part of the process of globalization. In this world, power exists beyond nation states in networks that transcend traditional borders. Networks might be based around academic, social or business interests but crucially, it is technology that allows for the exchange of knowledge. It is positive for Castells because it enables more people to be global. New forms of exclusion exist – those not part of these networks; (we could think about those people who cannot afford access to technology or are denied access. Older people who may not have grown up with these technologies might also be marginalized). Thus, for Castells, a global world is one undergoing significant re-stratification.

Information age

SNS allow peple to access networks and form groups whcih transcend national borders, becoming global citizens.

NAME TO KNOW: MOBILITIES AND FLUIDITIES

▶ ***John Urry (1946–2016), a British sociologist, argued that one way of understanding globalization and its impact is to analyze flows, or 'mobilities'. This includes who and what is allowed to cross borders, and importantly, where are the 'immobilities', or an inability to flow across borders. Such considerations allow us to see new forms of social exclusion.***

Glocalization

Some have argued that rather than being a source of homogeneity, or sameness and cultural domination, we can see heterogeneity – cultural diversity – at play on a global level. The argument here is that exposure to a new culture doesn't necessarily mean it is going to dominate. The point where the local meets the global can bring, according to some, hybridity. The Hindi spin on Hollywood – Bollywood – is a popular example. Roland Robertson coined the now famous term 'glocalization', a portmanteau of 'globalization' and 'localization', to describe the ways in which local people put their own spin on a global product.

RECONCEPTUALIZING PLACE IN A GLOBALIZED WORLD

When Jules Verne's *Around the World in 80 Days* was published in 1872, it was a fictional contemplation of what would have been an impossibility to most, other than the incredibly wealthy. Today, a significant proportion of people could feasibly travel the world in a few days, at a relatively cheap price (though that's not taking into account the cost at the expense of the climate or those working in the travel industry). Technological innovation also means you might order an item from the other side of the world, and it could arrive on your doorstep in a couple of days, without you ever having to have left your house.

We're all world travellers

Using the concepts of Urry's mobilities, Bauman's liquid modernity and Castells' network society, we can understand the above examples and the rise and prominence of global companies like Apple, Amazon or Google. Rather than making their own products, many of them offer a platform via technologies such as the internet, selling a range of goods made by others. It also means their employees and offices can be anywhere in the world with an internet connection and low (no) taxes. If, like Apple, they make things, it is often outsourced. Some companies deliberately choose places where labour is clearly exploitative but relatively cheap.

Outsourcing almost everything

JAGGERY LATTE

Companies like Starbucks and McDonalds allow local markets to adapt their products to reflect local tastes.

For instance, Starbucks in India might offer different flavours to suit the market there. Some question the extent to which this is positive glocalization, or just a small concession that allows the dominance of a Western/American product. Where companies don't acknowledge local culture and adapt their business model, there are examples of them failing. Starbucks in Australia, for instance, didn't understand their already vibrant coffee culture, influenced by Greek and Italian immigrants. The Australian cafe ethos is about sociability (and rather more sophisticated), whereas the US approach is much more about coffee as a commodity, a more anonymized culture (with sugary drinks less palatable for Australian tastes). Thus, the company lost millions of dollars and closed many of their venues.

THE MIGRANT EXPERIENCE OF GLOBALIZATION

On Falling (2024), a film by Laura Carreira, follows a migrant woman 'picker' in a fictional version of one of these global corporations' warehouses. As well as showing the precarious, dehumanizing monotony of working in the 'gig' economy (see Chapter 5), it is also a reflection on the impact of globalization and global consumerism, particularly on migrant workers.

MIGRATION

For Zygmunt Bauman (1998), inequality is a signature of globalization, in particular, inequality of movement. For the rich, mobility is a choice; for the poor, mobility is often forced and not welcomed. Migration is an example of this. There are many types and causes of migration, some of which is permitted and some not permitted (establishing these takes up a lot of government time). Some migration is voluntary, but much is still forced. The trafficking of humans for slave labour, in domestic and sex work for instance, is a pervasive feature of globalization. Many rich nations utilize connections with former colonies in order to source cheap labour. The NHS in the UK, for instance, has benefitted greatly from trained doctors and nurses from African countries among many others. This can also result in a brain drain in their home countries.

Types of migration

The issue of refugees or those seeking asylum is something that seems to particularly preoccupy governments and the media. Globally, many people are forced to seek asylum in order to escape from things such as war, conflict or climate crises (many of which are themselves caused by globalization, capitalism and colonialism – economics might be a shorthand term). As British sociologist Luke Martell (2017) has shown, media coverage of this in the UK often presents the numbers of people coming to the UK as a problem. As a result, many migrants face hostility and hate when they arrive. We are also often led to believe that migrants from poor countries are overwhelming rich nations. In fact, the vast majority of refugees (people given asylum) end up in neighbouring poor countries. Over

Refugees and asylum seekers

Migration is not just a contemporary issue. This image of American Tories (supporters of Britain) fleeing for Canada is a historical example.

70 per cent of the world's refugees live in poor countries, often in camps. When rich nations take in asylum seekers, they are less likely to grant them official refugee status. This is also an example of the power of rich nations to invisiblize their own migration (to colonize poor countries, for instance).

Creating moral panic

Stan Cohen's book *Folk Devils and Moral Panics* (1972) is useful here. He studied the way in which the government and media responded to what were very minor clashes between two youth groups – the Mods and the Rockers. The media depicted these young people as what he termed 'Folk Devils', a threat to established norms and values. In other words they became scapegoats, blamed for what was seen as wrong with modern society. This started a 'moral panic' about young people specifically and society more generally. In response to this, governments have to be seen to act and contain the 'problem' in some way. This is applicable to migrants seeking asylum in the UK: they are frequently portrayed as 'folk devils' taking our jobs and houses, or posing a threat to women and children, and we see a moral panic arise around migration. The people trying to escape often life-threatening situations are depicted as undeserving of our empathy and assistance. Prime Minister Keir Starmer recently announced that a 'tough new law' was coming to deal with the 'problem' of illegal immigration, which he argues is a significant cause of global insecurity – a discourse that conveniently ignores the aspects of globalization driving that very migration.

Migration is likely to become a bigger issue in the near future, as a result of the climate crisis, scarcity of resources and continued conflicts.

GLOBALIZATION OR CAPITALISM UNBOUND?

We're all migrants now

Contemporary social change is characterized by complex, interconnected processes operating at global, as well as national and local levels. From the far-reaching impacts of globalization and neoliberalism to the transformative potential of digital technologies and new social movements, these changes are reshaping societies in profound ways. Anthony Giddens argues that we are all migrants now – though we might not physically travel to other parts of the world, through technology most of us are in touch with a variety of cultures, ideas and opinions on a daily basis. Clearly, globalization brings with it many risks, but it also has the potential to afford opportunities to a great many people. Other chapters consider some of these further, for instance, in relation to digital cultures, the environment, race and ethnicity, violence and gender and sexuality. Some focus on 'globalization from below', whereas many more might argue that globalization happens 'from above', in particular, as a vehicle enabling neoliberal capitalism. At a moment when this world-system seems determined to continue apace, the impact of globalization is something that is going to occupy sociologists for a while yet. Globalization also presents a challenge to sociology, to go beyond the analysis of the nations and become, in Urry's words 'a sociology of mobilities'. As sociologists, our task is to continually refine our tools and perspectives to understand and engage with these dynamic processes of social change.

Chapter Eleven
VIOLENCE

In the eye of the beholder – Absent violence – Conceptualizing violence – Theorizing of violence – Forms of violence – Violent societies?

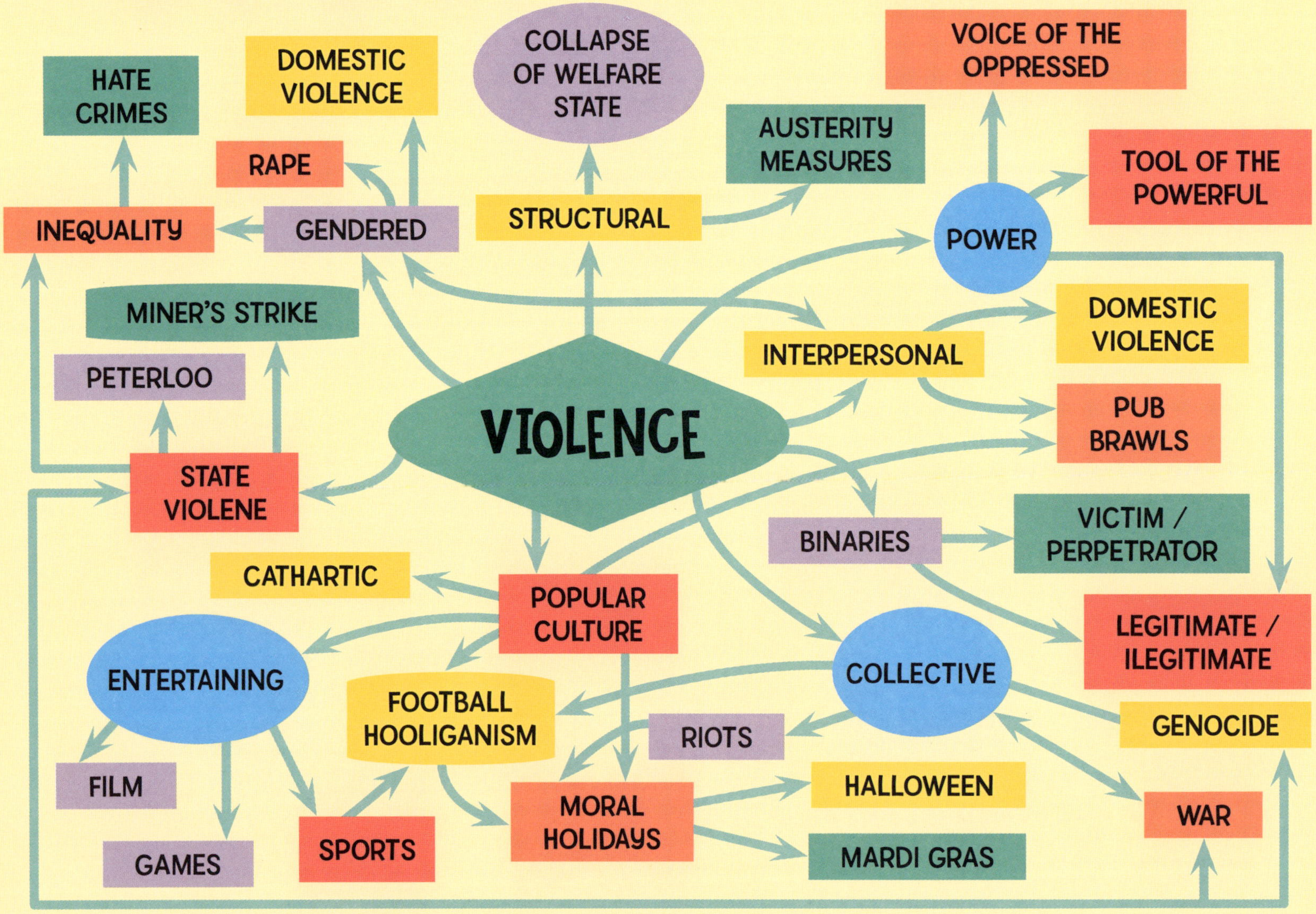

HATE CRIMES
DOMESTIC VIOLENCE
COLLAPSE OF WELFARE STATE
VOICE OF THE OPPRESSED
AUSTERITY MEASURES
RAPE
TOOL OF THE POWERFUL
INEQUALITY
GENDERED
STRUCTURAL
POWER
MINER'S STRIKE
DOMESTIC VIOLENCE
INTERPERSONAL
PETERLOO
PUB BRAWLS
VIOLENCE
STATE VIOLENE
VICTIM / PERPETRATOR
BINARIES
CATHARTIC
POPULAR CULTURE
LEGITIMATE / ILEGITIMATE
ENTERTAINING
COLLECTIVE
FOOTBALL HOOLIGANISM
GENOCIDE
RIOTS
FILM
HALLOWEEN
MORAL HOLIDAYS
WAR
SPORTS
MARDI GRAS
GAMES

IN THE EYE OF THE BEHOLDER

Does banging on someone's door, demanding 'trick or treat', constitute a violent act? Perhaps willingly engaging in contact sports, such as rugby, is violent; or maybe even any form of competition. Many would agree that war is a violent act but might struggle to see its connection with other forms of violence, such as domestic violence or bullying. For others, WRITING IN CAPITAL LETTERS is perceived as violent. Once we start thinking in this way, we can see how pervasive violence is. From this acknowledgement, we can also understand the ways in which aspects such as fear of violence structure our lives: from investing in security devices, to avoiding particular places at certain times. The range of products and services designed around safety and security also points to one of the many ways in which violence is commodified in contemporary society. These examples raise many questions that sociology attempts to respond to, including what constitutes violence, whether there are threads to help explain all forms of violence, and whether violence is ever appropriate or legitimate.

Defining violence

ABSENT VIOLENCE

Up until relatively recently, as US sociologist Mary Jackman (2002) observed, many sociological courses and textbooks might have looked at violence in a specific context (such as violent crime or domestic violence) and perhaps have left considerations of other forms of violence (such as war and genocide) to other disciplines like politics or history. Rarely, too, would you find a whole book or course devoted to violence per se. In some respects, this is because it is such a huge topic, which makes it tricky to find commonalities. It might also be because, as Yugoslav/Irish sociologist Siniša

Burning the Guy, mid-19th century, an act of symbolic violence and a reference to a violent period in history.

Malešević (2015) suggests, traditionally, sociology often focused on what was happening within one society, rather than across different territories. But that is no excuse for not trying to understand violence because, as we have already seen in this book, it has significant consequences. Sylvia Walby (2013), a UK expert on violence, has highlighted how it shortens lives, is a source of suffering and pain, and is often central to social change. Many of the institutions we have looked at – including the law, medicine, families, religion and the media – not only help to shape our view of violence, but they can also be violent themselves. Social processes – such as capitalism, patriarchy, globalization and climate change – can be understood through a lens of violence; violence can, for instance, play a key role in forming and maintaining social divisions.

Impacts of violence

CONCEPTUALIZING VIOLENCE

NATURAL-BORN KILLERS?

Defining violence is tricky and an ongoing debate. Many might argue that violence is natural, a biological drive and therefore inevitable, so perhaps we just have to learn to put up with it. However, even scientists – such as the evolutionary biologist Stephen Jay Gould – recognize that violence is a social phenomenon: 'violence, sexism, and general nastiness are biological since they represent one subset of a possible range of behaviours. But peacefulness, equality, and kindness are just as biological – and we may see their influence increase if we can create social structures that permit them to flourish' (1977). In other words, how we act is largely down to the social and cultural institutions, values and norms around us, rather than to some innate human 'nature'.

Is it biological?

STRUCTURAL

A ***common-sense*** understanding of violence often focuses on physical forms of violence, particularly inflicted by one person on another. The Dutch sociologist Willem Schinkel (2010) urges us to look beyond such views, because they obscure things like ***state violence***, and in fact, the common-sense understanding may in fact be state ideology, encouraging us to ignore the crimes of the powerful. Thus, sociological approaches often broaden this to include ideas of structural violence; the Norwegian sociologist Johan Galtung (1969), for instance, argued that violence is built into the very structures of society. When social arrangements systematically prevent individuals from meeting their basic needs or reaching their potential, this constitutes violence even without direct physical force. Unequal access to healthcare, education or legal protection can thus be understood as forms of violence. Galtung's work on this is seen as an example of 'slow violence' (a term first coined in 2011 by environmentalist Rob Nixon) occurring over centuries, as opposed to the 'quick violence' associated with wars, invasions and repression. Violence in this sense may result not only from intention but also from inaction. These forms of systemic violence include poverty, social inequality and institutional racism. Paul Farmer (2004), a physician-anthropologist, demonstrates how structural violence operates through examining health disparities. His research in Haiti revealed how poverty, racism

State violence

and historical inequalities create conditions where certain populations suffer disproportionately from preventable diseases and premature death. This form of violence operates without a clear perpetrator sometimes but through historic forces, individual agency is constrained.

The increasing need for food banks can be seen as a form of structural 'slow violence'.

HEGEMONIC

Antoni Gramsci's theory of hegemony is another useful concept to remember when considering violence. This understanding of power and domination argues that in democratic contexts, **coercive control** is not the main source of control. Instead, culture and ideology play a significant role in sustaining the dominance of the ruling class (which we can understand not just in terms of social class but also ethnicity, gender, sexuality and so on). Hegemony works mainly through consent, which means – in 'normal' times – it is not usually done through overt constraint and violence. For Gramsci, it is political, cultural and economic. By emphasizing the role of consent, we can see how conditions are created for a society to accept exploitation, sexism, racism and other inequalities – ideologies that benefit the minority ruling class but seem 'inevitable', 'natural' or 'common sense' to the majority. His *Prison Notebooks* also emphasized the 'armour of coercion'; what we think of as public opinion is in fact connected to political hegemony. In other words, civil society is closely connected to the state. This is a form of violence that for the most part replaces physical violence and coercion but can quickly become that if needed.

Armour of coercion

> **GRAMSCI'S INCARCERATION**
> The Italian Marxist activist and journalist Antonio Gramsci was arrested by the fascist authorities in 1926. Feared for his critical thinking, the regime argued 'we must prevent this brain from functioning for the next 20 years!' They were successful on one front: he remained in prison until 1934 when, because of his many untreated health problems, he was transferred – still a prisoner – to a hospital where his room was converted into a prison cell. Still not getting proper medical care, his health deteriorated further, and he was transferred to another hospital. He died of a brain haemorrhage in 1937. However, during his time in prison he wrote extensively, producing the influential *Prison Notebooks*.

SYMBOLIC

Symbolic violence

Pierre Bourdieu's (1991) work on symbolic violence potentially extends our understanding even further, by referring to the imposition of systems of meaning that legitimize and conceal power relations. In many ways, this is an extension of Gramsci's work on hegemony where dominant ideologies become seen as common sense. Dominant groups impose their culture and values on subordinate groups, who then internalize these as 'natural' or 'inevitable', and thus impact on their habitus. Such subordinate groups subsequently become marginalized and devalued in society more widely, and this relegation is viewed by the majority as legitimate or justifiable. In other words, inequalities are misrecognized.

Colonialism and cultural imperialism

Colonialism, cultural imperialism and systemic racism are often understood as being examples of symbolic violence. By linking violence to power in this way, some think this offers great scope for understanding violence. Others, however, warn that this approach is in danger of ignoring the specifics of violence and the harms done to victims. Sylvia Walby (2014), for example, argues that Bourdieu's suggestion that women internalize patriarchal values that diminish their worth or potential and experience symbolic violence that operates with their unwitting complicity is a harmful analysis. Bourdieu arguably ignores the specific effects of physical violence and implies that the oppressed cannot resist or fight back, a position refuted by Frantz Fanon (1961) (see Chapter 6).

GENDERED

Gendered violence

If we take the position that violence is a social construction, we can start to see the ways that, in many societies, it is constructed as gendered. It is gendered in terms of who we expect will be violent (men). Many have argued that violence is a facet of stereotypical ideas of what it is to be a man. Several of our myths and stories, such as tales from Ancient Greece about protagonists like Odysseus, Theseus and Achilles, to more contemporary figures such as James Bond, involve heroic violence – we might be disappointed if Bond wasn't involved in a few fights during the course of his adventures. Such violence is often portrayed as 'righteous', 'normal' and 'natural', as well as entertaining. When women have been violent (or accused of violence), either in fiction or in real life, rather than seeing this as an aspect of appropriate femininity, they are often depicted as being monstrous, evil or too masculine (for example Medusa and Myra Hindley). The toys traditionally given to boys and girls reinforce these stereotypes: boys might be given guns and swords, whereas girls might be given toys more associated with the mopping up of violent deeds, such as nurses' uniforms. As we shall see later, violence is also gendered in terms of who is likely to be a victim and who a perpetrator of what is termed gendered violence.

Violent playthings

UNPACKING DEFINITIONS

Official definitions can be a useful starting point for unpicking what violence is (and isn't). They are interesting, too, because they tell us something about how a nation, or organization, chooses to frame it, and these may differ over time or between cultures. We can also unpack these definitions to see what is perhaps missing, intentionally or otherwise.

VIOLENCE ▶ *The intentional use of physical force or power, threatened or actual, against oneself, another person, or against a group or community, that either results in or has a high likelihood of resulting in injury, death, psychological harm, maldevelopment or deprivation.*

(World Health Organization, 2002)

This is useful in that it asserts that violence need not be physical. However, by insisting that violence is intentional, it is perhaps missing out on some forms of structural violence that might not be intentional (though some may well be). It also misses, perhaps, those forms of violence that might be experienced as pleasurable, such as masochism. Many of us may take pleasure in viewing violent films or participating in violent sport. It could also be argued that this gender-neutral definition disguises the fact that most violence is commissioned by men (though conversely, there is an argument for gender-neutral definitions that allow for the fact that women do commission many forms of violence too, though not in such great numbers).

Is it intentional?

GOOD OR BAD?

Many definitions of violence take a moralistic stance, viewing violence as a negative act. US philosopher Allan Bäck (2004) has suggested that to call something violent almost always invokes opinions that it is morally wrong. Governments, for example, will often posit that the perpetrators of violent crime are somehow morally bankrupt or acting beyond the limits of morality – unless they themselves are the ones committing the violent crime. Alan Page Fiske and Tage Rai (2014), an anthropologist and psychologist respectively, however, argue that violence can be a virtuous act. Sometimes, if the social order is seen as unjust, for instance, it might provoke a violent action that is done for the best intentions. Indeed, Canadian psychologist Steven Pinker (2011) supports this, arguing that though we tend to think of perpetrators of violence as somehow pathological, often they are acting within a moral framework (though we might not necessarily agree with it).

A virtuous act

Violence is a c-word!

By considering several c-words in relation to violence we can start to understand violence – and people's responses to violence – through a sociological lens, and see some threads pulling all of this together:

- **Context** – intentional/unintentional, expected/surprising, legitimate/illegitimate, self-inflicted/external, location, victim/perpetrator, witnesses, type of violence, rationale for violence
- **Causes** – state conflict, hostility, prejudice, cultural
- **Consequences** – trauma, poverty/wealth, ill health, isolation, death
- **Categories** – interpersonal, institutional, structural, instrumental, expressive, symbolic
- **Contradictions** – violence might be public/private, pleasurable/painful, acceptable/unacceptable
- **Constructions** – what constitutes violence differs between nations; over time, what is deemed acceptable shifts too
- **Commodity** – violence can be a resource, a tradeable good, marketable

Power and violence

One thread that weaves through all forms of violence might be power. For instance, we can ask ourselves who has the power to define what is violent or what is legitimate violence, who gains from the commission of acts of violence, or whose violent actions are socially sanctioned. We can also clearly see that violence is a social act, which doesn't happen in isolation; even if an individual is violent, there are social explanations. We shall be considering many of these c-words as we go through the chapter.

Much competitive sport has violent elements, a form which is socially sanctioned and approved as entertainment.

Public executions were once considered 'normal' and appropriate in many countries, and still are in others.

VIOLENT TIMES?

A peaceful era?

According to some, such as Pinker, violence has declined throughout human history. Drawing on historical data, he suggests that despite media coverage that might indicate otherwise, we are living in the most peaceful time in our species' existence. Factors contributing to this decline, he argues, include:

- the rise of the modern state with monopoly on legitimate force
- increasing democratization and human rights values
- growing empathy and reason through literacy and education
- economic interdependence through global trade

Altruistic behaviours

For thinkers like Pinker, altruistic behaviours and ideas of human rights are becoming global norms. However, critics like John Gray (2015), a British philosopher, question Pinker's methodology and conclusions, arguing that violence has merely changed form rather than decreased. Contemporary violence includes new manifestations like cyber violence, terrorism and systemic economic violence that may not appear in traditional metrics. Zygmunt Bauman (1989), for instance, argued that violence culminated in the Second World War, with the modern bureaucratic state enabling horrors such as the Holocaust. US social critic Robert Kaplan (1994) warned that the end of the Cold War would result not in more peace but in increased terrorism, regional wars and environmental stresses that would lead to social violence.

These Ukrainian firefighters are responding to the violent consequances of their country's war with Russian.

The Cold War (1945–1990) was an ideological and political stand-off between Western countries, notably the US and the Soviet Bloc, in particular the perceived threat of Russia. Russia was depicted as a threat to the West when, at the time, the US had invaded far more countries, deployed more nuclear weapons and was founded on genocide. The British historian Eric Hobsbawm (1990) predicted that when the Soviet Union fell, whatever one felt about it, capitalism would be left 'unchecked', which would be disastrous for the rest of the world – including an increase in regional wars; the appearance of right-wing authoritarian states and a resurgence of anti-Semitism and racism in eastern Europe; and the dismantling of welfare states in western Europe.

THEORIZING OF VIOLENCE

The suggestion of a historical decline in violence, whether correct or incorrect, has been used to explain why violence wasn't central in sociological thinking. One argument was that when sociology as a discipline emerged in the late 18th and early 19th centuries, the Global North was relatively peaceful. However, this was not a view shared by all.

SOCIAL MURDER

Turning a blind eye

Friedrich Engels (1845), for example, saw the social relations of capitalism, and the bourgeoisie in particular, as being responsible for the social murder of the working classes. The terrible living and working conditions he witnessed in many towns and cities across England, he argued, were foreseeable and avoidable – but the bourgeoisie deliberately turned a blind eye in order to make a profit. Engels's concept is re-emerging in British sociology in response to events like the Grenfell Tower disaster and the ongoing effects of austerity measures. Regarding the latter, an early study estimated that, between 2010 and 2019 there had been 120,000 austerity-related deaths – leading one of the researchers, Professor Lawrence King of Cambridge University, to use the term economic murder; the most recent study, by the University of Glasgow (2022), has put the number of austerity-related 'excess deaths' at over 335,000.

These are examples of what criminologist Vickie Cooper and legal scholar David Whyte (2017) call ordinary and mundane bureaucratized violence.

More generally, sociology has considered violence as a phenomenon that is deeply embedded in social structures, cultural norms and social interactions.

STRUCTURAL FUNCTIONALISM

Influenced by the work of Émile Durkheim, ***structural functionalism*** was made famous by US sociologists such as Talcott Parsons (see Chapter 2). Though largely disregarded by contemporary social scientists, this approach remains popular in public discourse, especially that associated with conservative groups. ***Functionalism*** views society as a system of interrelated parts, working together to maintain stability and order. From this perspective, violence can be seen as a breakdown of the social order. Violence arises when social institutions such as the family or education system fail to function 'properly'. Members of society start to feel unattached to society – disconnected and frustrated – and recourse to violence in such conditions is understood as an attempt to assert themselves, or anger at not being accepted. One criticism of this approach has come from feminists, who argue that this explanation doesn't account for the fact that women, who are among the most marginalized in society, are not the ones who tend to act violently: it is those with relatively more power – men – who are most violent.

Functionalism

Robert Merton's (1938) strain theory is an example of a functionalist explanation of violence. He suggests that violence can result from the gap between culturally approved goals (such as home ownership) and the lack of legitimate means to achieve them. When individuals cannot attain success through approved channels, they may turn to violence as an alternative path to desired ends.

Strain theory

From a functionalist perspective, some forms of violence may actually serve useful social purposes. Durkheim (1893) identified how crime and deviance, including violent acts, can affirm social boundaries and norms, build solidarity among law-abiding citizens and create opportunities for social adaptation. Public outcry over an event, such as the felling of the tree in Sycamore Gap in the UK (see Chapter 12), provide an opportunity to build social ties around collective moral outrage and ideas about what is 'wrong' behaviour.

CONFLICT THEORY

Influenced by Karl Marx, this approach sees society as composed of groups with competing interests. Inequality creates conflict, which in turn creates an environment conducive to violence. Violence can thus be understood as a result of social inequality and power struggles. Dominant groups, for instance, use violence to maintain control and suppress opposition. It might also be a response to economic disparities, with marginalized groups resorting to violence as a means of survival. Violence is also viewed as being a potential catalyst for social change – for example through revolutions, uprisings and social movements.

Maintaining control through violence

Feminist approaches to violence can fit within this broad framework in their focus on gender inequalities. For US legal scholar Catharine MacKinnon (1989), violence against women is not merely individual pathology but systematically reinforces male dominance and female subordination. This perspective reveals how seemingly private acts of violence serve to maintain broader systems of patriarchal control.

SYMBOLIC INTERACTIONISM

When thinking about how and why violence emerges in society, conflict theory provides a useful broad context but perhaps doesn't always explain individual motivations, feelings and responses. Symbolic interactionism provides what might be seen as a complementary approach. It focuses on the meanings and interpretations individuals attach to their experience and interactions, including violent ones – it is a micro-level approach. Acts of violence can convey messages of power or resistance. Jack Katz explores in *Seductions of Crime* (1988) the sensual and emotional attractions of violence, arguing that some individuals find meaning and transcendence through violent acts.

Labelling theory, associated with Howard Becker (1963), is an example of this approach. Individuals might become 'deviant' because of societal reactions. For example, being labelled as violent can lead to the individual starting, or continuing, to engage in violent behaviour due to societal expectations and stigmatization.

Not naturally violent

Randall Collins argues in *Violence: A Micro-sociological Theory* (2008) that humans are not naturally violent but rather find violence emotionally difficult. Most violent situations are characterized by tension and fear, with successful violence requiring techniques to overcome these emotional barriers. However, some have accused micro-sociological accounts of ignoring the vital structural contexts within which such violence occurs.

FORMS OF VIOLENCE

Violence in popular culture

Just as there are many ways to theorize violence, there are also myriad approaches on how to group or categorize it, and we can only consider some of these here – but it should also be noted that several of these taxonomies of violence overlap. Wars are part and parcel of state violence; violence against women, some argue, should be seen as a hate crime; genocides can also be seen as hate crimes. We will start by looking at some examples of violence in popular culture, before moving from interpersonal through to collective forms of violence.

VIOLENCE, POPULAR CULTURE AND CONSUMERISM

Media madness

Our perception of violence is heavily influenced by media representation. And the media loves violence; like sex, according to UK criminologist Yvonne Jewkes (2004), violence sells.

In the 1990s, Stanley Cohen (1972) developed the concept of 'moral panics', where media coverage amplifies public anxiety about certain forms of violence, potentially distorting its actual prevalence. This process typically involves:

MEDIA ▶ *media, or mass media, refers to a broad range of forms of communication to a large number of people. It includes newspapers and magazines, social media and the internet, and television and radio.*

Impact of media stories

- identifying a threat to social values
- presenting it in a simplified form through media
- rapidly building public concern
- prompting response(s) from authorities
- often resulting in social change

One government response is often to encourage police forces to clamp down on a particular behaviour, thus crime statistics can suddenly rise, and the media may use this distorted figure to claim there is a bigger problem than there actually is. Moral panics will come and go but the processes are often very similar. Such panics about violence in the UK (which also tend to focus on the conduct of young people in particular) have included girls' participation in gang crime, the brief phenomenon of 'happy slapping', and attacks by dangerous dogs.

Amplifying behaviours

Algorithm agitation

Cohen largely focused on the impact of newspaper and television reporting. Contemporary digital media adds new dimensions to this analysis (see Chapter 9). Social media platforms allow violent content to spread rapidly, while algorithmic curation can create echo chambers reinforcing particular narratives about violence. Sonia Livingstone's (2009) research shows how young people navigate this complex media landscape where representations of violence are ubiquitous yet often disconnected from real-world consequences. More recently, studies have shown how young boys are being shown violent content, which might include fights or violent pornography, on platforms such as TikTok. In 2024, Andrew Kaung, an analyst who had worked at TikTok, highlighted the problems with how algorithms work and the ways in which AI tools, which are supposed to remove such content for platforms, fail to do this quickly enough.

Algorithmic distortions

Filmic fury

Violence in film can be a useful way to explore how ideas of gender are constructed. Laura Mulvey's (1975) 'male gaze' theory has been discussed elsewhere (Chapter 9); in brief, she argues that cinema puts the viewer into an assumed heterosexual male role. Within film, women become objects of sexual desire; the camera lens denies their subjectivity by cutting them up, focusing on bits of their bodies: feet, legs, breasts, and so on. Film also facilitates a separation of spectator and screen, which

Minor scuffles between Mods and Rockers in 1964 were exaggerated by the press at times where there was not much other 'news'.

Media concerns about dangerous dogs are a more recent example of a 'moral panic'. Attacks do happen but perhaps not to the exaggerated extent the media suggests.

indulges voyeuristic fantasy. Thus, in watching slasher or horror films, the audience is encouraged, or manipulated, into enjoying watching sexualized violence against women. Indeed, US scholar Carol Clover (1992) argued that horror films are in themselves 'monstrous' – we enjoy watching the victim's torture but, for female watchers, we are also coerced to enjoy our own fear and torture. Clover's 'Final Girl' theory (which became so famous a horror film was made in its name), argues that women's sexuality is punished in many horror genres – the women who have sex, drink or smoke are often the first to be killed off. The one who makes it to the end to slay the monster often displays qualities of virginal 'purity', but also 'masculine' traits of bravery and independence; in short, she becomes a convenient 'double' for male teenagers.

Gothic monsters such as vampires and werewolves, where traditionally the monster is male, also offer some interesting ideas about masculinity. In earlier versions of such films, we see an alignment of masculinity, sexuality and violence within the monstrous vampire or werewolf, a sort of proto-toxic masculinity. Women are often given the role of being victim or having the potential to 'tame' the beast within, through stereotypical ideas of female sensitivities and care. Becoming a werewolf, however, is often seen as a curse – typically, we see a nice, caring and thoughtful man, such as Larry Talbot in *The Wolf Man* (1941), suddenly having to wrestle with the fact he is driven to kill under the full moon. In this sense, such films can be seen as the struggle, or tensions, men face in having to perform the violent expectations of masculinity. The heroes of such films are themselves usually men, whose unquestioned displays of hegemonic masculinity (see Chapter 7) means they become top of the pecking order of the pack of potential victims, in order to slay the beast. We see, in these films, a process of masculinization through violence.

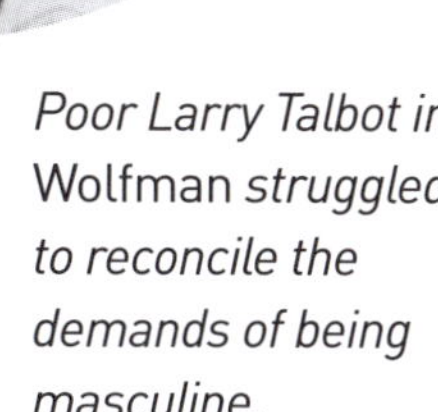

Poor Larry Talbot in Wolfman *struggled to reconcile the demands of being masculine.*

Not very sporting?

Sporting contexts provide useful sites for examining the social organization and meaning of violence. Sport traditionally is another gendered space – masculinity, arguably, has been one of its central organizing principles. In Ancient Greece sport was a form of training for war and battle, and thus was often very violent. Eric Dunning (1999), building on Norbert Elias's civilizing process theory, examined how controlled violence in sport now serves as a mimetic (representational or simulated) activity, providing excitement in societies where everyday life has become increasingly pacified.

Sports where violence is central to the activity, such as boxing or mixed martial arts, raise questions about the boundaries between legitimate and illegitimate violence. On-pitch, as well as off-pitch, sport can be another way of performing hegemonic masculinity. Misogyny and homophobia, for instance, have been observable aspects of sporting and spectator behaviour.

French sociologist Loïc Wacquant's (2004) ethnographic study of boxers showed how they develop a professional relationship to bodily harm, learning to use and receive violence within strictly controlled parameters. He suggests that most of the working-class men who box are familiar with violence, coming from areas rife with crime. The hypermasculine ethos of boxing and the controlled violence, he argues, provides a path to dignity and recognition for marginalized men. Such an analysis, of course, fails to account for women who box.

CASE STUDY: FOOTBALL HOOLIGANISM

British sociologists like Gary Armstrong and Richard Giulianotti have studied football hooliganism as a social phenomenon reflecting class identities, masculinity and territorial claims. Their ethnographic research reveals how apparently senseless violence serves important identity functions for participants, creating intense solidarity and meaning.

A pint, a pie and a fight...

Violence is a feature of the night-time economy. Many forms of violent crime, including sexual assault and harassment, occur within and outside pubs and clubs – hotspots for urban public violence. Some studies argue that alcohol has a role to play here, though not necessarily a causal one, as most people who are intoxicated do not become violent. Nonetheless, many of the violent incidents occurring over weekends, and at night, involve alcohol in some way. Promotions that offer cheap alcohol; extended drinking hours; venues that are cramped, hot and with little seating – and music so loud conversation is tricky – foster high levels of consumption and general agitation. Surveys conducted in British and Australian cities have revealed that over half, and perhaps as many as three-quarters, of people

who go to such places have witnessed some form of violence. Closing time, and the hours after, seem to be the time when most violent crime occurs in this context. Ethnographic research by UK sociologist Dick Hobbs (2000) suggested that this was particularly the case when everywhere closed at the same time. As a result, 24-hour licences were granted in 2005, though the only significant impact of this was that crimes happened a little later than they had previously. UK sociologist Simon Winlow and criminologist Steve Hall (2009) argue that consumer capitalism reinforces existing structural inequalities; participation in the night-time economy is felt to be compulsory for many young people, if they do not want to be ostracized. Involvement in violent cultures therein may not be so much to do with choice but rather instrumental adaptation.

Some argue the combination of alcohol, noise, heat and crowds is conducive to violent outbursts.

We're all goin' on a moral holiday

Influenced by the work of Norbert Elias, Randall Collins (2008) has looked at the moments when individuals or groups might loosen some of the usual constraints on their behaviour, thus becoming 'decivilized'. This relaxation of the usual rules is often temporally or spatially bounded. At such times, commonly emboldened by group participation, acts of disorder and disruption erupt. Such moral holidays might include socially sanctioned events, where there is a pleasurable sense of 'letting go' among group safety, such as trick or treating at Halloween, or Mardi Gras celebrations. Celebratory events, such as music festivals, often involve a lot of revelry people might not normally engage in, and these can, sometimes, tip over into violent episodes such as at Altamont in 1969 or T in the Park in 2016. More recently, the riots, looting and vandalism that occurred across the UK in August 2024, largely by far-right anti-immigrant protestors, is another such example.

Licence to violence?

GENDERED VIOLENCE

Much of this section might have appeared in the chapter on gender. However, as Sylvia Walby (2014) has argued, it is important that gendered interpersonal violence is mainstreamed in sociology and not sidelined as a separate issue, or just a concern of women and feminists. Over the last 40 years, feminists have charted and documented men's violence against women and girls. Feminists such as Liz Kelly (1988) see such violence as a consequence, and cause of, gender inequality. This understanding of the dynamic of violence being from the largely privileged (men) against the underprivileged (mainly women), challenges much mainstream criminological and sociological theory on violent crime more generally (such as the work of Robert Merton), and some approaches to domestic violence specifically, which has argued that

Violence against women and girls

violence is largely commissioned by the disadvantaged in society. Many feminists use the concept of patriarchy (see Chapter 7) to see the ways in which violence can serve to keep women subjugated.

The Hall of Names at the Holocaust Memorial encourages us to remember those murdered in the name of hate.

Gendered violence includes domestic violence, rape, sexual assault, homicide, stalking, female genital mutilation, forced marriage and sexual harassment. While often viewed as personal troubles, sociologists reveal their connection to public issues of social structure. Men can be victims of many of these forms of violence, usually at the hands of other men, though women can also commit some of these abuses too. Overwhelmingly, however, the pattern is gendered. In the UK, for instance, on average two women a week are killed by a current or former male partner, with these murders rarely making headline news. Between one in four and one in three women and girls are likely to be victims of domestic abuse committed by men. The majority of survivors of such abuse never inform the authorities, partly because the criminal justice system has such poor rates of conviction (which itself is seen as a form of violence by many scholars).

Hiding abuse

Evan Stark (2007) further developed this analysis with his concept of 'coercive control', noting how domestic violence often involves patterns of behaviour designed to dominate, rather than isolated incidents of physical harm.

Becoming invisible

Women's social class, age, sexuality, disability, ethnicity, gender identity and so on further impact the ways in which society responds to such violence and the access women have to justice and support. For instance, older women who experience domestic violence may be 'invisibilized' because society tends not to see their intimate relationships in quite the same way; instead, such violence is often misrecognized as elder abuse.

HATE CRIMES

Violence targeted at individuals based on their membership of a particular social group reveals how prejudice becomes enacted through harm. Canadian social scientist Barbara Perry (2001) defines hate crimes as 'violence motivated by prejudice, bias or hatred towards a particular group which has been subject to a long-term struggle for recognition and social inclusion'.

Types of hate crimes

In the UK, five types of hate crimes are legally recognized on the basis of race, religion, disability, sexual orientation and transgender identity. In 2024, in England and Wales, 14,657 hate crime defendants were prosecuted, with racial hate crime constituting by far the largest type of prosecution. Since the murder of Sophie Lancaster because she was dressed as a Goth, in 2007, there have been calls for hate crimes against the alternative community to also be recognized. Her murder was acknowledged

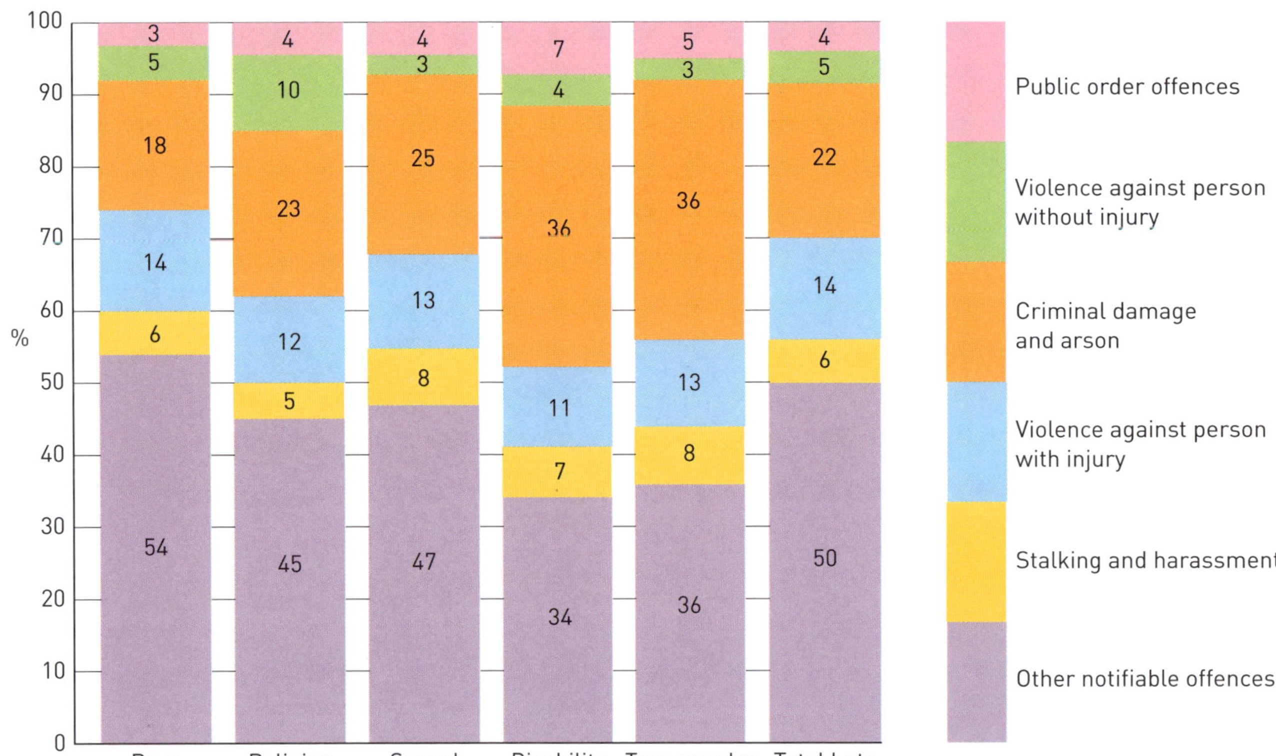

Graph to show rates and type of hate crime across different groups.

as a hate crime, as the judge deemed the motivation hateful but as yet, alternative subculture is not included in the legal definition.

Many feminists have also argued that misogyny, as expressed in male violence against women for instance, should also be a hate crime because they are targeted because of their gender. As yet, this is not legally recognized – one government argument being there are enough laws to capture these crimes. Feminists have suggested it has not been made a hate crime because the problem is so huge and would thus take up too many resources!

Is misogyny a hate crime?

Hate crimes serve multiple social functions beyond the immediate harm to individual victims, including:

- message crimes that communicate to all members of the targeted group that they are unwelcome
- reinforcement of social hierarchies and boundaries
- expressions of perceived threats to dominant group identity

Jack Levin and Jack McDevitt's (1993) typology identifies different motivations for hate crimes. These are:

- thrill-seeking (violence as entertainment)
- defensive (protecting perceived territory)
- retaliatory (avenging perceived wrongs)
- mission (ideologically driven)

Specific events can cause a rise in hate crimes. The UK's vote to leave the European Union (Brexit) in 2016 saw a rise in racist hate incidents. Similarly, the outbreak of the coronavirus pandemic caused a surge in racist incidents against people presumed to be Asian.

COLLECTIVE VIOLENCE, GENOCIDE AND WAR

Collective violence

Violence involving groups includes riots, terrorism, genocide and war. These forms raise particular sociological questions about how individuals come to participate in collective harm. These forms of violence seem prevalent and are never very far away from news headlines. Current conflicts between Ukraine and Russia, and Palestine and Israel, for instance, are both the result of long-standing social and economic geopolitical forces.

Creating harm together

Some social scientists are interested in the motivations behind individuals getting involved in collective violence. One, now largely discounted, theory that stills surfaces in popular discourse is the deindividuation theory associated with Gustave Le Bon (1895) (and later interpreted by Sigmund Freud). When we are part of a crowd, so the theory goes, conscious individuality lessens and we experience a convergence of thoughts and emotions. This in turn leads to a displacement of reason and rationality, which allows people to carry out their violent intentions as they develop.

Charles Tilly (2003) analyzed collective violence as a political process emerging from interactions between contentious claims and governmental responses. He identified mechanisms that transform ordinary social relations into violent encounters, including:

- **boundary activation** (heightening us/them distinctions)
- **brokerage** (connecting previously unconnected social sites)
- **category formation** (creating new identities that justify violence)

Genocide

A product of modernity?

Mass violence like genocide, such as in Rwanda and currently in Gaza, represents the extreme end of collective violence. Zygmunt Bauman argued in *Modernity and the Holocaust* (1989) that the Holocaust was not an aberration but a product of modernity itself, where bureaucratic rationality, technological efficiency and social engineering combined with deadly effect.

The Polish-US sociologist Jan Gross's study *Neighbours* (2001) details what happened on one day in July 1941, in Jedwabne, Poland, where 'half of the population murdered the other half – some 1,600 men, women and children'. Seemingly without much incitement from the new Nazi-occupiers, non-Jewish neighbours committed atrocities against their Jewish neighbours, people they had known well: such as playing football with the decapitated head of a girl, clubbing and gutting others, and burning many more in a barn. Awareness that the Nazis would not punish violence against Jewish people, nor disallow stealing their property – together with a long history of anti-Semitism in Poland – enabled the massacre.

Enabling genocide

While Zygmunt Bauman argued that genocide can be seen as a faceless, factory-like killing enabled by modern bureaucracy, Larry Ray (2011) argues that what is seen in events such as this is a grotesque intimacy that necessitates intimate dealings with bodies, and pleasure in knowing the suffering of victims.

War

A recipe for chaos?

Larry Ray has also suggested that a feature of modern warfare is that it has become more decentralized, chaotic and brutal, with unclear lines between militaries, paramilitaries and civilians. Ray highlights certain conditions for war and extreme violence, which are interrelated:

- **Politicization of war**: through mass mobilization, distinction between combatants and civilians disappears
- **Shame dynamics**: the enemy is devalued, their culture and history misrepresented
- Regime types: socioeconomic conditions – disorganization, high inequality – lead to authoritarian rule
- **Ideologization of conflict**: conflicts are resourced, extensive modes of economic growth where NGOs are seen as 'enemies within', context of nationalism/exceptionalism
- **Regime of gender heteronormativity**: masculinization, patriarchy (in Russia, for example same-sex relationships have been made illegal and domestic violence decriminalized. In Israel, same-sex couples cannot get married within a religious institution or have civil marriages.)

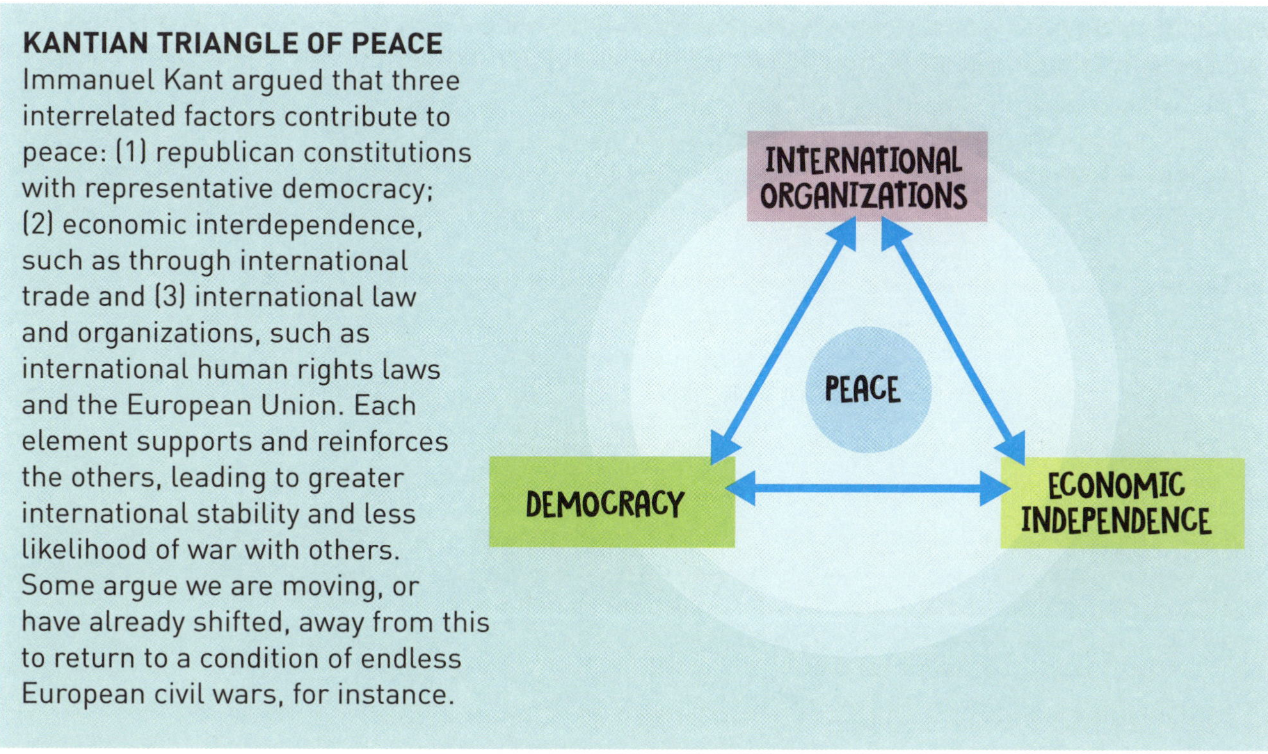

KANTIAN TRIANGLE OF PEACE
Immanuel Kant argued that three interrelated factors contribute to peace: (1) republican constitutions with representative democracy; (2) economic interdependence, such as through international trade and (3) international law and organizations, such as international human rights laws and the European Union. Each element supports and reinforces the others, leading to greater international stability and less likelihood of war with others. Some argue we are moving, or have already shifted, away from this to return to a condition of endless European civil wars, for instance.

- ***Scapegoating***: plus passivity of bystanders

All of which leads to extreme violence and possibly genocide

Ray's analysis allows us to see various social processes at play in war, something that is institutionalized, political and organized. We can also see the links between war-making and state-building.

State-sponsored violence also often comes under this category, for instance, when states such as the UK and Australia supported the US in its invasion of Iraq and Vietnam. Both these nations, and others, are also complicit in the conflict in Gaza.

STATE VIOLENCE

State-constructed violence

We might commonly think of the state as having a responsibility to protect its citizens. However, there are many examples of states acting violently against their populations; at times, in illegal ways, such as through torture. States also have the power to construct their violence as necessary, proportionate and appropriate. The state thus maintains a monopoly on legitimate violence within its territory, according to Max Weber's classic definition. This includes police forces, imprisonment and military action, making the state both a perpetrator of violence and the primary institution tasked with controlling it. The language, or euphemisms associated with such violence, also serve to hide it – police violence might be termed 'law enforcement' for instance.

The US sociologist Charles Tilly (1929–2008) famously said 'we made the state, and the state made war'; likewise, history, according to Michel Foucault (1977), is the history of violence. Every constitution is infused with past upheavals such as civil wars. Indeed, the various privileges we may (or may not enjoy) are the result of successful violence (such as women's and working-class men's right to vote). Rather than disappearing, violence became internalized through institutions that train obedient bodies and self-regulating subjects. Foucault's analysis of disciplinary power traces the historical shift from spectacular public punishments to more diffuse forms of surveillance and control.

Internalizing violence

At times of social unrest and (often peaceful) political protest, states will still take recourse to violent suppression. In the UK alone, there have been many such examples, from the Peterloo Massacre of 1819; the treatment of suffragettes campaigning for votes for women; the policing of the 1926 General Strike; the policing – by the now-disbanded Metropolitan Police's Special Patrol Group – of

Peterloo 1819. A peaceful protest about democratic rights ended with 18 people dead and many more injured by the cavalry at St Peter's Field, Manchester.

anti-fascist protests in 1974 and 1979 (which resulted in the deaths, respectively, of Kevin Gately and Blair Peach); or the anti-poll tax demonstrations of 1990. During the miners' strike of 1984–1985, miners in Yorkshire, Derbyshire and Nottinghamshire – among other counties – went on strike in protest at Margaret Thatcher's closure of coal mines. While reporting was suppressed or manipulated by the government at the time, documents later released reveal the ways in which the state intentionally used agents provocateurs to stir up violent conflict between strikers and the police. In addition, mounted police used batons against unarmed protestors who were on foot. The policing was so heavy-handed, especially by those from the South Yorkshire force, that officers drafted in from nearby counties such as Norfolk and Cambridgeshire were shocked at what they saw. More recently in the UK, anti-protest powers mean police are encouraged to treat peaceful protest as a threat rather than a right. According to groups such as Amnesty International, this violent authoritarian approach is a growing trend across the globe.

State responses to protest can be understood as violent, depending on context, such as the police response to Poll Tax protests in the UK in 1990.

Contemporary sociological analyses of policing highlight the uneven distribution of state violence across populations. Victor Ríos (2011) documented how young Black and Latino US men experience hypercriminalization, facing constant surveillance and policing that frames their adolescent behaviours as criminal. This creates a ***youth control complex*** that perpetuates marginalization.

RESISTANCE, REBELLION AND REVOLUTION: POLITICAL PROTEST

> *Those who make peaceful revolution impossible will make violent revolution inevitable*
>
> (John F. Kennedy)

Violence and social change

In the context of political struggle, there are some interesting questions sociologists ask, such as: what place violence holds in the quest for social change; what constitutes violence in such situations; are there examples of 'successful' violent protests; and who gets to define whether protests are violent. US sociologist William Gamson in *The Strategy of Social Protest* (1975) argues that violent tactics can be useful to social movements. In part, this is because they attract attention to the movement and to its goals.

Although revolutions tend to occur after decades of 'slow violence', people more often associate revolutions – rather than the preceding social conditions – with violence: in particular, with 'quick violence'. Historically, though, it has tended to be counter-revolutions that inflict by far the greater

TICK-BOX TACTICS

Legal scholar Lars Mosesson (1983) produced a list whereby we can trace whether a group's recourse to violence is justified and appropriate. If they have done everything on the list and not been heard, then violence might be seen as legitimate:

- Lawful public criticism of the law or policy, followed by submission to the processes of the law
- Taking test cases to the courts to have the legality or 'constitutionality' of the law or action determined
- Non-resistance or conscientious evasion
- Non-co-operation – involving a deliberate withdrawal from the state, renouncing benefits and burdens of membership
- Conscientious refusal
- Civil disobedience
- Violent resistance and protest
- Rebellion and revolution

violence. This is especially true if the changes resulting from a revolution are not far-reaching: in 1793, the French revolutionary Saint-Just observed that 'Those who only make half a revolution, dig their own graves.'

Given the extent to which states can be seen as violent, some protest groups have argued violence is the only language they understand. This was something that emerged in the research conducted by Karl von Holdt (2011) talking to protestors in South Africa. George Jackson, a member of the Black Panthers (see Chapter 6) argued that for social movements, non-violent action will fall on deaf ears in a context where authorities are not just and compassionate. Others have argued that violence is perhaps to be expected if groups are repeatedly ignored. Martin Luther King, Jr., for instance, though not espousing violence, said 'a riot is the language of the unheard'.

Making protest hostile

In the context of social unrest, states also have the power to change what actions are considered violent, in order to attempt to prevent public protest. Thus, what many might consider peaceful protest is read by public officials as a hostile and violent act.

VIOLENT SOCIETIES?

> *The practice of violence, like all action, changes the world, but the most probable change is a more violent world*
>
> Hannah Arendt

Rationalizing violence

Every chapter in this book could have had a subsection on violence – indeed, several do – and we have only considered a fraction of the different types of violence that exist in the world. This doesn't mean we are necessarily becoming more violent, though the ways in which violence is commissioned may change. We have also seen that seemingly distinct types of violence can have many commonalities. Perpetrators of violence often rationalize their actions and see them as justified: ideologies of hate – such as racism, homophobia and sexism – are frequently drawn on, for example. Victims, in other words, are frequently blamed. Power relates to violence in terms of who gets to define what is violent, who is able to act violently with impunity, and the consequences of violent acts. As the Australian social historian Inga Clendinnen (2005) said, 'every society is adept at looking past its own forms of violence, and reserving its outrage for the violence of others'. We can also see that sometimes violence begets violence, or as Macbeth said, 'blood will have blood'. For instance, war, an already violent act, uses other forms of aggression (such as rape and sexual assault), as part of the battery of weapons (some studies also suggest that the military has a higher degree of domestic violence). Others argue that the more a state justifies violence, such as war or capital punishment, the more forms of perhaps illegitimate violence (such as murder) proliferate within. However, given that many argue that the systems and institutions that impact on our lives are inherently violent, the fact that many of us are *not* violent shows that violence is not an inevitable act of nature, rather it is a choice. Randall Collins (2008) argued that violence is difficult, and humans are in fact 'hardwired for solidarity'.

Clashes between football fans and police turned violent during at match between PAOK and Olympiacos played at Toumba stadium in Thessaloniki in 2016.

Violence is a central concern for sociological analysis, and is likely to remain so in the future, as it reveals much about the complex interplay between individual agency, cultural norms and social structures. The study of violence demonstrates sociology's capacity to connect personal troubles to public issues, showing how seemingly individual acts of harm are embedded within broader social patterns. By examining violence through multiple theoretical lenses, and at different levels of analysis, sociology offers insights that can inform more effective responses to preventing harm and promoting social well-being.

As societies continue to debate what constitutes violence and who experiences it, sociological research can provide essential tools for understanding these fundamental aspects of social life. Whether examining interpersonal aggression, collective conflict or the subtle violence embedded in everyday structures, sociological perspectives reveal the deeply social nature of harm and the possibility of creating less violent futures.

Chapter Twelve
THE ENVIRONMENT

What crisis? – The social construction of nature – Social causes of crises – Consequences are unevenly distributed – So why aren't we doing anything? –The social construction of problems – Hope for change?

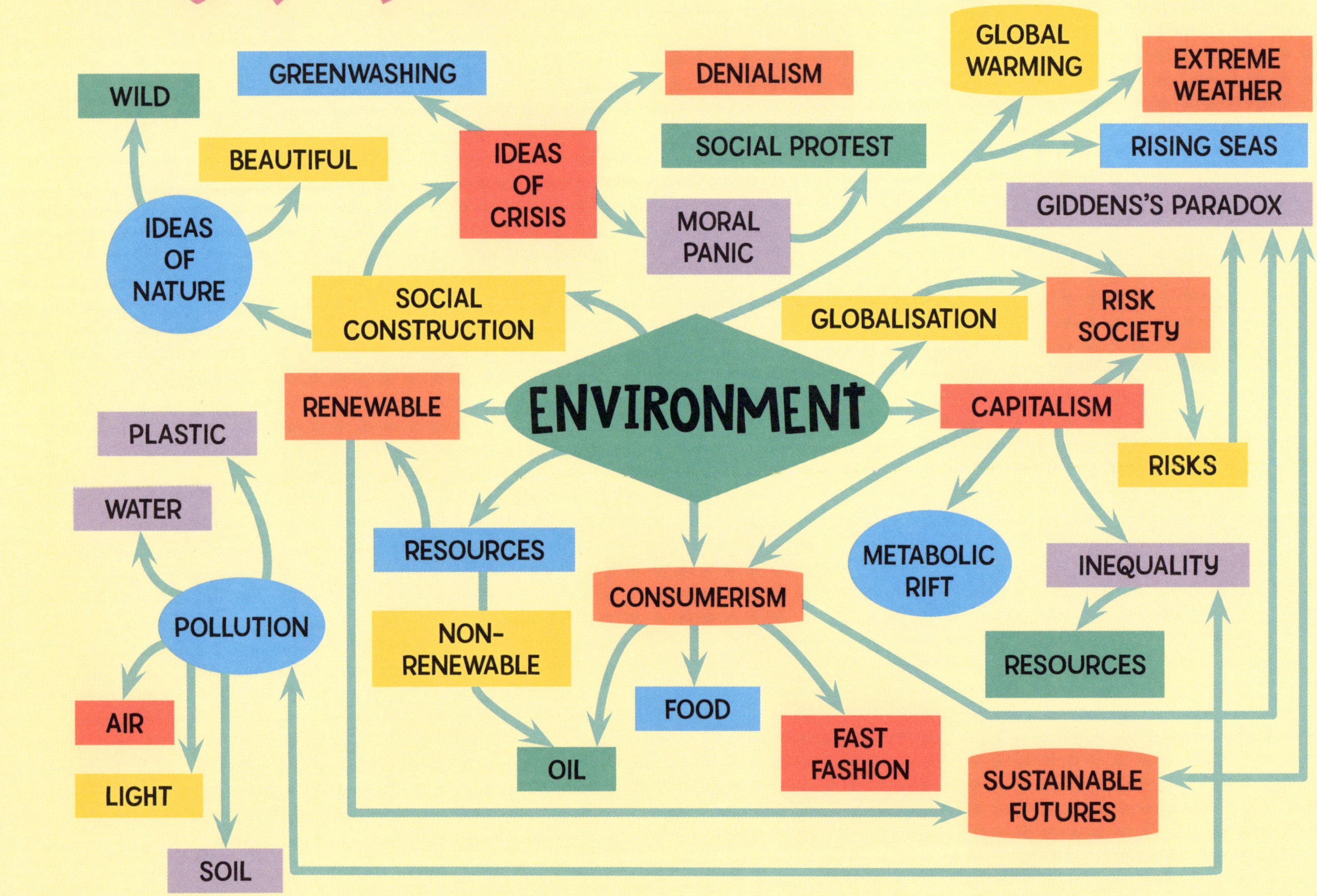

As you have probably guessed already, sociology as a discipline can't help but focus on suffering and so far, we have considered quite a few examples of 'man's inhumanity to man'. In this chapter we are going to extend that focus to look at our treatment of the earth we live on. The relationship between human societies and the natural (and built) environment has become one of the most pressing issues of our time. But is sociology appropriate to study this, you might ask? Surely sociology is about social relations and if anything, living in the late 19th, 20th and 21st century has been about how we are 'over nature' – 'man has conquered nature' – we can live comfortably in deserts (many of which, ironically, have been caused by human action in the past), we've created hybrid foods to cope with climate demands and so on.

Human action has deep and wide consequences, not just for other humans but for the environment we live and share with other species.

A closer look shows us this is anything but the case. While environmental challenges might appear to be purely scientific or technical matters, they are fundamentally social in nature. Martin Albrow (1996) has argued that the social sciences and the natural sciences have much more in common than traditional academic divisions would have us think. The US sociologist Dudley Duncan (1921–2004) had a schema he called POET (people, organizations, environment, technology), arguing that they were constantly interacting in complex ways, showing clearly that sociology has a role to play in understanding the environment and the mess we have sometimes made of it, and in providing solutions. This chapter posits the natural environment as a social issue and explores how sociological perspectives help us understand environmental issues, human-environment interactions and the social dimensions of things such as the current climate crisis, pollution, biodiversity loss and pandemics. It's not all doom and gloom though – we will also look at the ways sociology, as Duncan argues, can help reveal routes to social change for the better.

WHAT CRISIS?

Before going any further it might be useful to establish that there is a problem. It's not an easy read but bear in mind that many experts are hopeful we can avoid catastrophe if we take action – recognizing the extent of the problem is the first part of that.

There is not enough space to consider all the environmental concerns that we face. In fact, there are so many interconnected issues that words like permacrisis and polycrisis are becoming more familiar. Significant ones include the climate crisis; the ***ecological crisis***; threats from pandemics; and the increasing number of conflicts (often over depleted natural resources) that could lead to nuclear war. These are exacerbated by the rising social inequalities we have seen in previous chapters, and conditions such as the deterioration of public health and welfare provision.

Permacrisis and polycrisis

The planet is heating (driven largely by the burning of fossil fuels). The year 2024 was the hottest on record and 2025 looks set to be another very hot one. Greenhouse gases are also rising – carbon dioxide (CO_2), methane and nitrous oxide – trapping the sun's heat. As a result, the ice caps are melting and seas are rising. All of this impacts on weather systems (as well as the life of marine and land creatures) and creates extra competition for land. Extreme weather events, not just in the Global South but also the Global North, are becoming the new norm: 2019 saw the catastrophic Black Summer bushfires in Australia; in 2022 in East Africa, millions of people faced starvation because of severe drought, and in the same year devastating floods hit Pakistan. In 2023, Storm Babet, a tropical cyclone, devastated Northern Europe and that same year the Cerberus heatwave killed many. Southern California experienced disastrous wildfires in early 2025. Biodiversity loss as result of human consumption, population growth and so forth means that populations of mammals, fish, birds, reptiles and amphibians have experienced a decline of an average of 68 per cent between 1970 and 2016. Many species have gone extinct; many more are threatened by it. Plastic pollution is a significant problem – about 14 million tonnes of plastic end up in our oceans every year. This is entering the food chain and microplastics are now found all over the globe and in organs of fish, birds and mammals. Deforestation to accommodate our appetites for things like beef mean that every hour a space roughly the size of 300 football pitches is cleared. Intensive animal agriculture more generally is a significant contributor to greenhouse gases, water shortage and pollution and soil degradation.

Ecological destruction

Global institutions such as the United Nations (UN), and leading scientists, are in agreement that all this is caused by human action. It is a clear example of a truly global issue – every country on the globe will, to a greater or lesser degree, be affected by climate change. In 2024 the UN's climate chief predicted we have two years left in which to prevent catastrophic problems and avoid social and economic collapse.

OK, all that is pretty depressing, however, sociology is fundamentally about social change and social justice; in theory it can offer some explanations, answers and, potentially, some hope, so we will now look to how sociology has approached this problem.

THE SOCIAL CONSTRUCTION OF NATURE

Sociologists and nature

Sociology has perhaps been slow to consider the relationship between humans and their natural environment. Some have argued this is, in part, because those early key theorists – Karl Marx, Max Weber and Émile Durkheim (Liz Stanley's 'good ol' boys' from Chapter 2) – did not spend a great deal of time doing this. While this is possibly a fair justification in relation to Weber and Durkheim, it is perhaps a little less so in the case of Marx. They all had something to say about humans' relationship with the environment but what we think of as environmental problems, like climate change, were not the pressing issue they are today (which is not to say they didn't exist). Durkheim, in his enthusiasm to establish sociology as a well-regarded subject, was keen to distinguish it from other subjects such as science and so for him, sociology was firmly about 'social facts', not about things that might be considered 'natural' or 'environmental'. Thus began a long history of seeing these disciplines as outside of sociology's concern, a myopic approach that US sociologists William Catton and Riley Dunlap have described as anthropocentric (meaning humans are placed as the most important consideration). It was not until the late 20th century that sociology turned its attention in this direction. Gradually, academics acknowledged the impact that the natural world had on human society and vice versa, focusing initially on things like resource scarcity and its consequences, such as conflict over oil shortages.

Not our problem?

Thus, even with a short history of sociology as a case study, we can see that the way we understand and relate to 'nature' is deeply influenced by social and cultural factors. Daniel Defoe, the author of *Robinson Crusoe* (William Taylor, 1719), saw the Lake District as one of the 'wildest, most barren and frightful' regions. Yet, just a few years later, narratives and cultural responses to that area had shifted and the Romantic poets, such as William Wordsworth, thought it beautiful and inspiring. Environmental sociologists argue that our conception of nature as something separate from human society is itself a social construction. William Cronon's (1995) influential work 'The Trouble with Wilderness' demonstrates how the American idea of wilderness as anuntouched refuge emerged from specific historical and cultural contexts, a fantasy of those who have never had to work on the land and one that ignores the early history of the Indigenous Americans who were decimated, with those remaining forced on to reservations.

Environmental sociology

The Romantics, such as artist Caspar David Friedrich, in works like Wanderer above the Sea of Fog *(1818) changed our relationship to the natural world.*

DON'T PUT THE GOOD OL' BOYS OUT TO PASTURE

Metabolic rift

With respect to Marx, he saw capitalism's insatiable drive for profits as a source of exploitation not just for workers but also nature. He identified what he termed a 'metabolic rift' between cities and the countryside and between people and the rest of the natural world. Through this process, rural areas were stripped of their natural resources, which were fed into factories, producing wealth for the owners but also, as he highlighted, producing pollution for communities of people living in these urban areas. People in these urban areas also become estranged from nature, which he sees as damaging. His conceptualization of metabolic rift was influenced by a German soil scientist, Justus von Liebig (1859), who charted the degradation of the soil as a result of industrialization. By the 1860s, Marx had become interested in the 'greenhouse effect', as identified by US scientist Eunice Foote and a bit later, the Irish physicist John Tyndall. Marx's sometime writing companion Friedrich Engels had also written about capitalism's increasingly harmful impact on the environment, warning about the potential consequences of seeming 'victories over nature'. He stated 'for each such victory nature takes its revenge on us'. Max Weber, another prolific writer, produced bodies of work on China, India and the Middle East, as well as, a bit closer to home, considering capitalism and the protestant work ethic. He did include considerations of the environment, particularly in his writings on the Middle East. For example, he analyzed the ways in which events like drought promote social change. Despite Durkheim's insistence on 'social facts', his work has influence today. His *Division of Labour in Modern Society* (Félix Alcan, 1893) considers the role of population growth on social change – something that is prominent in environmental sociology today.

The 'greenhouse effect'

The impact of population growth

Marx's Metabolic Rift leads to increasing feelings of alienation.

TOWARDS A SOCIOLOGY OF THE ENVIRONMENT

What we recognize now as a sociological study of the environment emerged in the 1970s. Much of it drew on existing subfields of sociology such as feminism (in the form of ecofeminism) and the study of social movements. Important texts such as Rachel Carson's *Silent Spring* (1962), which showed the dangers of pesticides, and events such as the oil crisis in the early 1970s, saw a gradual 'greening' of existing sociological approaches and the development of new ones. Some early considerations mobilized around population growth and its related issues; US researcher Paul Ehrlich's seminal text *The Population Bomb* (1968) was a significant influence on sociological research at the time. Others began to focus on pollution and water shortages. Part of this involved a (slight) move away from what might be considered a human exceptionalism paradigm (HEP) towards what Catton and Dunlap call a new ecological paradigm (NEP).

Ecofeminism

A new ecological paragdigm

HUMAN EXCEPTIONALISM ▶ ***the idea that humans are both fundamentally different to other animals and also superior. This includes a belief in our innate right to 'plunder' the earth's natural resources for our own benefit. See Chapter 13 for more on this.***

What the Dickens?

One sociologist to challenge the idea that human societies and the natural environment were separate was British sociologist Peter Dickens (1992). He argued that we are connected in a range of complex and profound ways – not least in that humans are 'natural'. He also charts the ways in which much of what we consider nature is organized, controlled, managed, 'tamed' by humans – for instance the selective breeding of modern farm animals, forestry, land clearance and so on. In turn, this affects humans. He wrote about the reasons why bovine spongiform encephalopathy (BSE), or 'mad cow disease' as it was known colloquially, was a result of industrialized farming practices, which could spread to humans in the form of Creutzfeldt-Jakob disease. Since Dickens wrote that piece, we have had many other examples of human–animal diseases that are a result of both our farming practices, encroachment into wild zones, and loss of biodiversity, including Covid-19 and bird flu – examples of Engels's 'nature's revenge' perhaps (all part of the Sixth Mass Extinction that many scientists argue we are witnessing and is set to be the most devastating since the asteroid that wiped out the dinosaurs, unless we act now).

The management of nature

In 1990, John Selwyn Gummer, then UK Conservative minister of agriculture, tried to get his daughter to eat a burger to persuade the public that beef was safe following the 'mad cow disease' scare. She refused!

SOCIAL CAUSES OF CRISES

The treadmill of production

One of the key ways sociology can contribute to understanding (and solving) the climate crisis is to identify the ways in which certain human systems have led us to the state we're in, leading many to call this moment the Anthropocene (meaning human influence is driving climate change). Allan Schnaiberg's (1980) ***treadmill of production*** theory, for instance, explains how capitalist economies create a self-reinforcing cycle of resource extraction and environmental degradation – economic growth (which we are told is a good thing) inherently requires increasing resource use and waste production. Gidden's (1994) has even claimed that nature is now so thoroughly socialized we cannot assume anything is 'natural', so much have humans impacted on the natural world. As we have seen in this and previous chapters, capitalism and globalization have both been posited as drivers of this. Some argue this period would be better called the 'Capitalocene', to reflect capitalism's impact. John Urry (2010) argues capitalism is undermining itself through overexploitation of the natural resources it needs. Ulrich Beck's 'risk society' has been a useful way to consider this for many academics, where human actions have caused new levels, and types, of risk (see Chapter 10). Some trace the origins of the problem even further back. Tao Leigh Goffe (2025), a US academic, argues that the root of the problems lies in the colonization of the Americas. She argues that European colonialism created a 'dark laboratory of colonial desires and experiments'. The mass enslavement and displacement of people, racist 'science', the development of monoculture and exploitation of natural resources, among many other practices, were the foundation of capitalism and globalization, she argues.

Is over-exploitation undermining capitalism?

CONSUMERISM, CAPITALISM AND THE ENVIRONMENT

Buy new, buy more, buy now!

Many sociologists have argued that consumer culture has become a significant feature of everyday living, involved in things like identity formation. It is also crucial to the success of capitalism – it relies on lots of people buying lots of things. Alfred Sloan (1875–1966), chairman of General Motors, developed a number of approaches that became incorporated into manufacturing and ensured the continued 'success' of capitalism. Among these is the concept of deliberate or planned obsolescence – the idea that things are built to fail in the future. For instance, early light bulbs seemed to last a long time – the fabled Centennial Light in a Californian fire station has burned since 1901. Modern light bulbs last a fraction of the time. He also popularized the idea of a product regularly changing and 'upgrading' so that consumers will feel they need to buy the latest, and assumed-best, version. The numerous iterations of the Apple iPhone is an example of this.

Planned obsolescence

Many products are built to fail in order to encourage us to buy more of them.

Eat up!

Food fuels us but it also fuels social injustice and the climate crisis in a range of ways. For instance, 70 per cent of the food eaten globally is produced in Africa and Asia, often by smallholders and subsistence farmers whose ability to farm (and live) is impacted by climate change. The meat and dairy industries are responsible for more greenhouse gas (GHG) emissions than all forms of transport combined, and the Global North has a taste for meat. In 2023, the average American ate 149 kg (327.8 lb) of meat (equal highest position with Portugal). Much of our convenience food is based around meat – in the UK we have McDonalds, Burger King, Nando's, Wendy's, Subway,

Fuelling the greenhouse

Countries in the global North are the main drivers of meat production.

Average meat consumption (kg) in 2020	
United States	124.11
Australia	121.61
Argentina	109.39
New Zealand	100.90
Spain	100.26
United Kingdom	79.90
Sri Lanka	9.04
Sierra Leone	8.23
Nigeria	7.15
India	6.08
Ethiopia	5.40
Bangladesh	4.04

Source: Food and Agriculture Organization of the United Nations (FAO)

Greggs (many are US companies with a global reach), all of which are mainly known for their meat-based dishes. This is not 'normal' and historically is very new. Global average meat consumption is only 34.1 kg (75.2 lb) per year, which means some countries are eating very little meat. Some of this difference is because of affordability and accessibility but a lot of it is to do with cultural differences in taste.

Despite a rise in plant-based eating, globally, consumption of meat is on the rise. What has this got to do with the environment? You might have read a lot about the problem of food waste; arguably, a big part of this is feeding human-edible grain to industrially reared farm animals, because meat consumption is inefficient – for every 100 g (4oz) of protein fed to animals, humans get just 10 g (0.4 oz) from pork and only 5 g (0.2 oz) from beef. Farming animals also takes up a lot of land, necessitating deforestation, loss of biodiversity and high water usage (hello, pandemics!). In addition, all those animals produce a lot of waste; in the UK, industrialized farm animals produce more than 50,000 tonnes per day (over 100 double-decker buses' worth per hour), much of which ends up in our waterways.

The impact of our social milieu

Sociology teaches us that we can adapt. Pierre Bourdieu and Norbert Elias have argued that food is about cultural tastes and norms. Our social milieu has a big impact on what we view as 'normal', thus as people read more about and meet (pardon the pun) people who have transitioned to plant-based eating, it can provide a social tipping point. Tipping points are where there is a critical mass for behaviours (or ideas) to spread widely. Some recent examples are the ways in which sustainable lifestyle choices such as recycling (though you might want to read Samantha McBride's (2012) work on recycling, which argues it's not as 'sustainable' as we might like to think) and composting have become the 'new normal' fairly quickly in many countries.

FAST FASHION

Overproduction and overconsumption

We have looked briefly elsewhere about globalization's tendency to outsource (with examples of Coca-Cola in Mexico and garment factories in Bangladesh). Fast fashion is characterized by overproduction and overconsumption – the ideals of capitalism. As a business model that emerged in the 2000s with popular examples such as H&M, Zara, Boohoo and Shein, fast-fashion companies are able to produce trending styles quickly and cheaply. As a consequence, people are being encouraged to buy more items and it appears that increasingly, these items are being worn far fewer times before they are discarded – textile waste is becoming a big problem (again, much of it is outsourced to poorer countries such as Ghana where it might end up in landfill, or Chile's Atacama Desert, now home to a huge waste mountain). Making clothes, like making bottles or tins, uses a lot of resources (according to the European Parliament, making one T-shirt uses the same amount of water someone needs for two-and-a-half years). Many of the cheap materials are made from carbon-based resources and the process of making the item also contributes to a significant amount of pollution. It is one of the largest polluters globally: the oil industry has top spot, then intensive animal agriculture with fast fashion close behind (some reverse the order of these two).

A mountain of waste

Discarded clothing from the Global North often ends up in huge waste mountains in the Global South.

CONSEQUENCES ARE UNEVENLY DISTRIBUTED

We are seeing a pattern here – the greed and consumption of the Global North is driving detrimental impact on the globe, especially in the Global South. Various scholars and social movements, such as those for environmental justice, have pointed to the ways in which these issues have damaging effects on specific populations, particularly those on the margins of society, women and children, the poor and the Global South more generally. With regard to air pollution, low-income areas tend to be located near large roadways, leading to a variety of diseases and deaths. Robert Bullard's (1990) term, environmental racism, demonstrated how toxic facilities are disproportionately located in Black communities.

Is racism a factor?

When Hurricane Katrina hit the south-east of the US, it caused the deaths of over 1,800 people due to the hurricane and subsequent flooding. Social inequalities shaped both the vulnerability to and recovery from this environmental disaster. Research showed that ethnicity and class significantly influenced who was most affected and who could rebuild. Black communities, which tend also to be poorer, had less funding to repair levees (embankments to protect against flooding); there was also a notable slower relief response and evacuation from these areas. In addition, African American households received

Gideon Mendel at work making a portraits of flood victim Moo Baan Prapin in Bangkok. These photographs are part of his global Drowning World project.

Flood victims of Hurricane Katrina which struck New Orleans in August 2005, return to their devastated home.

an average of $8,000 less than white households in government aid, meaning they had to stay in unsafe housing for longer.

SO WHY AREN'T WE DOING ANYTHING?

GIDDENS' PARADOX

We saw in Chapter 10 that Ulrich Beck's concept of 'risk society' (1992) argues that modern societies are increasingly preoccupied with managing environmental and technological risks that they themselves have created. Climate change exemplifies this dynamic, where industrialization has created global risks that transcend national boundaries. Many theorists are interested in why, given all we know about what is currently happening across the globe and is predicted to happen, people and their governments seem reluctant to act in order to mitigatc against this. Anthony Giddens argues that anthropogenic (caused by humans) climate change is one of the most pressing dangers to have ever faced human societies. In 2009, he claimed that one factor involved in people not acting was that many of the impacts of human-induced climate change were not always obvious (though this didn't apply to many in the Global South). Certainly, the slow decline of insect numbers and diversity or soil degradation in the UK is an example of not immediately apparent change.

Waiting until these dangers are acute and impossible to ignore before acting, is too late. This is Giddens' Paradox. One explanation he presents is future discounting; when present rewards are balanced against future risks in such calculations, the present tends to win. A small reward now, rather than an even bigger reward later, often has the stronger pull. It is a concept with roots in psychology, where children's willpower has been tested with rewards of cookies or candies. Giddens also uses this to explain why people might choose to smoke (or vape), knowing the future health risks are potentially high. However, since Giddens was writing, extreme weather events – floods, storms, fires – have become much more common, and apparent, in the Global North too.

Imagine you're really hungry now... Which would you rather, one biscuit now or two if you wait five minutes?

THE AGE OF STUPID? DENIALISM

Another powerful framework to explain ongoing inaction, scepticism or outright denial in the face of the facts is Stan Cohen's (2001) work around denialism. Cohen was attempting to explain how and why people, institutions and states turn a blind eye to atrocities. He focuses on events such as the Holocaust, genocides, massacres and organized torture. Cohen identifies three forms of denial: (1) literal denial (denying facts); (2) interpretive denial (accepting facts but reinterpreting them) and (3) implicatory denial (accepting facts but minimizing implications for action). While he doesn't explicitly refer to climate change, his ideas can be usefully applied to thinking about this.

Literal denial

This involves rejecting the factual basis of climate change; it manifests as:

- questioning the scientific consensus on anthropogenic climate change
- claiming climate data is manipulated or exaggerated
- attributing climate change to natural cycles rather than human activity

For example, climate sceptics cite isolated cold weather events as evidence against global warming, despite the distinction between weather and climate.

This graph contrasts the 97 per cent plus scientific consensus with public perception of that consensus, illustrating the effectiveness of denial campaigns.

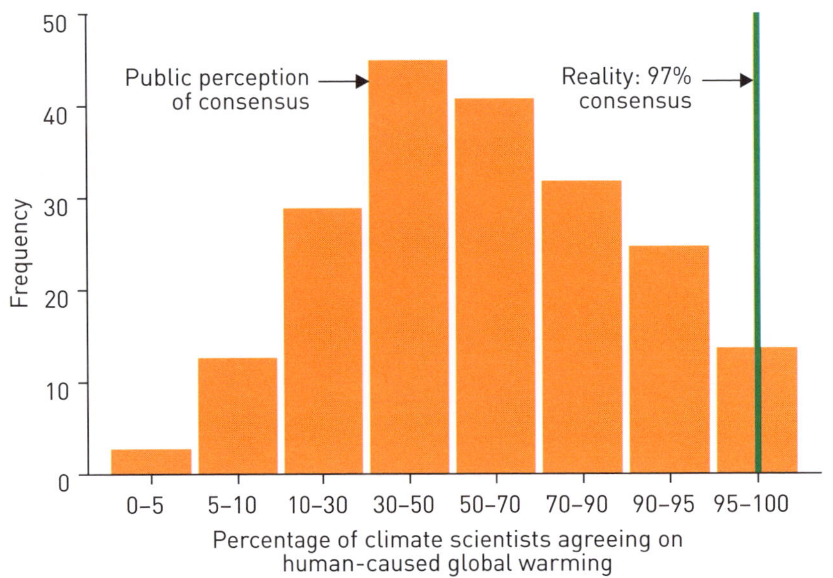

Interpretive denial

With this form of denial, people accept climate change facts but reframe them to minimize their significance by:

- admitting climate change exists but denying human causation
- accepting climate science but questioning predictive models
- reframing environmental damage as 'progress' or 'development'

When fossil fuel companies acknowledge climate change but emphasize uncertainty in climate projections to delay action, we see interpretive denial in action.

Implicatory denial

Perhaps most relevant to climate inaction, implicatory denial involves accepting the facts but denying their moral, psychological or political implications. Common arguments include:

Why not address climate change?

- 'It's too expensive to address climate change.'
- 'Other countries aren't doing their part, so why should we?'
- 'Future technology will solve the problem.'
- 'Individual actions don't matter.'

An example might be when governments set distant climate targets without implementing immediate policy changes, thus they are acknowledging the problem while managing to avoid immediate responsibility.

CULTURAL COGNITION, JUSTIFICATIONS AND PSYCHOLOGICAL DISTANCE

We can extend Cohen's framework and look at a few other theories that consider this issue. US critic Dan Kahan (2011) uses the concept of cultural cognition in relation to risk, suggesting that people process information in ways that protect their cultural identities. Climate attitudes often align with political ideologies, creating 'cultural cognition' where facts become tribal markers. For instance, conservative individuals may resist climate action not because they reject science but because accepting it might alienate them from their social group. 'System Justification Theory', associated with another US scholar, the social psychologist John Jost, argues that people have a psychological need to defend and justify existing systems, even when disadvantageous. Climate change threatens fundamental aspects of modern capitalism and consumption patterns. When people resist changing their consumption habits despite knowing their environmental impact, and they justify their current lifestyle choices as necessary or deserved, we see this theory in action. The notion of psychological distance (construal level theory) is also potentially useful for thinking about attitudes to climate change. The argument here is that climate change is often perceived as psychologically distant – temporally (in the future), geographically (affecting distant places), socially (affecting unknown people), and conceptually (difficult to grasp). This could be seen in the view that climate change is primarily a problem for island nations or future generations, reducing urgency for present action.

Edward Burtynsky's Oil Fields *photo series shows the vastness of the oil infrastructure.*

Psychological distance

THE CIVILIZING PROCESS?

Many aspects of day-to-day life for the affluent, particularly in the Global North – regular showering, using central heating and energy-heavy machines such as washing machines and dishwashers, leaving lights on in rooms we're not using – have become normalized. We don't often relate these practices to the ongoing crisis. They are part of what Nobert Elias (1939) termed the 'civilizing process', in part a symptom of the increased individualization and norms of cleanliness and comfort of modern living, and also behaviours encouraged in neoliberal consumer capitalism. He argues that humans

MIND THE GAP

In September 2023, the tree in Sycamore Gap on Hadrian's Wall, Northumberland, UK was illegally felled. There followed intense media coverage, which showed people crying or visibly angry that such an act of vandalism could take place. There was national, and international, shock and outrage. That same year, roughly 5,153 sq. km (1,989.6 sq. miles) of the Amazon rainforest was cleared to make way for cattle farming. Arguably, there was much less media attention about this loss. Why? Some scholars argue that such a contrast is explained thus: it is easier to embrace outrage about the chopping down of a single sycamore tree than it is the extensive destruction of a forest. More negatively some, such as Richard Stafford and Peter Jones (2019), might see it as a 'convenient distraction' from the bigger, more profound problem.

The sycamore tree that lay in a dip by Hadrian's Wall in Northumberland National Park.

Vast areas of Amazonian rainforest are cleared daily.

have a 'triad of controls'. These are sets of codes, or ways of thinking, humans have employed in order to allow their continued existence. These are: (1) control over non-human or 'natural events'; (2) control over each other through social processes; and (3) control of human beings over their internal selves, i.e. their impulses. When things seem overwhelming, he argues, they engage in myth-making or fantasy to make the world more manageable; often this is expressed in egocentric behaviours. The example of increased nationalism or stockpiling of goods during Covid-19 is an example of this. Again, social science offers an alternative route, enabling more 'cosmopolitan' (see Chapter 10) and co-operative visions.

UNCIVILIZED PROTEST?

There are many examples of social movements concerned with these, and other, problems. Some are global in reach and broad in scope, such as Greenpeace and Extinction Rebellion (XR). Others focus on narrower issues, such as Just Stop Oil. Many take part in acts of non-violent civil disobedience, as favoured by earlier protests such as the Black civil rights movement (these include slow walking, roadblocks and lock-ons). Our awareness of, and support for, them is very often mediated by the press and also shaped by state responses. In the UK, a series of policy changes, such as the UK Police, Crime, Sentencing and Courts Act 2022 and the Public Order Act 2023, which restrict people's right to gather in protest, demonstrate a lack of government support for peaceful protest. They also resulted in increased police powers to stop and search with and without suspicion and deal with public protest. Media responses to protests are also examples of Stan Cohen's (1972) concept of moral panics. Protestors are presented as 'scapegoats' – they become the problem, symbols of 'social breakdown', rather than a route to a possible solution. News headlines such as 'eco extremists could turn into new terror threat, police warn', 'eco fanatics' or 'Just Stop Oil threat to wreck hols' serve to position peaceful protestors as extremists who are potentially dangerous or at best pests who spoil people's fun.

CARBON FOOTPRINTS, CO-OPTION AND GREENWASHING – DISCOURSES OF DENIAL?

BP invented the term 'carbon footprint', the process whereby individuals are encouraged to be aware of their contribution to climate change. Some have argued this is an example of a discursive manoeuvre – a process that deflects attention from the much larger problem created by the fossil fuel industry. Others point to the ways corporations have enthusiastically got 'on board' with recycling because it's less of a threat to them than altering their production practices, and that they have managed to co-opt environmental groups into focusing on this approach. Greenwashing, according to the UN, is the process whereby companies mislead the public either to believe they are behaving with an environmental 'conscience', or they distract from, and delay, mitigating action.

Some argue the stockpiling of 'premium' goods such as pasta during Covid-19 was an example of a coping strategy when overwhelmed.

SUSTAINABLE LIVING

Many people are taking steps to change their consumer habits by becoming 'conscious consumers'. Sociologists such as David Evans and Philip Sutton have shown how sociology can help to understand lifestyle change and patterns of consumption, which in turn can be used to inform policy-making. We have briefly mentioned recycling and composting, but people are also taking a critical look at where their food comes from and how it produced. The awareness, for instance, of the ubiquitous palm oil and its role in the destruction of habitats for Sumatran orangutans is one example. Many actively seek products that are organic, local and Fair Trade and have not involved child labour. Shopping for second-hand clothes is becoming trendy; 'reuse' and 'upcycling' are also buzzwords. Plant-based lifestyles, and many of the previous examples, also become ways to create and maintain identity – identities that are aligned to ethics. More people are 'rewilding' their gardens and 'guerilla' planting. Others have eschewed flying. Groups and organizations enable this too. Landowners, with the aid of government funds, are replanting the hedgerows they were paid to remove. There are suppliers of 'green' electricity and gas, who use renewable sources of energy such as solar, wind and geothermal power, schemes to make solar panels and retrofitting of homes more affordable through government and local council incentives. Such individual and group action can become ***life politics*** and serve as a defence against anomie. Understanding the motivations behind these behavioural changes can be used to effect further change. We should not, however, 'offload' all the responsibility on to individuals (a common neoliberal strategy): while we all have a part to play, we should not forget that the biggest drivers of climate change are global systems such as capitalism and the oil industry.

The EU campaign 'You control climate change' poster shows how we all have a role to play but also how such campaigns can deflect attention from the 'big' polluters.

THE SOCIAL CONSTRUCTION OF PROBLEMS

Early on in this chapter, we considered the ways in which our understanding of nature itself is, in many ways, a social construction. The above example of responses to protest is an illustration of how a social constructionist approach can enable us to recognize the ways in which certain issues arise as social problems and others are ignored to perceive how society responds to certain possible solutions or viewpoints. We can see how the role of 'expert' opinion, state or governmental responses, media interpretations and economic incentives, among other things, can shape the ways in which such crises are presented. Crucially, it also helps us to look for the stories that have little platform and understand why this is so – are they a threat to dominant/hegemonic values, are they difficult to comprehend, do they challenge powerful institutions and organizations?

HOPE FOR CHANGE?

An ecological crisis materialized in the 1980s in the shape of a hole in the ozone layer. Decades of making and spraying aerosol cans had thinned the earth's ozone layer to the point where huge gaps emerged. The ozone is crucial for many things, including protecting humans and other animals from harmful UV rays (which can cause skin cancer and cataracts). The human-made compounds chlorofluorocarbons (CFCs), also used in cooling appliances such as refrigerators, were largely released in the Global North but their impact was visible over Antarctica particularly. If it had continued, experts are certain that by 2050 the holes would have appeared all over the globe and earth would have become uninhabitable. This prompted scientific investigation, and we saw governments on a global level collaborating in ways not often seen. By the early 2000s production and consumption of CFCs was minimal; the hole still exists but it is starting to slowly disappear. Though there are many risks we face, some of which we have seen and others we have not had scope to discuss, this example shows that when governments, institutions and individuals do act together, there is a chance to either slow those harms and in some cases, perhaps, improve situations.

The ozone layer that protects the Earth.

The environment is very definitely a social concern – sociology can reveal how societies produce environmental harms; who is most vulnerable to climate impacts; what solutions are considered feasible and why; and how different groups respond to climate threats. Sociology's role is crucial; the example of CFCs and the ozone hole is exactly what Dudley Duncan's POET framework shows – human action can cause a problem but through technology and coming together, it can also provide a solution. We need to do this quickly though; as the anthropologist Margaret Mead said, 'we don't have a society if we destroy the environment'.

Chapter Thirteen
HUMAN–ANIMAL RELATIONS

Animals are everywhere – Anthropocentrism to critical animal studies – Human/animal border – What's in a word – Religion – Childhood – My family and other animals: family values – It's just a pet? Companion animals and emotional capitalism – The boundary between pets and food – The industrialized animal – The rise of the vegan? – Beyond food: vegan identities – The meat paradox – What harms them, harms us

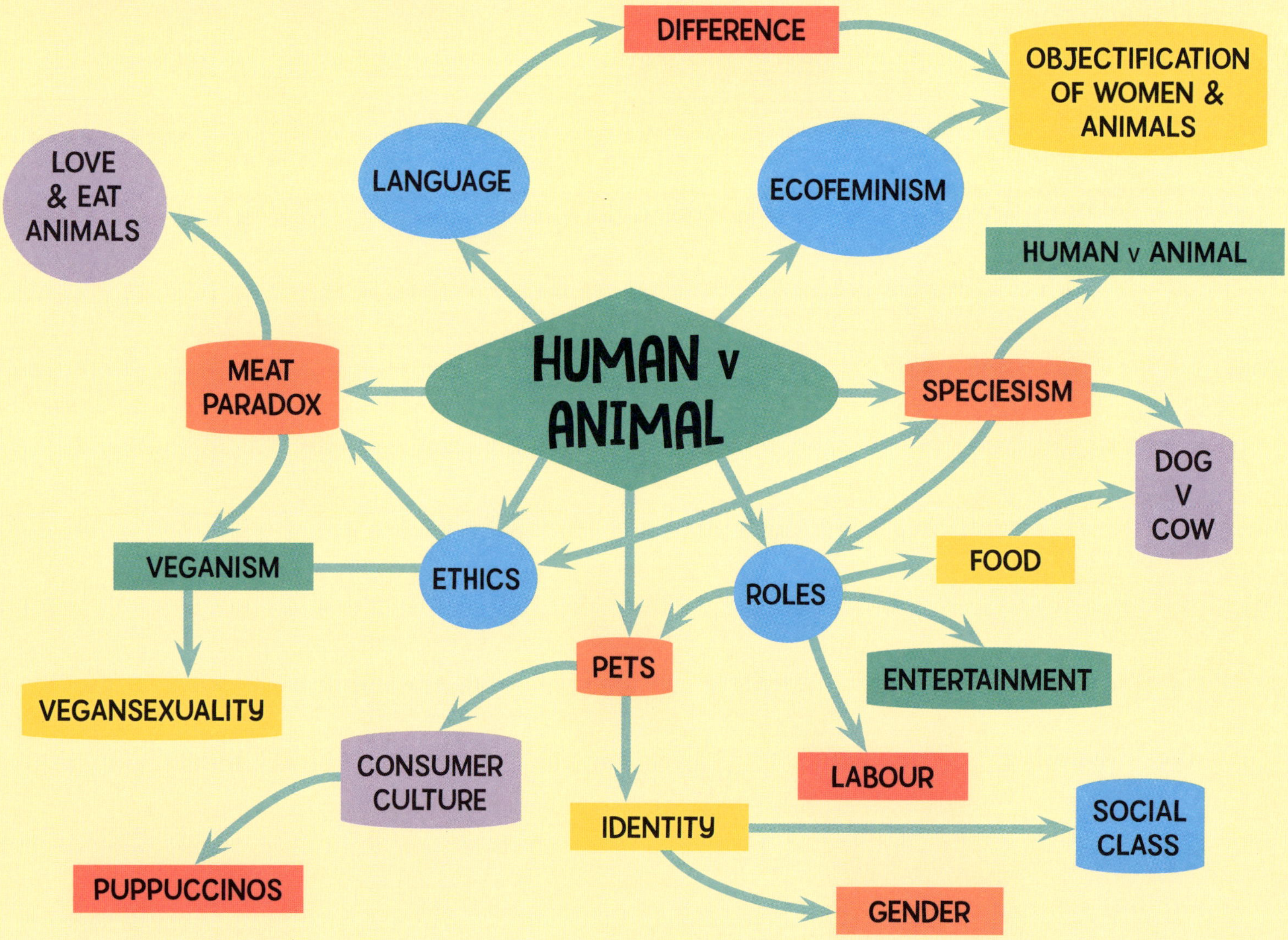

ANIMALS ARE EVERYWHERE

Historically, sociology has tended to be an anthropocentric discipline, one that concentrates on humans – their interactions with one another, the social institutions that shape our lives, and so on. For many of us, though, other animals (because, of course, humans are animals too) suffuse our lives even though we don't always notice it. In childhood, we might have had a favourite stuffed toy that was an animal – such as a teddy bear – while many of our childhood stories and nursery rhymes involve animals. Domesticated animals such as pets live with many of us, and we might also eat other domesticated, or wild, animals. We might clothe ourselves in their wool, fur or skin, or use cosmetics and medicines that have been tested on rabbits or beagles. For entertainment or leisure, we might ride a horse, place a bet on a dog or visit a safari park. Some people work with animals to help them find drugs or bombs, while others might rely on an assistance animal for visual or auditory assistance.

From the food on our plates to the companions in our homes, from wildlife conservation to animal testing, these relationships with other species are complex and often contradictory. They are not simply 'natural' or inevitable, but are socially constructed and vary greatly across time, place and culture. We tend to compartmentalize other animals – some are pets, some are food, some are pests – and perhaps we only notice other animals when those fragile boundaries are somehow breached. Our dealings with other species both reflect and reinforce social inequalities while shaping human identities and practices. By applying a sociological lens to human–animal relations, we can see how these interactions are structured by the same forces that shape other social phenomena: power, culture, economics and ideology. Thus, sociology reveals the roles they have played in human societies and the ways in which they are central to our understanding of ourselves.

Idealized and humanized animals appear in many children's stories and films.

Many of us profess to be animal lovers and argue that rationality is a key human trait – yet the way we treat other animals often doesn't meet either of those values. While this isn't a philosophy book, it might be worth considering some of the moral and ethical arguments that have influenced sociological thinking about animals. In recent years, other animals have legally been recognized as sentient beings – in large part, this is down to the work of philosophers such as Peter Singer.

MORALS AND ETHICS ▶ ***both of these refer to distinguishing between 'good' and 'bad', or 'right' and 'wrong'. Many define morals as being about an individual's internal compass as far as these are concerned, whereas ethics reflect wider group or cultural values.***

SENTIENCE ▶ ***the capacity to have feelings and experience suffering and pleasure. It denotes a degree of conscious awareness.***

Enlightenment philosophers such as René Descartes (1596–1650) and Immanuel Kant (1724–1804) were somewhat dismissive of animals, arguing that they do not require moral consideration in their own right. Descartes argued that animals were automata (mechanical and unfeeling) without souls. Some argued that animals lacked language, consciousness and the power of reflection: meaning they can't actually take part in mutual arrangements or reciprocate any moral consideration that's given to them. The issue was not about whether or not they could suffer, but that it didn't matter because they aren't rational. In short, their rights should be dependent on their likeness to 'us' (and we can see how dangerous that stance might be if extended). These were purely intellectual arguments and weren't based on any knowledge or understanding of animals. However, not all of their contemporaries agreed with them: Jeremy Bentham (1748–1832), for instance, argued that we should be concerned about their capacity to suffer, irrespective of their ability to talk or reason. He argued that while babies or disabled people can't always use language or reflect on their actions, they still have moral status. Australian philosopher Peter Singer developed this further. He argued that, as humans, we should aim to minimize suffering generally. He extends this to assert that animals are most certainly sentient and can make choices and have the capacity to suffer. If we want to farm, kill and eat them, we have to be able to answer the following three questions with a 'yes':

Capacity to suffer

Moral status

1. Have they had a good life, and one where they could satisfy their preferences?
2. Will they be replaced by other animals, who would not otherwise have been brought into the world, and will be given the chance to enjoy a good life?
3. Can they die painlessly and without suffering?

Singer ends by stating that at the moment, modern farming practices mean we cannot answer 'yes' to the above, thus we should not eat meat – the minimal suffering from converting to a vegetarian or vegan diet is far outweighed by the suffering of the animals we eat.

Philosophical questions asked about animals have shaped our attitude to them.

SPECIESISM

Many social scientists considering our relationship to other animals draw on the concept of speciesism, a form of **human exceptionalism**. The concept was coined in 1970 by a psychologist called Richard Ryder, and refers to both the assumed superiority of humans, but also to the hierarchy of other animals too, along a chain of significance. For instance, we might place pets higher up the chain than the animals we use for testing cosmetics. Within the category 'pets', dogs may well be placed above cats or rabbits depending on where you live. The less 'significant' the animal, the easier it is to cause it harm without guilt.

The chain of signification within speciesism may differ between cultures and subcultures but invariably puts humans at the top.

FROM ANTHROPOCENTRISM TO CRITICAL ANIMAL STUDIES

We tend to think of this as a *human* world, perhaps giving little thought to the other animals we share it with, and sociology can perhaps be accused of this too. Given the contribution of meat, fish and dairy farming to the climate crisis, however, and the related loss of biodiversity, and shrinkage of wild zones – with humans increasingly encroaching on these, leading to zoonotic diseases such as Covid-19 – sociology can no longer ignore animals.

We are all part of nature

Traditional sociology has been critiqued for being firmly anthropocentric, focusing almost exclusively on humans and human societies. When animals appeared in classical sociological works, they often served as mere contrasts to highlight supposedly unique human capacities for language, culture or rationality. George Herbert Mead (1863–1931), for instance, argued that animals lacked the symbolic capacity necessary for true social interaction. Karl Marx's (1844) early work, such as in the *Manuscripts*, was concerned with our relationship to nature and argued that we are part of nature; indeed, he believed that our relationship to nature was a key contingent in human emancipation. However, some have argued that his discussion of the metabolic rift that comes from industrial capitalism's working conditions (see Chapter 12) can be seen as somewhat ambiguous. Some, such as British sociologist Ted Benton (1942–), argue that his theorizing suggests capitalism reduces humans to the living and working conditions appropriate to animals, thus not only reaffirming the human/animal border discussed below, but also rendering animals inferior. Others, including UK political theorist Lawrence Wilde (2000), refute this reading of his work, arguing that Marx saw how non-human animals were debased under capitalism and that 'the creatures, too, must be free'.

Freedom for all

By the 1970s and 1980s, however, a shift began. The emerging field of environmental sociology (see Chapter 12) provided space for considering how human societies interact with the natural world, including other species. Early pioneers like Benton argued that sociology's human-centred focus was inadequate for understanding the full scope of social reality, which necessarily includes our relationships with other beings. Some of this work made links between human exceptionalism and the ecological crisis, with a particular focus on the role of capitalism in what are perceived to be exploitative relationships.

Critical animal studies

The development of critical animal studies in the late 1990s and early 2000s marked a significant turning point. Building on ***critical theory*** traditions, scholars like Mary Midgley, Carol J. Adams, David Nibert and Dinesh Wadiwel began examining how human exploitation of animals intersects with other systems of oppression like sexism, racism and capitalism.

ECOFEMINISM

An early, yet still useful, theoretical framework for understanding human–animal relations comes from ecofeminism, an approach that identifies connections between the domination of nature and animals and the oppression of women and other marginalized groups.

The term 'ecofeminism' was coined by French environmental feminist Françoise d'Eaubonne (1920–2005) in 1974, where she made connections between ecological concerns and feminist analysis. Ecofeminists argue that the same patriarchal thinking that justifies the control and exploitation of women's bodies also legitimizes the domination of nature and other animals. This builds on an earlier history of feminism and animal-rights movements having a meeting of minds. Campaigners such as Margaret Sibthorp and Edith Ward in the 19th century made clear the connections between the violent treatment of women and other animals.

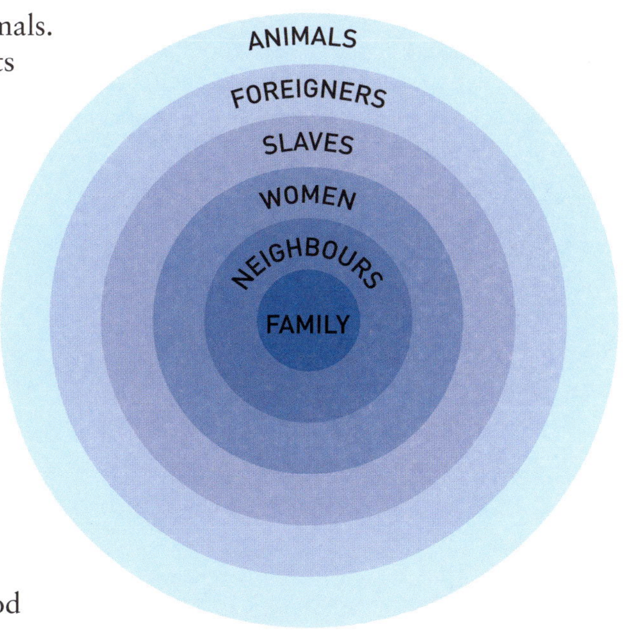

Early philosophical work by the British scholar Mary Midgley, who published her first book, *Animals and Why They Matter* (1978) when she was 59, showed the ways dominant concentric circles of 'us and them', though false, shape the ways in which people see kindness to other animals as sentimental or childish, rather than necessity. She considered many issues that have gone on to be fundamental in sociological thinking about animals – these include issues of speciesism, our relationship with pets and anthropomorphism. She also, crucially, identified connections between women and animals that influenced many ecofeminists.

One such is the US ecofeminist Carol J. Adams whose text *The Sexual Politics of Meat* (1990) revealed how the objectification of animals for food parallels the objectification of women in patriarchal culture. For instance, women's bodily parts are objectified and metaphorically dismembered – breasts, thighs, etc. – in a similar way to animals who are literally cut up into breasts, thighs and so on. Using the linguistics term absent referent, which broadly refers to a word or phrase that doesn't have a direct link to something in the real world, she shows how both animals and women are fragmented and made invisible through language and cultural practices that normalize exploitation. This happens in three ways:

According to Midgeley, false boundaries of 'us' and 'them' shape attitudes to other animals.

1. By eating meat, the animal is literally absent – it is dead.
2. The language used creates a conceptual gap – 'lamb' or 'veal' rather than talking about baby animals.
3. The ways in which animals become metaphors, they refer to something else, such as people's experiences.

Delicacy of feeling

Norbert Elias argues this process is part of the 'civilizing process' (see Chapter 4), where we distance ourselves from the violence of eating animals, by not being involved in rearing or killing animals; instead this is done in privatized spaces like slaughterhouses. In addition, this increasing 'delicacy of feeling' about animal suffering means we have meat products such as sausages and mince, which don't look like the animal they came from.

Adams goes on to show how nature, including animals, has been feminized, and vice versa (see Chapters 12, 7 and 8), with all seen as inferior/less rational and as something to be plundered by the masculine.

Adams's concept of the 'absent referent' reflects how meat packaging obscures the animal origin.

Greta Gaard (1993), a US ecofeminist, argued that hegemonic masculinity (see Chapter 7) was incompatible with environmentalism. She saw connections between heteronormativity and anthropocentrism, arguing that the same structures that enforce binary gender roles and compulsory heterosexuality also create artificial divides between humans and other animals.

Linked systems of oppression

Contemporary ecofeminist scholarship increasingly employs intersectional analysis to understand how multiple forms of oppression operate together. For example, US scholar Claire Jean Kim's (2015) concept of multi-species intersectionality examines how racial hierarchies and human/animal distinctions mutually reinforce each other. She highlights how ethnic minority people have often been 'placed' within a borderland between human/animal and historically have often been likened to other animal species.

Recent work by scholars like Lori Gruen explores how speciesism – the assumption of human superiority that justifies exploitation of other 'species' – operates alongside and through other systems of domination such as racism, sexism and ableism. These systems rely on similar logics of dehumanization and objectification. She questions the assumptions made around groupings of 'species' and shows how these definitions are not natural but rather they are fragile and fluid, and goes on to argue that the human/animal division naturalizes other forms of division.

FILM CLUB – 'I'M AN APE MAN…'

The films in the *Planet of the Apes* series offer some interesting ideas on human–animal relations, the idea of rights for non-human animals, animal testing and research, and also start to question speciesism. Many of the films in the franchise point to some of the key discourses and ideologies that emanate from science and religion and other key institutions, which have a profound influence on the way we respond to other animals, both human and non-human.

Planet of the Apes *applies the sociological imagination to rethink our relationship with other animals.*

KEY CONCEPTS IN ECOFEMINIST THEORY

- Dualistic thinking – the tendency to divide the world into hierarchical binaries (man/woman, human/animal, mind/body, culture/nature, straight/queer)
- Patriarchal domination – systems that justify control over both women and nature through similar logics
- The absent referent – language and practices make the exploitation of animals (and women) invisible
- Care ethics – an alternative moral framework emphasizing relationships and care rather than abstract rights

MEAT MAKETH THE MAN?

Sociological research has identified strong connections between meat-eating and constructions of masculinity in many cultures. Meat, particularly red meat, is symbolically associated with strength, power and virility – attributes traditionally linked to masculine identity. The French philosopher Jacques Derrida (1930–2004) argued that above all, the Western subject is a meat-eater, that there is some kind of connection between notions of virility and carno-phallogocentrism inherent in (hetero) masculinity. In part this is done through myths such as 'man the hunter' – actually, archaeology and anthropology have shown us that most early societies were more gatherers than hunters, and hunting groups would often be mixed, rather than just down to the men in the group. Contemporary carnivore and paleo diets hark back to this assumed way of eating.

Empirical studies support these theoretical connections. Research has found correlations between attitudes towards women and attitudes towards animals, with those holding more sexist views also more likely to support animal exploitation. A meta-analysis by Kristof Dhont and colleagues (2016) revealed significant relationships between social dominance orientation (the preference for hierarchical social structures) and both speciesism and nationalist and racist prejudice.

CARNISM ► ***a term used to describe the practice of eating meat. Phallogocentrism for Derrida is the way the masculine is privileged in discourse and constructions of meaning.***

Carol J. Adams and other feminist scholars have noted how advertisements for meat products often use sexualized imagery and language appealing to hegemonic masculine identity ('man-sized portions', 'beef up'). Conversely, plant-based foods are frequently feminized or portrayed as insufficient for 'real men'.

Studies by Emma Roe (2018), a UK human geographer, found that young men often express concerns about appearing 'weak' or 'feminine' if they choose vegan or vegetarian options, highlighting how food choices serve to perform and reinforce gender identities. Richard Twine, a UK sociologist, has also made convincing connections between human exceptionalism, masculinity and meat eating.

HUMAN/ANIMAL BORDER

One of the things we are very good at, as we have seen in many of the other chapters, is putting people into different groups, which often fall along false, yet persistent, binaries: masculine/feminine, rational/emotional etc. The same is true when we think of how humans have historically distinguished themselves from other animals. Various institutions, such as religion and science, have insisted that memory, emotions such as grief, depression or joy, communication through language, using tools, playfulness or the ability to act altruistically are just some of the things that make us different from (read 'better than') other animals. Yet, we now know that animals experience a range of emotions. UK zoologist Jane Goodall was the first to show us how chimpanzees make and use tools; crows are just one species of many who have been shown to act altruistically. An accusation of 'goldfish memory' is often used, yet relatively recently we have learned that fish have amazing memories – apart from anything else, they can distinguish between 44 human faces for six months and beyond – I wonder how many fish faces we could remember after that period of time? Other research reveals that dogs know many different human words (a border collie has been shown to understand 1,022 words), can remember them over a long period of time, and eavesdrop on conversations. Anyone who has seen the videos of Koko the gorilla will know that great apes can use and understand human sign language to effectively communicate with us. All of these attributes are measuring animals' capacities from a human-centric perspective of course, and don't even begin to chart the many attributes they have that we lack. The next sections will start to look at some of the ways we learn that animals are fundamentally different and lesser.

WHAT'S IN A WORD? THE POWER OF LANGUAGE

In a series of lectures entitled 'The Animal That Therefore I Am' (2006) Derrida points to the role of language in constructing difference. The very word 'animal', he argues, constitutes animals as 'other'. Peter Singer makes a similar point, highlighting how we might talk about 'people and animals.' Other

SOCIOLOGY AND ANIMAL ROLES

Some sociologists have charted the various roles animals play in human society:

- ***Food source*** – meat, fish, eggs, dairy, honey
- ***Clothing*** – wool, fur, leather, feathers
- ***Experimental objects*** – cigarettes have historically been tested on beagles because they have been bred to be passive, rabbits are often used to test cosmetics, many medicines are tested on animals first even though there is no guarantee humans will react in the same way as a mouse or a rat
- ***Pets*** – popular pets in many Western countries include cats and dogs but these may vary depending on nation, class, religion and gender
- ***Entertainment*** – zoos, safaris, circuses, stories, films
- ***Leisure*** – hunting (foxes, otters, hares, deer, lions, etc.), fishing (which someone once compared to drowning puppies for fun)
- ***Competitive sport*** – horse racing, dog racing, cock fighting
- ***Labour*** – horses and oxen plough fields, pit ponies, horses used in battle, dogs and rats sniff bombs, assistance dogs

From a broadly functionalist perspective, the inequalities involved in using animals for human gain might be seen as beneficial rather than problematic. A conflict theory perspective would see these injustices as arising from power differences and competition for resources. Symbolic interactionists would recognize the ways that ideas about species, including humans, are socially constructed and that through language, animals have been positioned as 'other' and marginalized.

Research has shown wolves to be altruistic, leaving food for those outside the pack, for instance.

discursive manoeuvres might hide what we are eating ('beef' not cow, 'veal' rather than baby cow) or distinguish between the murder of humans and the slaughter of animals. Phrases to demean other people such as 'dirty dog' or 'greedy pig', 'you bitch', 'you cow', 'sheepish', 'what a snake' and so on denote animals as inferior (many of these terms are also gendered). We often refer to animals as 'it' rather than 'him' or 'her', which, according to UK academic Arran Stibbe (2001) converts them into objects rather than subjects. The method of metonymy – replacing a name for someone or something by a word referring to its attribute – such as 'catching broilers' or 'killing beef', removes their individuality according to US philosopher Tom Regan (1996) and encourages us to think of animals as resources. A similar attitude was used by US soldiers in Vietnam when they referred to Vietnamese people as 'gooks' or 'ginks', which effectively distanced them from the humanity of the many civilians who were killed during the war. Reducing animals to inanimate objects is another common practice: near where I live, Herdwick lambs are frequently referred to as a lovely 'product', for instance. Detachment from animals and what happens to them is, according to Peter Singer, enabled through technical language – chicks might be 'processed', which disguises the methods of live crushing (termed 'maceration') or gassing (both RSPCA-approved methods of 'disposing' of male chicks in the UK).

Demeaning language

RELIGION

Many religions make reference to animals, as either things to be revered and worshipped, or to be avoided for the sake of purity. Various strands of Buddhism and Hinduism have the concept of ***ahimsa***, which means not harming any living creature. This ensures a degree of personal purity and helps to avoid suffering in future incarnations – a form of consequentialist thinking. Within Christianity, in the book of *Genesis*, before 'The Fall' (when Adam and Eve disobeyed God and ate from the tree of knowledge), God urged Adam and Eve to eat herbs and vegetables. However, after their expulsion from the Garden of Eden, God grants them right to have 'dominion' over animals. In *Isaiah*, after the Second Coming (the belief in both Islam and Christianity, that Isa/Jesus will return to earth after Judgement Day), humans are supposed to revert to not eating animals; some Christians, including many Seventh Day Adventists, follow a vegetarian or vegan diet because they feel this brings them closer to God. Friday night is still a popular fish and chip night because of the practice of abstaining from meat

'The lion and the lamb shall lie down together' – as represented in Briton Riviere's (1880) Una and Lion from Edmund Spenser's The Faerie Queene.

on Fridays. Christianity also drew on ancient Greek notions of the world as a 'great chain of being', with animals at the bottom because they cannot speak and are not rational. Judaism and Islam both have guidelines about the treatment of animals and the avoidance of, for example, pig meat.

CHILDHOOD

Relating to other species

Our understandings of, and relationships with, animals are not innate but are cultivated through socialization processes beginning in very early childhood. Through stories, toys, zoo visits and everyday family practices, children learn culturally specific ways of categorizing, relating to and treating different species.

Animals on screen and page

Children's literature, television and films are saturated with animal characters, from talking bears to adventurous rabbits. As UK sociologists Matthew Cole and Kate Stewart (2014) have shown, these anthropomorphized animals deliver complex and often contradictory messages about human–animal relationships.

Anthropo-morphism

Their concept of the anthroparchal childhood explores how children are simultaneously encouraged to love certain animals (usually cute, charismatic mammals), while being socialized into practices that harm others (like meat eating). For example, a child might cuddle and care for a stuffed pig toy while eating bacon for breakfast, with no acknowledgment of the connection between the two. In fact, they argue, the toy is a useful distraction from the reality of what they are eating.

ANTHROPARCHAL CHILDHOOD ▶
one where we learn to value human interest over other animal needs in such a way as to potentially lead to the exploitation of non-human animals in children's lives.

Children's book illustrations often show anthropomorphized farm animals, which contrast starkly with actual conditions on factory farms.

Children's entertainment often presents selective and idealized versions of human–animal relationships. Farm animals appear happy on idyllic family farms, rather than in industrial facilities; wild animals possess human-like motivations and emotions. These representations, according to Cole and Stewart, constitute a form of dysconscious speciesism – the uncritical acceptance of dominant, human-centric norms concerning animals.

MY FAMILY AND OTHER ANIMALS: FAMILY VALUES

Parents and other family members play crucial roles in shaping children's attitudes towards animals. Research by the social psychologists Kathryn Amiot and Brock Bastian (2015) shows how meat consumption is normalized through family meal practices, with parents often providing simplified or misleading explanations of where meat comes from when questioned by curious children.

In households with pets, children learn specific rules about which animals are family members deserving of care, and which are appropriate to eat or use. These classifications vary culturally but are rarely questioned within families. In Western countries, the stark moral distinction between pets and farm animals exemplifies what sociologist Arnold Arluke terms 'sociozoologic scales' – cultural ranking systems that determine how different species should be treated.

'DON'T TELL THE CHILDREN'

In 2013, UK sociologist Kate Stewart investigated parents' strategies for managing children's questions about meat. She found many parents deliberately concealed information about meat production from children or used euphemisms to avoid acknowledging animal suffering. This ***strategic ignorance*** helps maintain practices that might otherwise cause moral discomfort.

Disidentification

Gradually, according to media studies scholar Debra Merskin (2018), children start to conceptually distance themselves from other animals and to see humans as superior, through a process of dis-identification with animals. This process is exacerbated for children in urban areas, she argues, who may only come into contact with other animals in mediated ways such as via a trip to the zoo or interaction with companion animals – relationships, she argues, where the animals are often bred to be dependent on us.

Getting rid of guilt

Cultural distortions of food, depicting cartoon animals delighted at the thought of being eaten, enable this dis-identification. Termed 'suicide food' by US sociologist Lois Presser (2013), such images perhaps dampen any guilt that might be felt at eating animals.

IT'S JUST A PET? COMPANION ANIMALS AND EMOTIONAL CAPITALISM

While some animals face industrialized exploitation, others enjoy unprecedented levels of care and attention as beloved pets. Pet keeping has expanded dramatically, with approximately 60 per cent of households in countries like the US, UK and Australia having animal companions. Global spending on pet products and services exceeds £240 billion annually. In part, this is due to an historical evolution from a reliance on working animals to animals becoming family members. The growth of consumer capitalism has also had a big influence on how we see certain animals.

Power imbalance in pet ownership

THE GROWING 'PET-INDUSTRIAL COMPLEX'

The rise of what some sociologists call the pet-industrial complex includes:

- expansion of premium and speciality pet food markets, focusing on 'fresh', 'organic' or 'vegan' food
- pet versions of human rights and treats (puppuccinos, dog ice-cream, pawternity leave)
- growing pet healthcare and insurance industries
- luxury pet accessories and services (doggy daycare, pet spas, designer clothing)
- pet-friendly tourism and accommodation
- social media accounts and influencers focused on pets

This flourishing industry reveals how companion animals have been integrated into consumer capitalism, with human–pet relationships increasingly mediated through commercial transactions.

Yet many argue that even loving relationships with pets involve power imbalances, with humans controlling pets' reproduction, movement and basic bodily functions: such as what they eat and when, and even where and when they can go to the toilet. This power is often exercised through affection rather than force, but it remains fundamentally unequal. Yi-Fu Tuan's (2004) concept of 'dominance affection' helps explain this seemingly contradictory relationship. The language of 'having' or 'keeping' pets reflects this notion of ownership of another sentient being. The very word 'pet' reflects ideas of kindness, affection but also of taming, controlling and ownership.

Leslie Irvine's (2017) sociological studies of animal shelters in the US reveals how notions of animal 'personhood' are

PIGEON STREET

The habit of pigeon-fancying (referring to the practice of keeping, breeding and racing pigeons rather than anything else!) blurs many binaries. For instance, they are at once a working/sporting animal but they are also viewed as pets. The practice is also gendered in that most fanciers are men. In the 17th and 18th centuries, it was a pastime associated with the wealthy but by the 19th and 20th centuries, it tended to be a working-class leisure pursuit particularly associated with mining communities.

Pigeon fancying – just one of many classed and gendered forms of human-animal relationships.

socially constructed through human interactions, with pets increasingly viewed as family members with distinct personalities and emotional lives. This moral elevation of pets occurs simultaneously with the moral invisibility of farmed animals, producing what Irvine calls moral schizophrenia.

There are also classed and gendered dimensions to keeping pets. Certain breeds of dog, for instance, might be synonymous with ideas of masculinity (Rottweiler) or femininity (Chihuahua), of wealth and middle-class 'taste' (Cavalier King Charles Spaniel), or emblematic of working-class culture (English Bull Terrier). Of course, the very notion of breeding animals to our own design is yet another example of sometimes violent domination. Many breeds of dog with flattened faces have breathing difficulties, those with small craniums can suffer terrible pain, and some breeds such as Labradors and Alsatians are prone to hip pain.

Breeding to design

THE BOUNDARY BETWEEN PETS AND FOOD

The divide between animals categorized as companions and those designated as food is not natural but is culturally determined. Which species fall into which category varies dramatically across cultures and historical periods.

US sociologists Arnold Arluke and Clinton Sanders (1996) have shown how these classifications reflect arbitrary cultural preferences rather than inherent qualities of the animals themselves. For example, both pigs and dogs are intelligent social mammals, yet Western cultures overwhelmingly view one as food and the other as friend.

Maintaining these boundaries requires considerable cultural work. Food animals are typically kept invisible. For instance, I worked on a farm as a teenager: one of the jobs was to grade eggs and I never questioned the fact that I'd never seen any chickens roaming the farm – they lived their whole lives within huge industrial barns. Similarly, during milking we took some of the milk to make cream and cheese. A by-product was skimmed milk, and the highlight of my day would be to feed the calves kept in a shed. Again, I never once questioned why they weren't with their mothers, drinking their milk, nor why they were never released in the fields, save for the ones kept as dairy cows. Pets, on the other hand, are highly visible but separated conceptually from their species counterparts used for food. When these categories blur – for example, when a particular cow, pig or chicken becomes individually known and named – the contradiction becomes difficult to maintain.

Invisible animals

THE INDUSTRIALIZED ANIMAL

The scale of modern animal agriculture is unprecedented. Over 70 billion land animals are raised and killed annually for food, with the vast majority living in intensive systems known as factory farms or concentrated animal feeding operations (CAFOs).

Intensive farming

Sociologists like David Nibert have applied Marxist analysis to understand how capitalism has transformed animals into living commodities. His concept of animal-industrial complexes highlights how interlocking economic, political and cultural institutions facilitate the large-scale exploitation of animals for profit.

Again, we can also go back to Derrida (2008), who described the violence of factory farms thus:

> *such a subjection... can be called violence in the most morally neutral sense of the term...No one can deny seriously, or for very long, that men do all they can in order to dissimulate this cruelty or to hide it from themselves, in order to organize on a global-scale the forgetting or misunderstanding of this violence.*

Detached concern

Rhoda Wilkie's (2005) sociological research on livestock farmers shows how workers in animal agriculture develop 'detached concern' – professional emotional management strategies that allow them to care for animals they know will be slaughtered. These emotional labour processes help workers navigate the contradictions inherent in caring for creatures destined for consumption. I can remember being puzzled during the foot-and-mouth crisis in 2001 when farmers were in tears over the mass slaughter of sheep and cows – I would travel home from the school I taught in and see huge pyres of burning animals. I had assumed they would only be concerned about the loss of profit but many seemed genuinely upset at having to kill healthy animals, even if they would have been sent to the abattoir at a later date.

ANIMALS KILLED FOR FOOD EACH DAY

1.4 million goats

900,0000 cows

1.7 million sheep

12 million ducks

3.8 million pigs

202 million chickens

Hundreds of millions of fish

Huge numbers of animals are slaughtered each day for human consumption.

THE RISE OF THE VEGAN?

Rejecting animal products

Once considered fringe, or even freaky, plant-based eating patterns have moved towards the mainstream in many countries in the Global North. Surveys have shown steady increases in those identifying as vegetarian or vegan, particularly among younger generations. In the UK, the number of vegans almost trebled between 2014 and 2019 according to the Vegan Society and in 2022, an Ipsos survey revealed that 46 per cent of Britons aged between 16 and 75 were wanting to reduce their consumption of animal products.

VEGETARIANS ▶ ***by definition, vegetarians do not eat meat or fish, but they often consume honey, eggs and dairy. Some might wear wool and leather, others choose not to.***

VEGANS ▶ ***people who eschew all animal products. However, their diet might include ultra-processed foods.***

'PLANT-BASED' ▶ ***generally refers to vegan diets but ones based on wholefoods, such as fruits, vegetables and nuts, rather than any ultra-processed food. Some plant-based eaters might include limited amounts of eggs, honey or dairy.***

Sociological analysis reveals that there are many reasons for choosing a vegan diet, including being motivated by health or religious concerns, awareness of the environmental impact of meat, fish and dairy (see Chapter 12), as well as ethical considerations for animals. However, veganism also encompasses broader lifestyle choices beyond diet.

BEYOND FOOD: VEGAN IDENTITIES

Contemporary veganism extends far beyond dietary choices to include rejection of animal products in clothing, cosmetics and other consumer goods. Richard Twine (2018) has examined how veganism functions as what Anthony Giddens would call a 'lifestyle project' – a means of constructing identity through consumption choices.

A whole lifestyle

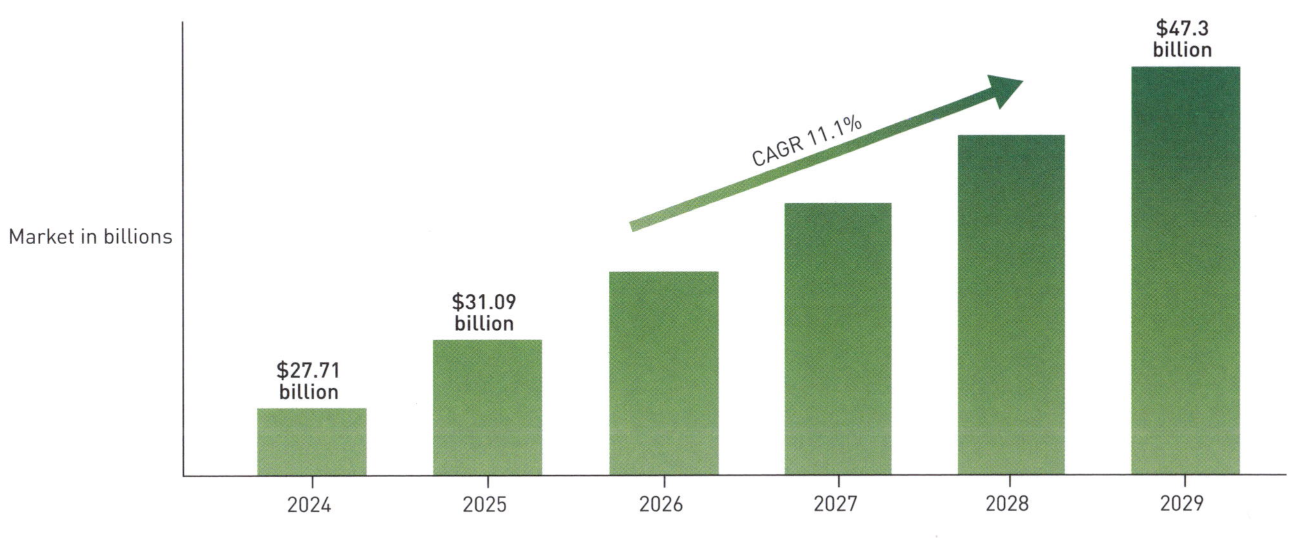

The graph shows the exponential growth in the market for vegan products during the 2020s.

This expansion of veganism into multiple consumer categories has created substantial markets for plant-based alternatives, from faux leather fashion to cruelty-free cosmetics. Major corporations have responded with product lines catering to vegan consumers, though their non-vegan products might involve animal-testing or products, raising questions about whether ethical consumption can meaningfully challenge systems of animal exploitation.

Plant-based substitutes

Veganism and sexuality

The intersection of veganism and sexuality represents an interesting area of research that illuminates how ethical dietary choices can influence intimate relationships. Annie Potts and Jovian Parry (2010) have explored how veganism can shape sexual preferences and partner selection through their work on vegansexuality – a term describing vegans who prefer sexual and romantic relationships exclusively with other vegans. Potts and Parry observed that some vegans experience embodied ethical reactions to the bodies of meat-eaters, reporting discomfort with things like perceived 'meat breath', bodily fluids or even the different smell they attributed to non-vegan bodies. Perhaps even more significantly, they felt deep cognitive disappointment or even repulsion towards those who are able to eat animals.

Many vegans use vegan dating apps to find like-minded partners.

Other recent sociological investigations by Jessica Greenebaum and Brandon Dexter (2018) have explored how vegan dating apps and social networks facilitate connections between like-minded individuals, creating communities where shared ethical commitments to animals form the foundation for romantic partnerships. These platforms represent technological solutions to what many vegans experience as a significant barrier to intimate relationships across dietary divides.

The concept has sparked considerable debate, with some viewing vegansexuality as a legitimate extension of ethical commitments, and others critiquing it as a form of 'lifestyle discrimination'. Media coverage often sensationalized the phenomenon, revealing deep cultural anxieties about the relationship between food choices and sexuality.

My own (2023) research examined vegansexuality in the context of the climate crisis, exploring how food choices intersect with both interpersonal relationships and environmental concerns. Using ecofeminism and the ethics of a vegan perspective enables us to recognize the suffering of those most affected by climate change, both human and non-human. By connecting vegansexuality with broader climate justice issues, we can see how intimate relationships, including friendships, become sites where environmental ethics and personal attachment converge.

THE MEAT PARADOX

Despite growing concern for animal welfare, and the growth in veganism, meat consumption remains high in most wealthy nations. This contradiction has been termed the 'meat paradox' by psychologists Steve Loughnan, Nick Haslam and Brock Bastian (2010) – most people express concern for animal welfare while continuing to eat animals.

Sociologists have built on this concept to explore how social structures and cultural practices help manage this cognitive dissonance. Strategies include:

- physical and linguistic distancing (slaughterhouses located away from population centres, euphemisms like 'beef' instead of 'cow')
- cultural narratives justifying meat eating (appeals to tradition, nutrition or naturalism)
- institutional arrangements that hide production processes from consumers

How do you eat yours?

WHAT HARMS THEM, HARMS US

Our lives are tethered with those of other animals in complex and contradictory ways. They played a role in the success of industrialized capital through their labour in fields, pits and towpaths. Animals are present in many of our formative narratives, they are our companions, and also our prey. They have infected us with disease, but they have also been tested on to prevent our own ill health. We use them for our entertainment. Our relationship with animals is informed by consumerism and it plays a role in identity formation. In large part, our relationship with them is one characterized by violence and domination.

As we face unprecedented environmental challenges and growing awareness of animal sentience, traditional ways of relating to other species are increasingly questioned. As the Indian social activist Mahatma Gandhi (allegedly) famously said: 'the greatness of a nation can be judged by the way its animals are treated'. These challenges require not just new ethical frameworks, but also new sociological understandings of how human societies are always already multispecies communities.

By applying sociological analysis to human–animal relations, we gain insight not only into how we treat other species but into the nature of human society itself. Our treatment of animals reflects our values, power structures and social arrangements. In this sense, the sociology of human–animal relations is ultimately about understanding what it means to be human in a more-than-human world.

Many might be shocked at the thought of puppy meat though they eat piglet meat. This is the meat paradox.

Chapter Fourteen
FUTURE TRENDS

Sociology of crises – Sociology of the past, present and future – Future focus: speculative sociology – Sociological principles – The role of sociology – Wanting to change the world

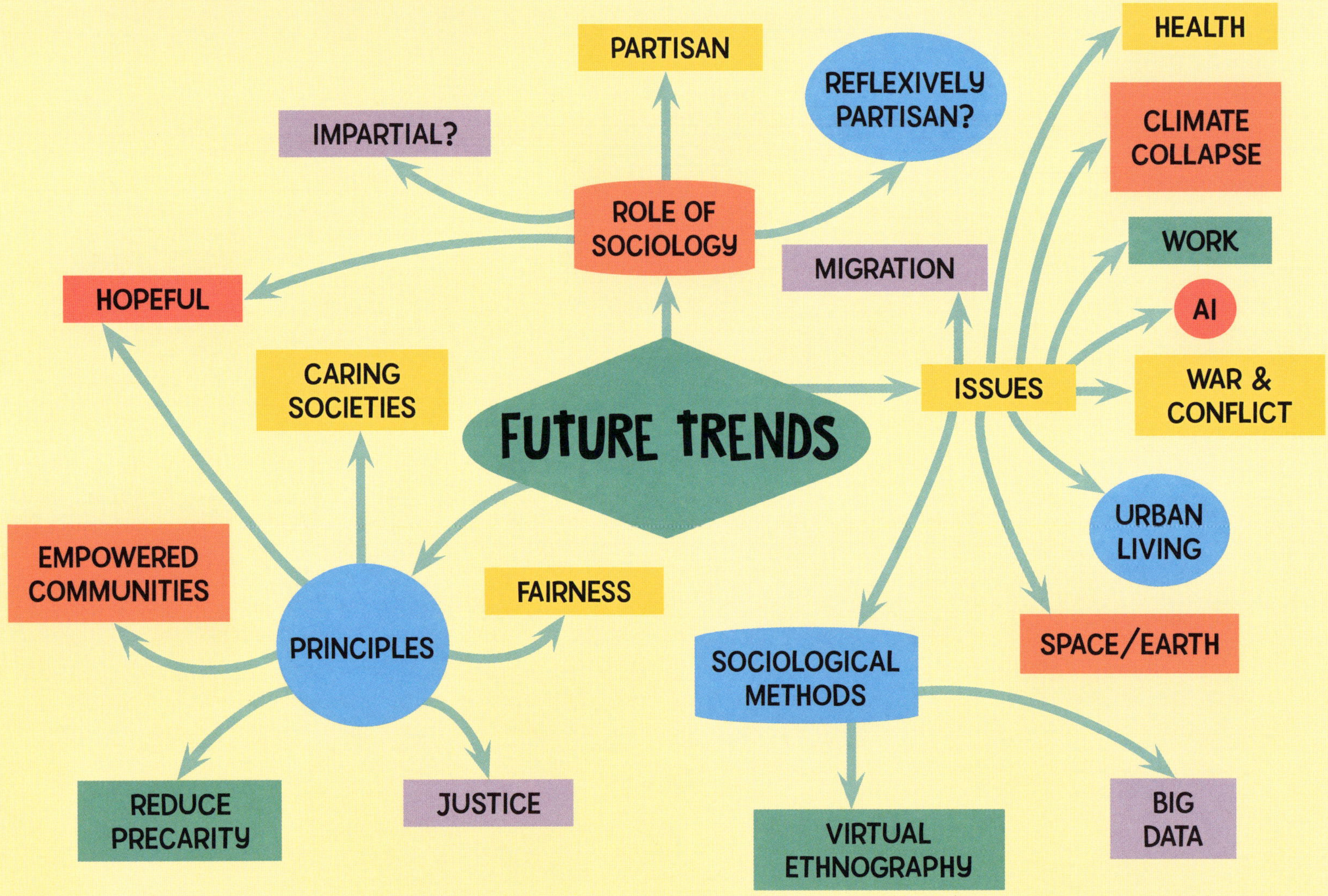

FUTURE TRENDS

ROLE OF SOCIOLOGY
- PARTISAN
- IMPARTIAL?
- REFLEXIVELY PARTISAN?
- HOPEFUL

ISSUES
- HEALTH
- CLIMATE COLLAPSE
- WORK
- AI
- WAR & CONFLICT
- URBAN LIVING
- SPACE/EARTH
- MIGRATION

SOCIOLOGICAL METHODS
- VIRTUAL ETHNOGRAPHY
- BIG DATA

PRINCIPLES
- CARING SOCIETIES
- HOPEFUL
- EMPOWERED COMMUNITIES
- FAIRNESS
- REDUCE PRECARITY
- JUSTICE

People in the UK gathered every evening to publicly celebrate NHS workers during Covid-19.

A heavily protected worker supervises the mass burning of bodies in India during the Covid-19 outbreak.

A volunteer hands groceries to an elderly man who is shielding (staying at home) during Covid-19.

SOCIOLOGY OF CRISES

The Covid-19 pandemic showed how an event such as the spread of a disease can become huge very quickly, partly as a result of factors associated with globalization. We witnessed significant changes in behaviour becoming the new 'norm' in a short space of time, whether that was wearing a face mask, standing metres away from people, or touching elbows to say hello during social distancing. A sociologically positive take from the way that the overwhelming majority of people quickly followed such public health measures – for prolonged periods of time – is that the pandemic crisis underlined the fact that most humans are essentially social and co-operative.

Another result of the pandemic crisis was that sneezing in a public space became an embarrassing and stigmatized behaviour. In addition, working patterns changed as we increasingly worked from home. Our methods of communication, aided by new technologies, altered and many of us spent a lot of time 'Zooming' or 'Face Timing' with friends and family under lockdown. Decisions had to be made about who to form a 'bubble' with. Restrictions on how far we could travel meant we left cars behind, and our leisure pursuits changed; walking from home became a new or renewed pleasure. Consumer patterns altered, with many more relying on online shopping, again aided by new technologies. Long, slow queues at supermarkets were to be expected, with priority for shopping given to those who were key workers for that particular crisis. Gig workers and health care practitioners, among others, were briefly recognized for the important roles they played at that time. Wildlife came out to play while we were locked away – Kashmiri goats grazed the gardens of Llandudno, dolphins frolicked in the usually busy Bosphorus, and wild boar foraged in the city centre of Haifa. Loo roll became gold dust!

However, we also saw how existing patterns of inequality associated with 'race', class, health, age and gender, for instance, were reaffirmed in stark ways. Those who were poorer or more marginalized, the elderly and the already sick, were more likely to die. This was especially the case when those infected with coronavirus were sent back into care homes equipped with little appropriate support. Those with underlying health issues were encouraged to self-isolate throughout. Victims of domestic abuse

Resistance to racist, anti-migrant discourse in the UK reflects an inclusive response to a social issue.

were shut in with their abusers and found it harder to access help. Changes in the education of young people meant that those from poorer households struggled to have access to the digital technologies necessary for remote learning. Economic impacts were unevenly distributed with, for instance, young people and women among the first to be furloughed or lose their jobs. Collective grief and guilt, among other emotions, were felt as we saw the rising numbers of deaths. In response, we also saw collective action in the form of volunteers who made PPE equipment or administered vaccines. Sociology helped us to understand all of these, and more, aspects of that pandemic.

We don't know what the next extraordinary event for any of us will be, or when or where it will occur, but some of the things we have learned might help us anticipate how it might impact on our social lives, and we can plan for a more inclusive response in the future. We already know who are among the most socially vulnerable in society – the homeless, the disabled, the poor, the marginalized, the socially isolated. Sociological knowledge can also help in predicting how we might behave and respond as a society.

It can also help to anticipate what is likely to be important in the coming years. Already the Anthropocene and related interconnected challenges are pressing for many of us across the globe. Climate change, migration, war and violence are likely to continue to be big issues. Consumption patterns, indeed, even economic structures such as capitalism, may well be put under pressure. Current global political shifts to the right will also have an impact. At the same time, resistance to these issues can be extremely powerful and bubble up very quickly. The role of AI and its impact on our social and working lives is something to watch.

SOCIOLOGY OF THE PAST, PRESENT AND FUTURE

In many respects, sociology might be considered a social history in that it spends a considerable time mining the past in order to understand the present. Arguably, much sociology of the 20th century was firmly embedded in the present. Though Marx, at its origins, had the future in his sights, the future was largely bracketed-off. Perhaps that is no surprise, given sociology's focus on empirical research – the future is hard to quantify! That has shifted in recent years: sociology is also concerned, now, with the future. As Lisa Suckert (2022) argues, imagined futures are also useful for understanding the present – and even for envisaging a better world. However this can present challenges because, as we have already seen, Giddens points out that people find it hard to give the same level of reality to the future as they do to the present. Some go so far as to say speculative sociology is risky. Whether or not it is risky, it is certainly an endeavour that involves our sociological imagination and emotions such as nostalgia, fear, hope and excitement, just as much as it requires calculations and predictions.

As we stand on the cusp of unprecedented global changes and challenges, the role of sociology in understanding and shaping our collective future has never been more crucial. Throughout this book, we've explored how sociological perspectives help us make sense of the complex web of human interactions, institutions and social structures that form the fabric of our societies. Now, as we look towards the future's horizon, we need to consider how these perspectives can illuminate the path forward.

FUTURE FOCUS: SPECULATIVE SOCIOLOGY

Imagined futures

The future is not a fixed destination but a realm of possibilities shaped by the choices we make today. Sociology, with its unique toolkit for analyzing social patterns, power dynamics and cultural shifts, is well-positioned to anticipate future trends and contribute to positive social change. In this chapter, we'll explore some of the key areas where sociological inquiry is likely to play a vital role in the coming

SPACE BUBBLE

Making a new society elsewhere

At the time of writing, singer Katy Perry and friends had just been shot into space by Amazon owner Jeff Bezos, in the first all-female space flight. Whatever we might think about the climate impact of such a flight, or question whether this is a failed attempt for Bezos to address claims of rampant sexism in his company, it does lead to other interesting questions about our social futures. While sociology has been focused on life on earth, as it becomes increasingly uninhabitable, life here is likely to change drastically. Perhaps for the 'super-rich' this will be less of a concern, as they can afford to colonize another habitable planet, or space station. Eventually, we might see sociology of social life on another planet. The sociologist's task then will be an interesting one: will similar social structures emerge? Will humans have learned lessons from life on earth?

decades. We can begin this endeavour by listing the issues that might be the most pressing. With this in mind, I'm going to put my head above the parapet and provide a 'top ten' list of what I think these issues are likely to be, many of which are interlinked in complicated ways:

Sociology is crucial

- **Climate crisis and environmental sociology** – this might include a focus on justice, inequality, sustainability, ecological economics, 'degrowth'/radical abundance, ecosocialist/anti-capitalist movements
- **Migration and global mobility** – climate refugees and migration, transnational identities
- **Political polarization and democracy** – the rise of authoritarian populism, 'creeping fascism', and Fromm's idea of *folie à millions* (2002); social media ***echo chambers*** and fake news; new forms of civic engagement and activism
- **War and conflict** – competition for resources, civil resistance, post-conflict societies
- **Digital technologies and society** – AI and its impact, surveillance and digital rights, digital divides, fake news and deep fakes (what is 'truth'?)
- **Health and society** – lessons from global pandemics, mental health in rapidly changing societies, ageing populations
- **Work and employment** – gig economy and precarity, impact of automation, work–life balance
- **Urban futures** – as more of us live in urban areas this will have to include a consideration of sustainable urban planning, urban inequalities, 'smart' cities and technology
- **Space exploration and off-world societies** – tech billionaires such as Elon Musk, Jeff Bezos etc. are already considering such futures, but what will it mean for the rest of us? Earth–space relations and inequalities (new forms of global inequality based on access to space resources), impact of space-related technologies on earth-bound societies
- **Sociological methodologies** – using big data and AI to uncover social patterns, virtual ethnography

Hyper-individualism

Another issue for future sociological exploration, which relates both to the individual and to society as a whole, could be the question of hyper-individualism in a consumer society. Building on the earlier sociological concept of alienation, hyper-individualism focuses on the growing impacts of social media (such as Instagram and TikTok) on consumer identity, the need for 'validation', fragmentation and feelings of isolation/loss of social connection. This would require further study of the effects of consumerism – which is increasingly both enabled and celebrated by neoliberalism – on both individuals and the planet.

As regards the wider environment, such consumerist attitudes link to lifestyles that see conspicuous consumption – despite the impacts of overconsumption on a finite planet – as the way for individuals to achieve a happy and fulfilled life. Increasingly, as Veblen (2005) has noted, the possession of consumer goods has become linked to personal identity; Carole (2005) sees things as having evolved even further, with consumers moving beyond *having* 'nice things' to *wanting to become* 'nice things'. Yet, as noted by Grace Lee Boggs (2003, 2012), change doesn't come about unless people take responsibility for it – to do that, people need to feel connected to one another, to society, and to the world. If people can create 'loving relationships with one another and with the Earth', then a different future becomes possible.

This, in turn, might suggest another area for sociological exploration that is, in part, connected to hyper-individualism: the idea of radical abundance or an alternative hedonism. Such ideas, associated with writers such as Kate Soper (*Post-Growth Living*, 2020) and Jason Hickel (*Less is More*, 2020), point to a future in which social 'commodities' – such as healthcare, education and leisure – become more important than 'stuff'. Sociology – if it remains open and critical – can undoubtedly play a key part in helping to envisage a better future.

SOCIOLOGICAL PRINCIPLES

However, as we've already noted, in many ways, the future is unpredictable and unknowable, thus such a list might very quickly become outdated. I could very well end up looking like those who predicted the internet was just a fad, or that we would all be living a life of leisure because of technological advances! Rather than trying to pinpoint what our future(s) might look like, we could instead focus on what core tenets we think should be worked on – here and now – for a fair and just future. For example, many of the sociological theories we have looked at in this book advocate for more empowered communities, whether that be in response to the climate crisis, to economic breakdown or living in impoverished areas. Some research has highlighted increased precarity in social life, for example in the lives of workers in the gig economy, so reduced precarity might be a logical aim. A condition of care, community and solidarity, whatever the circumstances, might be an admirable goal. This leads to us to go back to the beginning of this book, to consider what sociology is and, fundamentally, what its role is. Much of the book has looked at the causes, and impacts, of intolerance and prejudice; in a world where we are likely to meet more migrants, and perhaps become migrants ourselves (*Families like Ours*, a Danish TV mini-series shown recently on BBC4, imagines the impacts on families when Denmark and the Netherlands have to be evacuated because of rising sea levels), a culture of tolerance or cosmopolitanism might be another quality or principle that sociology should advocate for.

To do so, sociology will have to be, as it's always been: radical in its approaches. As Angela Davis said, 'Radical simply means "grasping things at the root"'.

Empowered community living offers ways of adopting a more cosmopolitan culture.

A masked man brandishes a Union Jack flag at a far right demonstration against migration in Leeds, UK in March 2024. Sociology can help us to understand why movements, both positive and negative, develop.

THE ROLE OF SOCIOLOGY

> *Not everything that is faced can be changed, but nothing can be changed until it is faced*
>
> James Baldwin

Above all, perhaps, sociology needs to address what its role is in the future. The issues that I have predicted might be pressing, may differ; other issues I haven't anticipated will no doubt arise – but sociology can prepare us for such eventualities. How it does that is up for debate.

As we have seen throughout, sociologists are often not in agreement about the topics and issues we have addressed – that includes ideas of what sociology's purpose is. Some, like Steve Bruce (1951–), are of the belief that the sociologist's task is to be dispassionate, to observe and map a situation, or event, to find patterns, or predict the future from an impartial perspective. In some ways, this might be an admirable goal to avoid bias. On the other hand, according to Liz Stanley and Sue Wise (1983), objectivity is a word that men have used to describe their own subjectivity. Ken Plummer has suggested that perhaps being 'objective enough', or 'reflexively partisan', might be a better goal. Others, such as British sociologist Michael Burawoy (1947–2025), are more partisan in their approach. Burawoy was an advocate for what is known as Public Sociology. In 2004 he gave a speech at the American Sociological Association conference that caused quite a buzz (you can view this engaging and accessible speech on YouTube: **https://www.youtube.com/watch?v=8NxvPKGtkUQ**).

From this perspective, sociology has a duty to engage with social issues and to speak for the voiceless, to promote a fairer and more just society. He argued it should work with social movements, to counter the rise of the far-right and growing inequalities. Bourdieu claimed, referenced early on in this book, that sociology is like a martial art, one to be used to defend those with less power. Sociologists like Ken Plummer and Mary Holmes have also argued that sociology must remain hopeful – be mindful of harms and inequalities but also remember that not everything is changing for the worse, and that we should also be able to focus our sociological attention on the things that give us pleasure too. Such an approach allows us to work for change – Gramsci, after all, argued for 'pessimism of the intellect, optimism of the will'.

WANTING TO CHANGE THE WORLD

We have considered some challenging topics in this book, but hopefully you will have seen there is scope and hope for change.

Thinking about the future can be hard: it might present as an imagined 'unknowableness'; it can seem distant or scary. But British sociologist Barbara Adam (1945–) reminds us that we are constantly living in the future: it is enacted in everyday lives, through events like birth, marriage, death. We are living in yesterday's future. We can all play a small (or large) part in changing the world around us – now and in the future – whether it be through how we treat other people, vote (or not vote) in an election, signing petitions, or thinking about what we wear, eat or buy. Young people, in particular, have been involved in many important social movements from Black Lives Matter, the Arab Spring, the Occupy movement, Extinction Rebellion, Just Stop Oil, Stand Up To Racism, and Youth Justice Now. Having conversations with other people about difficult subjects, politely challenging common-sense viewpoints by drawing on evidence, can be another way of effecting change.

CONCLUSION

As we've explored in this chapter, the future presents both unprecedented challenges and extraordinary opportunities for sociological inquiry. From the existential threat of climate collapse to the transformative potential of AI, the coming decades will require us to rethink fundamental aspects of social life.

The sociological perspective, with its emphasis on understanding the complex and contradictory relationship between individual experiences and broader social structures, will be crucial in navigating these changes. By cultivating our sociological imagination, we can better anticipate future trends, understand their implications, and work towards creating more just, sustainable and inclusive societies. It will also help us to adjust to these changes.

As we conclude this book, we encourage you to carry forward the sociological torch in your own life and work. Whether you're a student, a policymaker or simply a curious observer of social life, the insights of sociology can help you make sense of our rapidly changing world and contribute to shaping a better future for all.

Remember: the future is not predetermined. It is shaped by the collective choices and actions we take today. By understanding the social forces at play, we can make more informed decisions and work towards the kind of society we wish to create. Sociology was born of social change; its critical tools have been forged to help us understand it and thus, with a little adaptation and sociological imagination, it can carry us forward on the continuing tide of change. The future of sociology is inextricably linked with the future of society itself – and you, armed with sociological insight, have a role to play in shaping both.

GLOSSARY

Agency: The capacity of individuals to act independently and make their own free choices, often constrained by social structures.

Alienation: A concept developed by Karl Marx referring to the estrangement workers experience from the products of their labour, themselves and others in capitalist systems.

Anomie: Durkheim's concept describing a condition of instability resulting from a breakdown of standards and values or from a lack of purpose or ideals in a society.

Austerity: Government policies designed to reduce public spending, often leading to cuts in welfare and public services.

Big data: Extremely large data sets that can be analyzed to reveal patterns, trends and associations, especially relating to human behaviour and interactions.

Bourgeoisie: In Marxist theory, the capitalist class who own the means of production (factories, resources, technology). They employ others to work for them, profiting from the surplus value of workers' labour.

Bureaucracy: A system of organization characterized by hierarchical authority, defined roles and formal rules and procedures. Max Weber identified bureaucratization as a key feature of modern societies.

Capitalism: An economic system based on private ownership of the means of production and the pursuit of profit.

Cartesian dualism: Distinction between mind and body derived from René Descartes's philosophy, which valued the mind as the rational part of human subjectivity while rendering the body an animalistic appendage.

Civilizing process: Norbert Elias's theory describing how changes in sleeping, eating habits, and ideas of shame resulted from processes of socialization, rationalization, and individualization.

Colonialism: The policy or practice of one country invading and taking over land to exploit it economically, and imposing settlers on it, often resulting in the subjugation of Indigenous populations and the imposition of the colonizer's culture, language and governance systems.

Compulsory heterosexuality: Term coined by Adrienne Rich referring to the idea that heterosexuality is positioned as the default or obligatory sexuality in society.

Cosmopolitanism: A theoretical perspective that emphasizes global citizenship, transcending traditional boundaries of nation-states.

Critical theory: An approach that argues research should critique and change society, not just understand it, with emphasis on power relations.

Cultural capital: In Bourdieu's theory, non-financial assets that promote social mobility beyond economic means, such as education, intellect, style of speech, dress or physical appearance.

Cultural racism: A form of racism that emphasizes cultural differences rather than biological inferiority as the basis for discrimination. Cultural aspects like language, religion or customs are seen as threatening to mainstream culture.

Denialism: The rejection of established facts, often manifesting as literal denial (rejecting facts), interpretive denial (reinterpreting facts) or implicatory denial (minimizing implications for action).

Disciplinary power: Foucault's concept of subtle, ubiquitous forms of discipline that operate through self-regulation and surveillance, often using reward as well as punishment.

Disenchantment: Weber's concept describing the loss of mystery, magic and spirituality in modern rationalized society.

Division of labour: The specialization of co-operative labour in specific tasks and roles, as studied by Durkheim in relation to social solidarity.

Dramaturgical theory: Erving Goffman's framework that views social interactions as theatrical performances where individuals manage impressions using 'frontstage' and 'backstage' behaviours.

Economic capital: Financial assets, money and property ownership.

Ecological crisis: The critical disruption of earth's ecological systems, including biodiversity loss, habitat destruction and ecosystem collapse.

Elite: In the Great British Class Survey, the highest social class with abundant economic, cultural and social capital.

Embourgeoisement: The theory that the working class was adopting middle-class values and lifestyles due to increasing prosperity.

Epistemology: The theory of knowledge concerned with what counts as valid knowledge and how it can be acquired.

Ethnicity: A broader concept than 'race' that refers to the ways groups are marked, or construct themselves, as 'different' based on shared cultural heritage including elements like language, religion, nationality and traditions.

Ethnography: A qualitative research method involving immersion in a particular social setting to observe and sometimes participate in the daily lives of the people being studied.

False consciousness: A Marxist concept describing the ways in which material, ideological and institutional processes in capitalist society mislead members of the proletariat about their own class interests.

Feminist theory: Theoretical framework that examines gender inequality and the social, political and economic aspects of gender relations.

Focus group: A qualitative research method involving facilitated discussions among small groups of participants to explore collective views on a topic.

Frankfurt School: A school of social theory and critical philosophy associated with the Institute for Social Research at Goethe University in Frankfurt; known for developing critical theory.

Functionalism: A theoretical perspective that sees society as a complex system whose parts work together to promote stability and solidarity.

Gender: The socially constructed characteristics, behaviours and attributes associated with being male, female or other gender identities.

Gender binary: The classification of gender into two distinct, opposite categories of male and female.

Gender fluid: Identity describing a person whose gender identity varies over time or in different contexts.

Genocide: The deliberate killing of a large number of people from a particular nation or ethnic group.

Gig economy: A labour market characterized by short-term contracts or freelance work rather than permanent jobs, often mediated through digital platforms.

Globalization: The increasing interconnectedness and interdependence of societies, economies and cultures worldwide through communication, trade and migration.

Grand narratives: Overarching explanations or stories that seek to make sense of historical experience or knowledge.

Habitus: In Bourdieu's theory, a system of embodied dispositions, tendencies that organize how individuals perceive and react to the social world. These are shaped by one's history and include tastes, preferences and bodily comportments.

Hate crimes: Violence motivated by prejudice towards a particular group that has been subject to long-term struggle for recognition and social inclusion.

Hegemonic masculinity: Concept developed by Raewyn Connell referring to the culturally dominant form of masculinity that legitimizes men's power over women and other men.

Hegemony: Gramsci's concept describing how dominant groups maintain power through ideological means, winning the consent of subordinate groups.

Heteronormativity: Term coined by Michael Warner that describes the ways in which heterosexuality is normalized and privileged in society, including the assumption that everyone is heterosexual unless proven otherwise.

Hierarchy: A system or organization in which people or groups are ranked one above the other according to status, authority or power.

Historical materialism: Marx's theory that emphasizes the importance of economic structures and class relations in shaping history and society.

Ideological State Apparatuses (ISAs): Louis Althusser's term for institutions like education, family and media that reproduce dominant ideologies and power relations through subtle influence rather than force.

Ideology: A system of ideas and ideals that forms the basis of economic or political theory and policy; in Marxist theory, it often refers to ideas that serve the interests of the ruling class.

Industrial Revolution: The transition to new manufacturing processes in Europe and the US in the late 1700s through the 1800s, characterized by the shift from manual to machine-based production.

Inequality: The uneven distribution of resources, opportunities, outcomes or status within a society or between societies.

Informed consent: The ethical principle that research participants must be fully informed about the nature of the research and voluntarily agree to participate.

Institutions: Established social structures that shape or govern the behaviour of members of a society. Examples include education, family, law, media, religion, economy and healthcare.

Intersectionality: A theoretical approach developed by legal scholar Kimberlé Crenshaw that examines how multiple dimensions of inequality ('race', class, gender, sexuality, disability etc.) intersect to create unique forms of disadvantage or privilege.

Intimacy: Close personal relationships and private experiences, increasingly mediated and transformed by digital technologies.

Life politics: Political and personal choices related to lifestyle and identity, often aimed at creating ethical ways of living.

Lifecourse: Sociological concept emphasizing how age-related bodily experiences are shaped by historical context, social location and institutional arrangements.

Looking-glass self: Charles Horton Cooley's concept suggesting our self-identity develops through how we imagine others perceive us, like seeing ourselves in a mirror through others' reactions.

Macro sociology: The study of large-scale social structures, patterns and systems.

Means of production: In Marxist theory, the physical, non-human inputs used in production: factories, land, tools, infrastructure etc.

Meritocracy: A social system in which advancement is based on individual ability or achievement, rather than on class privilege or wealth.

Methodology: The theory and principles guiding the choice of research methods.

Methods: The specific techniques or tools used to collect and analyze data in research.

Micro sociology: The study of human behaviour in contexts of face-to-face interaction.

Modernity: A period characterized by industrialization, urbanization, secularization and rationalization, typically contrasted with traditional or pre-modern societies.

Moral panic: Stanley Cohen described how media coverage amplifies public anxiety about a perceived threat to social values, potentially distorting its actual prevalence and resulting in disproportionate responses.

Nationality: Being recognized as a citizen of a nation, typically through birth, marriage or naturalization.

Network society: A social structure organized predominantly around networks rather than vertical hierarchies, enabled by digital communication technologies.

Non-binary: Identity describing a person who does not identify exclusively as a man or a woman.

Norms: Informal rules that govern behaviour in groups and societies, such as covering one's mouth when coughing. According to Durkheim, they play a key role in maintaining social order.

Ontology: The philosophical study of being, dealing with the nature of reality and what exists.

Paradigm: A distinct set of concepts or thought patterns, including theories, research methods and standards for practice.

Passing: Strategy used by individuals with stigmatized identities to present themselves as members of non-stigmatized groups to avoid discrimination.

Patriarchy: Social structures and practices in which men dominate, oppress and exploit women. Sylvia Walby identifies six structures: paid work, household production, culture, sexuality, violence and the state.

Perspective: A particular way of thinking about something, especially a theoretical approach.

Positivism: An approach to social research that applies the methods of natural sciences to study society, seeking to discover objective social facts and laws.

Postcolonial theory: A theoretical approach that analyzes the cultural legacy of colonialism and imperialism.

Postmodernity: A late 20th-century movement characterized by broad scepticism, subjectivism, relativism and a general suspicion of 'reason'.

Poststructuralism: A movement in philosophy and social sciences that rejects the self-sufficiency of structuralism and often emphasizes the importance of language in structuring our experience of the world.

Power: The ability to influence others and control resources, often distributed unequally in society based on factors like class, gender and ethnicity.

Prejudice: A preconceived opinion not based on reason or actual experience, often involving hostility directed against particular racial or ethnic groups.

Proletariat: In Marxist theory, the working class who must sell their labour power to survive, as they do not own means of production.

Protestant work ethic: Weber's concept describing how Protestant values of hard work, frugality and prosperity influenced the development of capitalism.

Public issues and private troubles: Terms coined by C. Wright Mills to distinguish between personal difficulties and broader social problems. The sociological imagination connects individual experiences to larger social structures.

Queer theory: Theoretical framework that challenges binary thinking around gender and sexuality, arguing that such binaries serve to maintain social hierarchies rather than reflect natural categories.

'Race': A socially constructed classification system that attempts to group people according to surface, visual traits or differences such as skin colour or hair type. There is no genetic basis for this grouping. The inverted commas around 'race' indicate its contested/troubled origins and usage.

Racialization: The process by which different groups in society are categorized based on ideas of 'race', attributing racial meaning to relationships, social practices or groups that did not previously identify themselves in racial terms.

Racism: The prejudice and discrimination based on 'race', often involving the belief that different 'races' possess distinct characteristics, abilities or qualities that distinguish them as inferior or superior to one another.

Random sampling: A method of selecting participants where each member of the population has an equal chance of being chosen.

Rationality: The quality of being based on reason rather than emotions; in Weber's work, associated with modernity and bureaucracy.

Rationalization: A concept developed by Max Weber referring to the process whereby traditional and emotional actions are increasingly replaced by actions based on calculation and efficiency.

Reflexivity: The practice of critically examining one's own role in the research process, including how personal biases and positions may influence the research.

Regression analysis: A statistical method examining relationships between dependent and independent variables.

Reliability: The consistency or stability of research findings across different measurements or time periods.

Respectability: A concept related to class that emerged in the 19th century, referring to moral authority associated with belonging to a higher social class, particularly pertaining to the behaviour of women.

Risk society: Ulrich Beck's concept describing modern societies increasingly preoccupied with managing risks they themselves have created through industrialization, modernization and globalization.

Scapegoating: Blaming a person or group for problems not of their making.

Scientific racism: The use of ostensibly scientific techniques and hypotheses to support or justify racial prejudice, often involving misapplications of anthropology, biology and genetics.

Self-fulfilling prophecy: Robert Merton's term for how a false definition of a situation evokes behaviours that make the originally false conception come true.

Sex: Typically refers to the biological characteristics (chromosomes, hormones, anatomy) used to categorize individuals as male, female or intersex.

Sexual identity: How individuals define themselves in terms of their sexuality, often in relation to the gender of those to whom they are attracted.

Sexuality: Refers to identities, practices, relationships and desires related to sexual attraction and intimacy.

Slow violence: Term coined by Rob Nixon referring to violence that occurs gradually and out of sight, such as environmental damage over centuries.

Snowball sampling: A sampling technique where existing participants recruit future subjects from among their acquaintances.

Social action: Behaviour that takes into account the actions and reactions of others, demonstrating how individual choices are influenced by society.

Social capital: Resources based on group membership, relationships, networks of influence and support, that enable individuals to function effectively in society; concept developed by Bourdieu and later by Putnam.

Social class: A division of society based on social and economic status, affecting life chances and access to resources.

Social construction: The idea that many aspects of our social world are created and maintained through social practices rather than being natural or inevitable.

Social contract: A theory, associated with philosophers like John Locke, suggesting an implicit agreement among members of society to co-operate for social benefits by sacrificing some individual freedoms.

Social Darwinism: A misapplication of Charles Darwin's evolutionary theory to justify racial inequality, suggesting that certain 'races' were more 'evolved' or 'fit' than others.

Social identity: The aspects of an individual's self-concept based on their group memberships and the value and emotional significance attached to those memberships.

Social mobility: The movement of individuals, families or groups through a system of social hierarchy or stratification.

Social stratification: The classification of society into groups based on socioeconomic factors such as wealth, income, 'race', education, ethnicity, gender, occupation, social status or derived power.

Social structures: Relatively stable patterns of social relations that influence or limit the choices and opportunities available to individuals.

Social tipping point: The moment when a significant portion of a population adopts a new belief, behaviour or technology, leading to rapid widespread adoption.

Sociological imagination: A term coined by C. Wright Mills to describe the ability to see the connection between individual experiences and larger social forces.

Sociology: The systematic study of society, social relationships and social institutions, analyzing how they develop, interact and change.

Sovereign power: Foucault's term for external and often violent forms of bodily control from authority, generally relying on punishment.

Speciesism: A form of human exceptionalism that refers to both the assumed superiority of humans and the hierarchy of other animals along a chain of significance, with some animals considered more valuable than others.

Standpoint theory: A feminist theoretical perspective arguing that knowledge is always situated and research should acknowledge the social position of the knower.

State violence: Violence perpetrated by the state against its population or others.

Stigma: Erving Goffman's term for attributes that are deeply discrediting and reduce the bearer 'from a whole and usual person to a tainted, discounted one'.

Structural functionalism: Theoretical approach viewing society as a system of interrelated parts working together to maintain stability and order.

Structural racism: Systems and institutions that perpetuate racial inequality without requiring individual prejudice, operating through policies, practices and cultural representations that reinforce racial advantage and disadvantage.

Structural violence: Violence built into social structures, where social arrangements systematically prevent individuals from meeting basic needs or reaching potential.

Surface acting: Arlie Hochschild's term for when service workers display emotions they don't genuinely feel, to please customers or meet workplace expectations.

Surveillance capitalism: An economic system based on the commodification of personal data with the core purpose of profit-making, pioneered by Google and later Facebook/Meta.

Survey: A research method involving collecting data from a large number of respondents through standardized questionnaires.

Symbolic interactionism: A micro-level theory, developed by Herbert Blumer (building on Mead's work), that focuses on the way that people create meaning through social interactions, interpretations and symbols: words, gestures, rules and roles.

Symbolic power: The ability to influence or shape reality through symbols; the capacity to impose one's vision of the social world.

Symbolic violence: Pierre Bourdieu's term for the imposition of systems of meaning that legitimize and conceal power relations, where dominant groups impose their culture and values on subordinate groups.

Technical middle class: One of the seven classes identified in the Great British Class Survey, characterized by high economic capital but relatively few social contacts and limited cultural capital.

Technological determinism: The view that technology drives social change independently of social factors, following an internal technical logic.

Territory of the self: Erving Goffman's concept describing the various physical and symbolic spaces that individuals claim as extensions of themselves and defend from intrusion.

Theory: A set of ideas that explains why something happens or exists in society; a systematic explanation for observations that relates to generally understood principles.

Thick description: A detailed account of a human behaviour that explains not just the behaviour but its context as well, making it meaningful to an outsider.

Treadmill of production: A theory explaining how capitalist economies create a self-reinforcing cycle of resource extraction and environmental degradation through the constant pursuit of economic growth.

Triangulation: Using multiple methods or data sources to enhance the validity, reliability and credibility of research findings.

Uneven development: The unequal distribution of development across different geographic areas, often as a result of the way capitalism operates globally.

Unfinishedness: Chris Shilling's suggestion that bodies are in a state of constant evolution throughout the lifecourse.

Validity: The extent to which research methods or instruments measure what they claim to measure.

Variables: Measurable aspects of concepts that may vary in quantity or quality and are used in hypothesis testing.

Virtual community: Groups of people who interact primarily through digital communication rather than face-to-face, often developing social bonds despite physical distance.

Welfare state: Government system providing healthcare, education, housing and financial support to ensure citizens' well-being.

White supremacy: The belief that white people constitute a superior 'race' and should dominate society, typically to the exclusion or detriment of other racial and ethnic groups.

Youth control complex: Victor Ríos's term for the system of institutions, practices and relationships that criminalize everyday youth behaviours.

Zombie categories: Ulrich Beck and Elisabeth Beck-Gernsheim's term for traditional social concepts (like class or family) that continue to exist in theory but have lost much of their meaning in people's everyday lives.

SUGGESTED READING

1. What is Sociology

Bauman, Z. and May, T. (2019) *Thinking Sociologically*. Wiley Blackwell. An engaging introduction to the 'adventure' of sociology.

Mills, C.W. (1959/2000) *The Sociological Imagination*. Oxford: Oxford University Press. The first chapter, 'The Promise', sets out how sociology can help us understand social issues.

Plummer, K. (2010) *Sociology: The Basics*. Abingdon: Routledge. A great starting point which considers what sociology is and introduces some key themes, theories and approaches.

Websites: https://www.britsoc.co.uk/ The British Sociological Association's website offers a peak into current research and researchers. There are some free resources and it's a useful place to see what is trending in sociology. Similarly, The Economic and Social Research Council (ESRC) fund sociological research and on their website: www.ukri.org/councils/esrc/ – you can access papers and information about past, present and future research.

2. Sociological Ways of Thinking

Inglis, D. with Thorpe, C. (2024) *An Invitation to Social Theory*. Cambridge: Polity. A useful introduction to classical and contemporary social theory, showing links between schools of thought.

Ritzer, G. and Stepinsky, J. (2022) *Contemporary Sociological Theory and Its Classical Roots: The Basics*. London: Sage. Looking at key classical and contemporary scholars, this explores major theoretical approaches.

Scott, J (2023) *Sociological Theory: Contemporary Debates*. Cheltenham: Edward Elgar. An engaging text which examines some of the pressing issues in contemporary sociology.

Website: https://www.bbc.co.uk/programmes/b006qy05 An opportunity to explore a range of programmes from the BBC Radio 4 series 'Thinking Allowed', which introduces many new and classic sociological works.

3. Doing Sociology

Becker, H.S. (1998) *The Tricks of the Trade: How to Think about Your Research While You're Doing It*. Chicago: University of Chicago Press. A great help if you're planning to do some research or want to know more about research more generally.

Bryman, A. (2015) *Social Research Methods*. Oxford: Oxford University Press. A comprehensive exploration of all the stages of research for quantitative and qualitative research.

Silverman, D. (ed) (2021) *Qualitative Research*. London: Sage. Great practical advice but also explores the theories underpinning the methods.

Website: https://methods.sagepub.com This methods website includes tools, guides and case studies.

4. Identities and Society

Giddens, A. (1991) *Modernity and Self Identity: Self and Society in the Late Modern Age*. Cambridge: Polity. Traces the ways in which modernity has impacted on ideas of the self.

Jenkins, R. (2014) *Social Identity*. London: Routledge. Looks at the processes of identity formation from individuals through to institutions.

Woodward, K. (ed) (2004) *Questioning Identity: Gender, Class, Ethnicity*. London: The Open University/Routledge. Looks at how social identities are made, with a focus on key social divisions.

5. Poverty, Class and Inequality

Bhattacharyya, G. (2017) *Rethinking Racial Capitalism*. London: Rowman & Littlefield. Shows how racial division and exploitation were, and continue to be, part of capitalism's 'success'.

Skeggs, B. (1997) *Formations of Class and Gender: Becoming Respectable*. London: Sage. An empirical study of the ways in which people try to fit into social positions.

Wilkinson, R. and Pickett, K. (2018) *The Inner Level*. London: Penguin. Argues that inequality in society negatively impacts on all of us.

Website: www.poverty.ac.uk research, data, news relevant to the UK and worldwide. A useful resource.

6. 'Race' and Ethnicity

Anthias, F. and Yuval-Davies, N. (1993) *Racialised Boundaries: Race, Nation, Gender, Colour and Class and the Anti-Racist Struggle*. Looks at why sociology needs to consider a range of factors in addition to 'race'.

Back, L. and Solomos, J. (2022) *Theories of Race and Racism*. London: Routledge. A range of important texts considering theories in relation to 'race', ethnicity and nationality.

Hill-Collins, P (2000) *Black Feminist Thought: Knowledge, Consciousness and the Politics of Empowerment*. London: Routledge. An important text focusing on the intersections of 'race' and gender, which includes considerations of other key thinkers such as bel hooks and Audre Lorde.

7. Gender and Sexuality

Connell, R. and Pearse, R. (2014) *Gender*. Oxford: Polity. A very useful introduction to the sociology of gender which includes historical and global discussions.

Richardson, D. and Robinson, V. (eds) (2020) *Introducing Gender and Women's Studies*. London: Red Globe Press. A useful range of important topics in feminist and gender theory.

Todd, M. (2021) *Sexualities and Society: An introduction*. London: Sage. An accessible consideration of research and theories into sexualities.

8. The Body and Society

Creggan, K. (2006) *The Sociology of the Body: Mapping the Abstraction of Embodiment*. London: Sage. Looks at social processes 'shaping' bodies and engages with a range of theories including those of Elias, Bourdieu and Butler.

Howson, A. (2012) *The Body in Society*. Cambridge: Polity. An accessible discussion of bodies in various social contexts.

Shilling, C. (1993) *The Body and Social Theory*. London: Sage. Looks at bodies in relation to a range of issues including ageing, sexuality and disability. Provides interesting examples involving sport, leisure and consumer society.

9. Digital Cultures

Bell, D. and Kennedy, B. (2000) *The Cybercultures Reader*. London: Routledge. Introduces a range of key theorists and concepts, offering useful interpretations for the reader.

Lupton, D. (2015) *Digital Sociology*. London: Routledge. Considers a range of ways that digital technologies have impacted on social and cultural life. Also asks some interesting questions about the direction of sociology in the future.

Selwyn, N. (2019) *What is Digital Sociology?*. Cambridge: Polity Press. Addresses the role and impact of digital technologies on society and how they have influenced sociological research.

10. Globalization, Culture and Society

Giddens, A. (1990) *The Consequences of Modernity*. A now classic text which still asks very useful questions about modernity and its relationship to globalisation.

Harvey, D. (2019) *Spaces of Global Capitalism: A Theory of Uneven Geographical Development*. London: Verso. An engaging consideration of contemporary capitalism and its uneven distribution across the globe.

Martell, L. (2016) *The Sociology of Globalisation*. Cambridge: Polity Press. An accessible and wide-ranging introduction to key issues such as capitalism, inequality, technologies and migration

11. Sociology of Violence

Boyle, K. (2004) *Media and Violence: Gendering the Debates*. A really interesting look at how the media in various forms depicts violence and impacts on attitudes. Includes analysis of horror films, pornography and serial killers.

Collins, R. (2009) *Violence: A Micro-Sociological Theory*. Westport, CT: Greenwood Publishing. Using symbolic interactionism as a framework, this looks at a broad range of types of violence.

Walby, S. (2013) 'Violence and Society: Introduction to an emerging field of sociology', *Current Sociology* 61(2): 95-111. Explores the current state of the sociology of violence and suggests new areas for research.

12. The Environment

Brechin, S. and Lee, S. (eds) (2025) *Routledge Handbook of Climate Change and Society*. Abingdon: Routledge. This includes chapters from key thinkers in a broad range of areas. Includes useful sections on how climate crises impact on marginalised communities and health.

Dunlap, R.E. and Brulle, R.J. (eds) (2015) *Climate Change and Society: Sociological Perspectives*. Oxford: Oxford University Press. Looks at how key institutions and cultural practices are related to issues of climate change. Considers the causes and impacts of climate change and responses to it.

Sutton, P. (2007) *The Environment: A Sociological Introduction*. Cambridge: Polity. An accessible text which introduces key issues.

13. Human-Animal Relations

Adams C.J. (2018) *Neither Man nor Beast: Feminism and the Defense of Animals*. London: Bloomsbury. Makes links between the cultural attitudes about women and other animals in the Global North.

Demello, M. (2012) *Animals and Society: An Introduction to Human-Animal Studies*. New York: Columbia University Press. Looks at the construction of the human-animal border, the role of animals in sport and consumerism and issues to do with violence against animals and meat-eating.

Peggs, K. (2012) *Animals and Sociology*. London: Palgrave. Shows how sociology can help us to understand our relationship to other animals.

14. Future Trends

Becker, H (1967) Whose side are we on', *Social Problems*, 14(3): 239-247. An important essay which looks at what sociology's role is.

Holmes, M (2016) *Sociology for Optimists*. London: Sage. Critical optimism has long been touted as essential (think Gramsci) and here Holmes continues this to look at how it can be used to understand contemporary social life, particularly for current and future challenges such as climate change.

Plummer, K (2010) *Sociology: The Basics*. Abingdon: Routledge. Has a useful final section which summarises how sociology can be useful for understanding social life into the future.

INDEX